D0762245

The Technique of Clear Writing

The Technique of
Clear Writing

Revised Edition

ROBERT GUNNING

McGraw-Hill Book Company

New York   London   Toronto   Sydney

Fourth Printing, 1973

Library of Congress Catalog Card Number: 68-9047
07-025206-8

To Mary, my partner

Preface

In 1944 Robert Gunning Associates launched a business not listed among more than 35,000 job classes of the United States census. This work was readability counseling or, as we have come to call it, counseling in clear writing. Our aim was to help people make better use of the written word.

By the time the first edition of this book appeared, we had already been working for eight years with writers in five chief groupings:

—Authors of books and members of magazine editorial staffs.

—Staffs of newspapers.

—Staffs of business and trade magazines.

—Those writing memos, letters, and reports in industry, government, and the armed forces.

—Scientists and engineers writing technical reports, particularly those in research laboratories.

Now, 16 years later, as we survey these fields again, we can report more readable writing in all—with a qualifying word regarding magazines.

Time magazine and *Reader's Digest*, which we have long used to illustrate standards of readable writing, are somewhat more complexly written today than they were 20 years ago. The increase in reading difficulty that we observe may not be enough to interfere with the popularity of the publications. One may even argue that increased schooling in the United States justifies more complex writing. We do not take this point of view. Rather we feel that the writing standards of many popular magazines have been relaxed. The standards of which we speak are those of readability, based upon the sentence length and complexity of vocabulary. In any case, when Henry Luce and DeWitt Wallace held a firm hand in building *Time* and *Reader's Digest,* the writing in them was more simple, concise, and concrete.

In the women's-magazine field, reading difficulty has likewise risen. This probably results from more articles being staff written. Twenty years ago we found that what magazine staffs wrote themselves was harder reading than what they bought from free-lance writers. Like other writers, those working on magazines tend to indulge themselves in words. But, like other readers, they rarely put up with complexity in reading that they buy.

Magazines have become harder reading generally, but newspapers are another story. All across the country, newspapers are more readable today than they were 20 years ago.

Unfortunately, saying they are more readable is not the same as saying that newspapers are better. Many newspapers, we find, are slighting important local news. There are conspicuous exceptions, but most local news staffs fail to dig as deeply into problems as they did in the past. A lessening of competition among newspapers, the increase in one-newspaper cities, is no doubt a chief cause. So news writing is more readable than it was, partly because dailies do not deal with as challenging concepts. Columns about personalities, amusement, and froth are on the increase. Newspapers become more an entertainment and less an informative medium.

Let us quickly distinguish between local and wire news. National and international news is as deeply or more deeply reported than it was 20 years ago. Furthermore, news-service writing has much improved. The background of this development is worth reviewing.

During the 1940s, the war led many newspaper staffs to write carelessly. Even editors relaxed standards of craftsmanship. In a talk before the American Society of Newspaper Editors, I threw on the screen the following original and a suggested revision of an article from the ASNE bulletin:

Original	*Suggested Revision*
DIFFICULT READING FOR COLLEGE GRADUATES	EASY READING FOR YOU, ME AND EDITORS
Looking forward to the restoration of international communication on a peace basis, the American Society of Newspaper Editors today invited reciprocal declarations by the United States Government and all other governments, press, radio and other media of information, embracing the right of the people to read and hear news without censorship.	The American Society of Newspaper Editors today called upon all nations to speak out against news censorship after the war.
The Society urged the removal of all political, economic, and military barriers to the freedom of world information.	The Society hailed a recent step by Edward R. Stettinius, Jr., the new Secretary of State. He has suggested talks with other nations to open the way for free exchange of world information.
The Society notes with satisfaction the recent statement of Edward R. Stettinius, Jr., newly-appointed Secretary of State, that the United States . . .	The editors are for this plan. They want statements from the United States and other nations pledging free radio and press. They call for an uprooting of all political, economic and military censorship.
	These moves are vital to a lasting peace, the editors declare . . .

Between 1944 and 1952, Robert Gunning Associates made surveys for and worked with the staffs of newspapers in New

York, Philadelphia, Washington, San Francisco, Dallas, Houston, and a score of other cities. Even in such quality newspapers as the Hartford *Courant* and Louisville *Courier-Journal* we found more than half the text harder reading than average writing in the *Atlantic Monthly*. Such writing we consider above the danger line of reading difficulty. Readers, no doubt, *can* read more difficult material, but judging from what they buy, they don't prefer it.

Through rewrites, we showed newsmen that the complexity we found was not needed. It resulted from tangled sentences and wordiness that could be avoided; it was fog that interfered with meaning rather than helped convey it.

The newspapers we worked with improved greatly in readability overnight. We were working with professionals. All they needed was a warning and concrete evidence of error.

As we surveyed newspapers across the country, editors began complaining to the news services that they were delivering much foggy writing from Washington and abroad. Presently Earl J. Johnson, then General News Manager of the United Press, retained us to survey the U.P. daily report. Slightly more than half the news put on the U.P. wire tested above college reading level. Johnson issued a series of memos to the staff, later combined in a booklet, "Readability and the News."

Two months later, further tests showed only 10 per cent of the daily report testing above college reading level. More than half was below the danger line of reading difficulty, a big improvement. Following this work, the Associated Press hired Dr. Rudolph Flesch to survey its report. Improvement followed there also. Wire news continues markedly more readable than it was in the early days of our work.

All this effort obviously has not resulted in excellent newspaper writing. Readability research did, however, bolster standards of good writing. It has become increasingly difficult in the news field to write horribly and get away with it.

Probably the greatest writing improvement of the past 20 years has occurred in the business and industrial press. Two models did much to raise these standards—the *Wall Street Journal* and *Business Week*. The story of our work with the former is told in an early section of this book, "What Every Writer Should Know about Readers."

The business press gained its great momentum during the 1940s. Before then a typical pattern was one publication reporting the news for each field from optometry to auto repairing. After World War II, many publishers rushed into this rich, growing field. Circulation and advertising revenue climbed. Soon there were several publications in each field. Better writing and easier reading became important competitive tools.

Staff members of the magazines of business and industry are in special need of a warning system against foggy writing. As we have already noted, salaried staff writers tend to indulge themselves with words. One writing for a scientific or technical field is further tempted to use specialist language to impress rather than ordinary language to express. Furthermore, many such publications reach readers through controlled circulation plans. Magazines are given away to those who hold key positions within a company. This assures the advertiser of a select audience. But, when a publication does not have to be bought to be read, writers tend to be relieved of the need to write readably.

Good, readable writing was one of the lesser interests of the business press in its early days. Today it is a necessity if a publication is to survive in competition.

Aside from the *Wall Street Journal,* we worked with Chilton Publications, the American Chemical Society Applied

Publications, Fairchild Publications, Watson Publications, and the MacLean-Hunter Publications of Canada, about a hundred publications in all. In every instance readability improved. In a few instances, failing papers were turned into money-makers, and the change could be traced to improved writing.

Of the millions of words placed on paper each day, most are the product of the offices of corporations and government agencies. So it was natural for our work to turn to these areas. Since 1950 Robert Gunning Associates' chief effort has been to aid those who write memos, letters, and reports in industry and government. The largest corporations have the biggest communication problems. The most extensive jobs we have done were for headquarters staffs of Standard Oil of New Jersey and International Business Machines. In the field of defense industry there was probably no effort more complex than the Minute Man program. Hundreds of engineers writing reports were involved, and typical engineering jargon had become so heavy with fog that many memos were incomprehensible. If we did nothing else, we reminded them to keep writing on a human scale and direct it toward persons rather than filing cabinets.

Judging writing improvement in industry and government is not the clean-cut task it is in working with publications. Rarely do we work with an entire industrial group or government division. Also lacking are those ideal "before-and-after" samples that issues of a publication furnish automatically.

Managers of Ethyl Corporation research laboratories did make a survey on their own which we considered objective. We had held training programs for most of their research staff. The report showed writing of their chemists and engineers averaged above college reading difficulty before the training. After training, most reports dropped below the danger line of reading difficulty. A control sample composed of those who had not taken the training showed no change in readability.

Similar improvement was experienced at scores of other research laboratories with which we worked, among them Lawrence Radiation Laboratory, Battelle Memorial Institute, Argonne National Laboratory, Chevron Research Corp., Esso Research and Engineering, General Motors Technical Center.

Improving writing in industry, in government, and the armed forces is, of course, a never-ending job. Although we have conducted training for more than one hundred corporations and government and military units, there is no hope of reaching them all. We have granted use of copyrighted materials to the Army and Navy, to the General Services Administration, and the Department of Agriculture. The last has made extensive use of our Fog Index, as have many other organizations with which we have had no direct training contact.

Although we have often given permission for reprinting the Fog Index, our means of measuring reading difficulty, we have sometimes cringed at the use made of it. In our work, we emphasize that the Fog Index is a tool, not a rule. It is a warning system, not a formula for writing. Testing without the support of analysis based on experience can be detrimental.

I well remember my first introduction to a readability yardstick. The idea of applying such measurement to writing made me furious. After years of newspaper work, I had become editor of an educational publication. The head of the firm walked into my office with a readability report on my writing from the Columbia University Readability Workshop. They had tested my articles with a complex calculation called the Vogel-Washburne formula. The report said my writing had too many different words per thousand, too many prepositions, not enough simple sentences, too many words outside the Thorndike list of 10,000, and was too difficult writing for the intended audience. In anger, I drafted a scathing rebuttal. But, as I wrote, I found myself giving closer attention to the mechanics of my prose. Sentences were held in check and not allowed to ramble. Each word I weighed carefully, favoring the simple ones. The warning of the yardstick people was taking effect. I had to admit they were influencing me to improve my writing for the sake of readers.

But the means of measuring readability in those days were intolerably burdensome. Applying a yardstick often required four or five times as long as the time required for the original composition. And the measurements bordered the absurd in their scientific pretensions. (Carrying figures to the fourth decimal place, as an example.)

As a professional writer, I knew writing to be an art—first, last, and always. But also, as a writer who had started out to be a chemist, I did not despise a scientific approach. Early readability research made it clear that successful writing is somewhat systematic. There are limits relating to long sentences and long words that the craftsman does not go beyond. The writer's restrictions may be conscious or unconscious, but they are there. If not, he does not win an audience. (James Joyce and William Faulkner, who wrote experimental complexity later, won their original audiences, you can be sure, with quite simple, direct, and beautiful English.)

The Fog Index resulted from our efforts to produce a measure that would be sufficiently reliable and still easy to use. Apparently this effort has succeeded.

Of the Department of Agriculture campaign for better writing, William R. Van Dersal writes:

"On the basis of many years of study of hundreds of people and their reading comprehension, various formulas have been developed. We use here a formula developed by Robert Gunning. It is by all odds the simplest to use."

The General Services Administration has also been extended permission to use the formula in its training work.

Ritchie R. Ward, an author and teacher with many years

of industrial experience, studied seven readability formulae from the point of view of the "professional technical man" and came to the conclusion:

"The test recommended here is the Fog Index. . . . It is easy to apply . . . and it has proved widely useful in practical applications in industry and government." *

Blaine K. McKee of Colorado State University surveyed companies and business publications in regard to their use of readability yardsticks. He reported in *Public Relations Journal* of July 1967 that the Fog Index was mentioned most often.

Since 1944 I have sat down with thousands of writers to help them analyze and improve their writing. About half these were men and women working on staffs of newspapers and magazines. The other half were not professional writers but persons who had to write as part of their professions or specialties—in business, industry, government, or the armed forces.

I am grateful to them for the concrete examples of writing problems and writing improvement that form the basis of this book. If they should recognize samples of their writing among the following pages, I hope they will be pleased to have been able to contribute to this crusade against foggy writing.

Clear writing is hard for anyone to achieve. It results only from clear thinking and hard work. We are all in the same boat. We need constructive criticism. Usually my comments have been received as such. I treasure the response of one able newspaperman of New England. He had written an article about a difficult federal-court subject. His lead and my suggested revision follow:

* *Practical Technical Writing*, by Ritchie R. Ward. Alfred A. Knopf, 1968.

| *Original* | *Suggested Revision* |
| HARD READING FOR COLLEGE GRADUATES | NEWS MAGAZINE READING LEVEL |

Original

HARD READING FOR COLLEGE GRADUATES

An experimental policy in which federal prosecutors will make a full disclosure of all government evidence to defense lawyers before trial will go into effect in Connecticut today.

In a move that is believed to be the first of its kind in the nation, U. S. Atty. Jon O. Newman has directed all six assistant government prosecutors to completely unveil their evidence to the defense providing that the defense lawyer also disclose his evidence to the prosecution.

Newman directed that the complete disclosure be made at a meeting of the prosecution and defense lawyers a week before trial.

In an important exception to the policy, however, Newman told his assistants . . .

Suggested Revision

NEWS MAGAZINE READING LEVEL

In Connecticut federal courts today prosecutors will begin testing a policy of opening their files of evidence to the defense before trial.

The move is believed to be the first of its kind in the nation. U. S. Atty. Jon O. Newman has directed his six assistants to unveil all evidence to the defense if the defense lawyers will do the same in return. Such disclosures are to be agreed upon in a meeting of lawyers a week before trial.

The "open file" move is an effort to make a trial more a search for truth than a contest between lawyers.

An important exception to the policy . . .

After the clear-writing session he wrote me:

"When my story appeared on your screen, I'm sure you knew my reaction. I was embarrassed and irrritated. I am writing to tell you, however, that Gunning wasn't the target of my irritation. It was the author of that gem.

"I have been resident in this estate for about a dozen years and it was an eye opener to see this story dissected. It may be hard to believe, but I learned to write news using most of the tools you demonstrated in your talks. It was a shock to see how the cobwebs had settled.

"Thanks for the refresher course. It was the best two hours I've spent at my trade in a long time."

I replied: "In your story I rewrote, I recognized the hand of a professional. At the same time I detected either: work under pressure, or momentary lapse of that necessary intense sense of contact with the reader."

The price of good writing, as that of liberty, is eternal vigilance. This book is intended as an alert to excellence.

Possibly, as a fashionable pundit implies, the day of the written word is fading. Possibly books and magazines are giving way to pictures and TV. Possibly the written word will not be important in forming our actions and supplying our pleasures in the future. Possibly craftsmanship in use of English is no longer a matter of deep concern. But if this is the case, I don't want to hear about it.

ROBERT GUNNING

Blacklick, Ohio, 1968

Contents

Part Three: Causes and Cures

Appendixes

"Except ye utter by the tongue words easy
to be understood, how shall it be known
what is spoken? For ye shall speak into the air."
1 Corinthians—14 : 9

"Variety in human beings is the pleasure
of the Lord."
Kinzy Payne

PART ONE

What Your Reader Wants

The Fight against Fog

This book is based on several propositions:

One: Writing is an art. But when it is writing to inform it comes close to being a science as well.

Two: Far more than half of what is now written is heavy with fog. Most writing you meet in business, in newspapers, and in schools is harder reading than it should be—or need be.

Three: Those writers who gain a wide audience and those who have wide influence obey definite principles of clear statement that promote easy reading.

Four: Readability research of the last 30 years has analyzed these principles from a new viewpoint. It has developed "yardsticks" with which you can test your own writing. Anyone can improve both the form and the force of his writing by building these principles into his own personal style.

As a reader you are sharply aware of the daily waste of words that results from poor writing. Readers as a group suffer much. Heads buzz and eyes burn trying to read:

> Tax forms, reports of Congressional committees, memos from the legal department, instructions on how to assemble a boy's work bench.

Perhaps you have fallen asleep over news or magazine articles you really wanted to read. Their complexity drugged your attention. And, at the office, if you are as poor a mind-reader as I am, you have made mistakes because of the unclear writing of others.

As a reader, therefore, you are opposed to:
　　　—words that don't say what they mean
　　　—words that don't say anything
　　　—words that are used merely for display.

But do you look at your own writing from the point of view of the reader? Do you know how many different words and what sort your readers are likely to understand? Do you know what sort of words work best in transferring facts and ideas from reader to writer? Do you know what mixture of hard words readers will tolerate?

Do you know what patterns and lengths of sentences people read without tiring? Do you know what sort of writing is most likely to make the other fellow take action? Do you know how to hold his interest? And do you have a means of measuring your own writing against that which has proved successful?

If you possess and use this knowledge you are a rare and valuable human. Even among those earning a good living at writing there are too few who obey this Golden Rule—

"Write unto others as you would be written to."

That guide was laid down years ago by managing editors at the American Press Institute of Columbia University, and it is a good one.

The reader in each of us grumbles over the mass of difficult verbiage we are expected to read. But the writer in us turns to the typewriter or to the stenographer with bland disregard of what makes reading easy.

The attitude of a certain Washington newspaper correspondent makes the point. I lunched with him during the early New Deal when many of the confusions of our present day were hatching. I was telling him of readability yardsticks developed early in the 1930s by Dr. William S. Gray of Chicago University.

As gently as possible, I broke the news to him that what he was writing for the general public about NRA and RFC was hard reading for college graduates. On the other hand, I showed him that popular newspaper writing, such as that done by Ernie Pyle, was on the sixth- or seventh-grade reading level —so far as mechanics of style are concerned. Pyle's column was easy reading for nearly anyone who could read at all.

I mentioned a score of factors that made news written in Washington hard reading. Then I talked of principles of clear statement which he and other writers could follow to make even their difficult subjects easy to read.

The correspondent was a man very sure of himself—a valuable attribute in his profession.

"I get the facts down," he said after listening quietly. "I see that they are accurate and I try to put them into English. After that I figure my job is done. If the reader can't get what I am saying, he's just dumb."

The writer in most of us responds to that statement. Sometime or other we have all felt the same way. It is the *easy* way of looking at a job of writing.

But watch out! The word "dumb" is a boomerang. Throw it at the reader and it spins back to whack the writer. If a reader doesn't understand what you write, he is dumb—in the *slang* sense of the word.

But, in the proper sense of the word, if the reader misunderstands what you write—*you* are dumb. You have failed to communicate. And you have wasted time, energy, ink, and good white paper.

Good writing goes beyond the mere recording of facts. To have effect, writing must communicate facts to readers.

The gulf between writers and readers is very great. Readers

want careful organization in what they read. They desire concreteness to help them picture and apply ideas. They like variety; it maintains their interest. They prefer short but variable sentences and not too rich a mixture of hard words.

Writers, on the other hand, enjoy *self*-expression. They would rather use abstractions to which they give their own special meanings. And a writing job goes easier and faster if you can simply set down the facts, without the exacting thought needed for careful organization.

Thus many a writer fails because he makes in his own writing the same mistakes that irritate him in the writing of others. As a *writer* he has never analyzed these faults and does not know how to avoid them.

This book aims to give you the means of finding in your writing the factors that tend to make it difficult reading. It aims to show you how to clear the faulty structure from your writing and put in its place the means of attracting and holding readers. The book will also give you a yardstick, one that is most easy to use, with which you can check your writing and gauge it to your audience.

This training method has been tested and has met with marked success in fighting fog. The results are particularly easy to measure in the periodical field, where writing staffs of newspapers and magazines turn out a product that can be compared from issue to issue. We have tested more than two hundred magazines and large city dailies repeatedly since 1944—some of them month after month regularly for more than five years. Staffs of these publications have all been trained in the readability principles set forth in this book. In many instances the writers have markedly altered their styles. Before training we have often found that more than half the articles in a publication are harder reading than average material in the *Atlantic Monthly*. After training, an article that goes above the *Atlantic Monthly* level of reading difficulty is an exception.

There is still much room for improvement in the writing of newspapers and, particularly, industrial magazines. Our tests indicate that about half the articles in a large city daily are still more complex than average writing in *Time* and *Newsweek*. The newspaper sentences are longer on the average and the mixture of long words is greater. They are comparatively hard reading and are skipped by the average newspaper reader.

Writing produced in business and industry is still further out of line with reading abilities and tastes. We have made surveys for leading companies in the aerospace, steel, oil, food, utility, rubber, railroad, chemical, and retailing fields. In each instance, the story of abuse of the written word is similar.

More than a third of the writing intended for employees and customers is above college reading level. Writing of that degree of difficulty is usually skipped by both customers and employees. And the few who do pull on their hip boots and wade through, waste time and run the risk of mistakes and misunderstanding.

The pity of this waste is more dismal in view of the fact that even the most complicated business prose can be made easy reading if the writer pays heed to principles of clear statement. Most complexity in writing is the fault of the writer rather than of the subject matter.

One office worker meets another in the hall. "Joe," he says, "if you need more stickers ask us for them."

His message is 9 words. They deliver his thought simply and directly. Anyone can understand. What more is there to say?

But let the same man write this message and he fills it with business jargon:

"If the supply of stickers sent you is not sufficient to meet your requirements, apply to this office for additional copies."

The 9 words have grown to 21 and the sentence has become

heavy reading. But it can be tortured still more by twisting the verb forms. This is the way the written message actually appeared in business copy:

"*Should* the supply of stickers sent you *not be sufficient* to meet your requirements, *application should be made* to this office for additional copies."

A message that in simple form required but 10 syllables has now grown to 37.

Business writers quite often disregard their audience. An example of such writing follows. It is from a form to be filled in by those "budget" customers of a certain chain-store system who are unable to meet their weekly payments. Typical examples would be teen-agers who need more time to pay for their bicycles and poor housewives trying to hold on to their washing machines. They are asked to read this with comprehension:

"Except for a change in the Schedule of Payments, all the provisions of the Sale Agreement shall continue in effect without any modification. The contemplated refinancing is necessary in order to avoid undue hardship to me or my dependents resulting from contingencies which were unforeseen by me at the time of obtaining the original credit or which were beyond my control. This statement is made in good faith and I certify that the contemplated refinancing is not pursuant to a preconceived plan or an intention to evade or circumvent the requirements of Regulation W."

Most of those who befog the written word do so because of careless habits or poor training or because of wrong ideas. Bad habits and training can be corrected and wrong ideas can be wiped out with accurate information.

If you wish to write clearly you should set yourself straight on one distinction at the outset. You must be able to draw the line between dignity on the one hand and pomposity on the other.

Nowadays nearly every trade and profession vies with others in coining a complex jargon to set itself apart. As a result scientists have difficulty talking with engineers. Engineers are puzzled by accountants; accountants can't follow physicians, who, in turn, are confused by language of psychiatrists.

Many new terms are necessary, of course. But much of this special jargon is designed to impress rather than express. It rests on the most ludicrous of follies—the concept that complexity is the badge of wisdom.

Quite the contrary is true, of course. Wisdom goes arm in arm with simplicity. The keen mind is one that can absorb a complicated problem, then state it in simple direct terms that will transfer the idea quickly and accurately to the minds of others. To put complicated ideas in simple language is not child's work. It calls for sophistication. Such skill requires the simplicity one associates with Abraham Lincoln. Lincoln was a man of high intelligence and of deep understanding and feeling. He was also a great master of English. Because of these traits he was able to pierce to the heart of problems and state them in language which, though it can be understood by children, fires the imagination of adults.

To write well and simply you must train your mind to cut through surface details and get at the bones of your thought. And you must constantly polish your English. But have a care along what lines you polish it. See that the improvements are along the clean, smooth lines of good modern design. Don't get the idea that you improve your writing by adding glittering gewgaws. Good writing is based on the right word in the right place. And, of course, in order to have the right word at hand at the right time you must know many words. But don't use a big one when a little one will do.

Clarity of style cannot replace clarity of thought. But the two do go hand in hand. Clear thinking will lead to a clear style, on the one hand. On the other, a will to avoid foggy words in your writing and speech is one of the best paths to better habits of thought.

A complex writer will often defend himself in this way:

"I am writing for a special audience. Nearly all the readers I intend to reach are college graduates. I musn't write grade-school English for them. I mustn't write down to them."

Quite right. You mustn't write *down*—not even to children. But it is equally true you should never write *up*—not even to college professors.

No one prefers writing that contains unnecessary complexity. That goes for college professors as well as for Joe Doaks and the rest of us. The preferred writing is that which delivers the intended thought most clearly in the fewest words possible. Don't write down. Don't write up. Write *to*.

In addressing an audience of superior intelligence you may deal with more difficult concepts but this does not necessarily mean that your language will be more complex. Actually your effort should bear in the opposite direction. If your subject is deep you should make all the more effort to keep your language simple.

Herbert Spencer made this point most ably more than a century ago in *The Philosophy of Style*. A reader, he explained, brings to your writing limited mental power. He uses it in three ways: (1) in understanding the words you use, (2) in getting their relationships, and (3) in realizing the thought conveyed.

Be sparing, therefore, in your use of hard words and marathon sentences, so your reader will have energy left for your complicated ideas.

The special audience, like any other audience, is annoyed by fog in writing. But the special audience will have special appreciation for a polished piece of simple, direct writing.

The key problem of clear writing is much the same as that of running a business or living a balanced life. You succeed if, from moment to moment, you are able to be careful of details without losing sight of the whole. Clear writing is based on clear thinking. One must organize his thought first, see the whole fairly clearly, then outline, build the skeleton of his message, either in his head or on paper. Then choose the words and form the sentences.

Many are poorly trained because their study of language has been so mired in detail they have lost sight of its chief aim. English has been considered too much as a subject for analysis and too little as an instrument to communicate meaning. Writing is closely linked with life. Pull it to pieces and it dies.

Writing should be learned with the emphasis on the meaning to be communicated and practice in getting that meaning transferred clearly from one head to another. Wendell Johnson put it well when he wrote, "You can't teach writing; you can only teach how to write *something* to *someone*." A quarterback learns the forward-pass by practicing with a good coach at hand. Writing likewise is learned through practice and sound advice rather than through the sort of dissection that so often produces "grammar-fear."

Shakespeare did quite well with English before its grammar was formalized. Not until many years after his time did scholars succeed in fencing in the lively, sprawling English language with a set of rules. The first English grammars were written in the middle of the eighteenth century. Franklin and Jefferson (both of whom wrote very well) had completed school before English grammars appeared.

Grammar, of course, aims at clearer speech and writing. And so long as it clarifies communication it deserves respect. But meaning overshadows grammar in importance. The first step of grammar is to center your attention on the meaning you wish to convey. Don't freeze up, as some do, from fear of breaking a "rule." Take care to make your meaning clear and, for the most part, your grammar will take care of itself. We'll have more to say of this later.

The chapters that follow give detailed facts about the writing people want to read and are willing to pay for. These chapters analyze the writing of those who have succeeded.

Underlying all this is the lesson of simplicity. In general you can define successful writers as *those who have something to say and who have learned how to say it simply. No writer ever gained a large audience by making his style more complicated than his thought required.* The writers who gain an audience—the writers you read and can name—write surprisingly simply. They observe a strict discipline, but they introduce within that discipline much variety. They write simply but they don't get caught at it. To a great degree, that is the key to writing craftsmanship.

You may be one of the hundred thousand or so who earn a living writing. You may be one of the millions whose job success depends to a degree upon the quality of letters or reports you write. Or you may be one of the other millions who merely wants to write better because the skill is one of the best aids we have to getting along in the world.

Whatever your interest you are invited to join the fight against fog for the sake of your own writing and earning power —and for the sake of us all. For you can be certain of one thing:

If the world is in more peril than usual (and people keep telling me it is) foggy language is at the root of much of the trouble.

What Every Writer Should Know about Readers

Chancellor George Stoddard of New York University used to teach young people who hoped to become teachers themselves. He tells this story:

"I used to display a child about three and a half years old as a guinea pig for a class of juniors and seniors. 'How old is this child?' was the first question. The answers would run from ten months to eight years! 'What is his vocabulary likely to be?' Answers ran from 50 to 10,000 words. 'What does he weigh?' Anywhere from 15 pounds to 100 pounds."

Chancellor Stoddard was making the point that students know no more about children than they do about rocks, birds, or stars until they observe them with system.

Lack of knowledge about readers is equally astonishing among the writers of business letters, booklets, and news articles.

If you would know about readers study their habits. It is not enough, for instance, to ask, "What *can* people read?" If a person's motive is strong enough, he will plow through any complexity of words, signs, or hieroglyphs. Once I watched a twelve-year-old boy reading a radio repairman's manual. The volume was not only clogged with technical terms; it was atrociously written as well. I doubt if I would have read it with a whip over me, but he went through it from cover to cover.

One newspaper editor of experimental mind tried to hide some of the news stories about a sensational paternity case involving a widely known figure of the entertainment world. He would print the articles with small headlines on page 28. Still, readership surveys showed, subscribers sought the stories out and read them. The editor considered printing them in Sanskirt to see how many would still decipher and read them. After all, archaeologists with sufficient motive learned to read picture writing of the Pharaohs in a language that had been dead for centuries.

No, it is not enough to ask, "What can people read?" They can read the most complex material if forced to do so. But the material they prefer to read is written simply. The question for study, then, is, "What *do* people read?"

For the United States, here is the answer:

The Bible has sold better in America than any other book. The runners-up are a varied lot. At mid-century, Dr. Frank Luther Mott made a tabulation.* He found the following to have won the largest American audience at that time:

> *Shakespeare's Plays*
> *Mother Goose*
> *Ivanhoe*
> *Uncle Tom's Cabin*
> *Ben-Hur*
> *Gone with the Wind*
> *How to Win Friends and Influence People*

These books spread over three and a half centuries. They are very different in subject. Several are chiefly for entertain-

* *The Golden Multitudes* by Frank Luther Mott, The Macmillan Company, New York, 1947.

ment. One is aimed at the reform of slavery. Another is purely a self-improvement book.

The authors are also varied. One was an actor, another a nobleman, another a housewife, another a general, and still another a teacher. And the styles of the books vary from the greatest of English poetry to the conversational anecdote of Dale Carnegie.

But with all their differences these books have one thing in common. Each is written in comparatively simple language —language less complex, for instance, than you will find on the front page of your daily newspaper. The first two are poetry and do not lend themselves to testing by the readability yardstick. None of the others, however, except *Ivanhoe*, require more than eighth-grade reading skill. *Ivanhoe* tests tenth grade.

I won't try to convince you that Shakespeare's plays are easy reading. But I will ask you to recall that they were written 350 years ago and that many words have changed in meaning since. Also remember that those who first enjoyed the plays were the Elizabethan equivalent of the movie crowd. It is a fact that the sentences are shorter and there are far fewer long and abstract words in Shakespeare than in the average business writings we have tested. In a later chapter we will discuss the language of Shakespeare along with another old best-seller, the Bible. Meanwhile, how about modern best-sellers?

Since the middle of the century, paperbook editions have swelled greatly the number of books sold. Alice Payne Hackett is now America's best-seller authority. In her book *70 Years of Best-Sellers, 1895–1965** she shows the most widely sold book to be Dr. Benjamin Spock's *Baby and Child Care*. By 1965 it had already sold more than nineteen million. Dr. Spock writes in a simple conversational style. Although dealing

* Published by R. R. Bowker Co., New York, 1967.

with many complicated problems of child care, his writing maintains an eighth-grade reading level.

Mrs. Hackett found *Peyton Place* by Grace Metalious, with a sale of more than ten million, to be the best-seller among novels. A test of the sentence length and long words, show it to be fifth-grade reading level. Remember, these mechanics of writing style are something other than the concepts treated. Miss Metalious's book was hardly intended for fifth-graders. Simplicity of language is necessary to win a large reading audience although there is no question that sexy subject matter helps. The second most widely sold novel in America is *In His Steps*, forgotten by today's public. Around the turn of the century it sold an estimated eight million copies. In contrast to *Peyton Place* it had a religious theme. Its writing style tests eighth-grade level.

Other novels with sales between five and ten million Mrs. Hackett ranks thus: (The figure in parenthesis is our calculation of the grade reading level.)

> *God's Little Acre* by Erskine Caldwell (6)
> *Gone with the Wind* by Margaret Mitchell (6)
> *Lady Chatterley's Lover* by D. H. Lawrence (6)
> *The Carpetbaggers* by Harold Robbins (5)
> *Exodus* by Leon Uris (6)
> *I, the Jury* by Mickey Spillane (5)
> *To Kill a Mockingbird* by Harper Lee (5)
> *The Big Kill* by Mickey Spillane (5)

The writings of Grace Metalious, Harold Robbins, and Mickey Spillane are not greatly admired by literary critics. On the other hand, Harper Lee's book won a Pulitzer Prize, D. H. Lawrence is widely recognized as a master among English novelists. Another novel next on Mrs. Hackett's list and at the time just short of five million sales is *Catcher in the Rye* by J. D. Salinger, who many believe among the best of those writing English today.

Aside from cookbooks, atlases, and dictionaries, Mrs. Hackett lists only two books of nonfiction as selling more than five million. One is Dale Carnegie's *How to Win Friends and Influence People* which tests 7. The other is John F. Kennedy's *Profiles in Courage* which tests 12. This last is an excellent book, but one written by a great public figure who was not primarily a writer. All the other best-sellers are eighth-grade reading level or lower.

All are full of people, action, and concrete, picturable language. Each shows excellent use of readability principles discussed in this book.

To get a specific idea of how simple best-selling prose is, let's take samples from two men—John Steinbeck and John Gunther. Both have appeared regularly on best-seller lists since the early 1930s. I choose them from among scores of writers because their styles and subjects contrast sharply.

Steinbeck's novels are written in extremely simple language. From page to page, samples will test fifth, sixth, and seventh grade. Still his average of 7 is not markedly lower than that of other leading novelists, whether they be the late greats, Somerset Maugham, Sinclair Lewis, and Ernest Hemingway, or more recent successes such as J. D. Salinger, John Cheever, and Truman Capote. All these test easy reading for high-school freshmen.

The opening passage of Steinbeck's *The Pearl*, which scores the same as the average for the book—7—goes like this:

> Kino awakened in the near dark. The stars still shone and the day had drawn only a pale wash of light in the lower sky to the east. The roosters had been crowing for some time, and the early pigs were already beginning their ceaseless turning of twigs and bits of wood to see whether anything to eat had been overlooked. Outside the brush

house in the tuna clump, a covey of little birds chittered and flurried with their wings.

Both the subjects and the style of Gunther's writing are more complex. Still his writing stays within the easy-reading range of the average man as do other best-sellers.* His average is 10.

Here is a quotation from *Inside South America*, which tests 11, the average for the book.

Industrialization is, however, still a subject of considerable controversy. Critics say that South America has no "right" to industrialize when it still cannot feed its own people. And the cost is high. Most South American businessmen will not touch an investment unless it pays off at what their counterparts in the United States would think is an abnormal rate—20 percent or more. Foreign investors coming in are also expensive, because they want to insure their risks, compounded by the fear of political instability, and ask for a quick and high return. But as a matter of fact foreign investment is falling off compared to the lush 1940's. I met a Chicago industrialist who said recently, "I wouldn't touch South America with a ten-foot pole. They squeeze you dry, then chuck you out."

* Our organization has not, of course, tested all best-sellers. Therefore, this statement is an opinion. It is based on tests of many scores of books that have sold widely. Individual differences being what they are, I would not be surprised to find a best-selling book that tests as hard reading (above twelfth-grade level). But I haven't found one yet. If you run across one I'd like to hear about it. [After this footnote appeared in the 1952 edition, a Christian Science reader wrote, "I would like to ask about *Science and Health* by Mary Baker Eddy. Although it has sold millions of copies, some of the language seems to me complex." We drew the book from the library and tested it, anticipating an exception. On the contrary. Although tests showed some passages to be rather heavy reading, the average for the book was 11, still within the easy-reading range. Most of the book has a readable, vigorous style.]

Gunther uses a number of big words and a great variety of sentence structure. Some sentences are quite complex. Possibly you would consider this passage rather heavy reading. It is, compared to the Steinbeck quote. But compared to the prose most of us are expected to read each day it is as clear as spring water.

Compare, for instance, the report from *The New York Times* that appears below.

Try reading only the italicized words. Each is an abstract term which brings only a vague picture, if any, to the mind. There are 24 such abstract words per 100 in this piece. No reader can wade through such foggy words and come out with clear understanding. There are other faults in this story, but its abstraction is probably the worst. No one could be sure of the precise meaning of the author, and more facts would be necessary before it could be written in concrete and readable fashion.

LONDON, Dec. 8.—The long-range foreign *policy* of the present British *government* desires not only to foster *restoration* of world *peace* and *economic stability* in *cooperation* with the United States but *eventually,* by *establishment* of a firmly based Socialist *system* here, to make of Britain a bridge between *capitalistic* America and the Communist Soviet belt which might tend to facilitate *global understanding.*

That these are *eventual aspirations* of this *government,* this correspondent is in a *position* to state authoritatively. Naturally at present Britain, like most other *powers,* finds itself devoting more *attention* to the shorter range *tactical aspects* of such *objectives* than long-range *strategical aspects* because of the *exigencies* of the chaotic world *situation.* But the *fundamental hopes* remain.

But it is usually possible to wring the fog from a complex passage quite quickly. Some sentences from materials of our business clients follow. To the right are "translations":

Hard Reading
for College Gradutes

Consumer elements are continuing to stress the fundamental necessity of a stabilization of the price structure at a lower level than at present.

Easy Reading for Most People

Consumers keep saying prices must go down and stay down.

* * *

The finance director related that substantial economies are being effected in his division through increasing the time interval between distributions of data-eliciting forms to employing business entities.

The finance director said his division is saving money by sending fewer questionnaires to employers.

* * *

The establishment of a uniform level of freight rates on wool no higher in relation to distances to Southern consuming points than those to Eastern and New England consuming points is necessary in order to avoid imposition against Southern consumers of an added disadvantage of higher level rates over and above the normal disadvantage attributable to their greater distance from source of this raw material.

If freight rates on wool are higher in the South than in the East and New England, the Southern consumer will have a double handicap. For, even with the same rates, the Southerner pays a larger hauling charge because he is farther from the source of supply.

One of the puzzles of our business is how prose like that in the left-hand column above ever gets into print. Certainly no one ever approved it *as a reader.*

The veto of readers is a very healthy pressure. When it is exerted, reading material remains within the easy-reading range. The best-seller books just considered offer a good example. But, unfortunately, only a small portion of written material depends for its existence upon acceptance and absorption by the reader.

What business writes for the public is given away. The public may misunderstand it or drop it unread into the wastebasket. But such vetoes as these are not felt directly.

Most of the writing in newspapers also escapes the veto of the reader. Readership surveys show that a large portion of each paper goes unread. But newspapers continue to sell in increasing numbers. People buy them for the headlines, the comics, the sports pages, and the ads.

Trade and professional publications also escape the full force of reader veto. What they contain usually cannot be found elsewhere, and people buy them from necessity or duty. Professional journals are usually included as part of dues. Many business publications come free of charge to persons holding certain positions within a company. Your experience with such periodicals may be the same as mine. I find many articles in my own field go unread. I start them; if they prove tough going, I often lay them aside to read another time. Only by force of will am I able to return to them.

When writing does not depend directly on the reader for its existence, it tends to become needlessly complex. Some writers are pompous. Others write complexly because they *think* complexly and will not take the time or trouble to card out their thoughts before trying to communicate them. Almost any writer, if he can get away with it, will write less simply than readers prefer.

In the general magazine field, however, we find a very different situation. Here the direct veto of the reader is constantly expressed and its results are easy to see. If reading material goes above a certain level of complexity readers will not buy it. There is a rather clearly drawn line beyond which a magazine depending upon text cannot go and remain in circulation. We call this line the danger line of reading difficulty. It corresponds with the reading skill of high-school seniors (12 years of schooling). The Fog Index number is 12.

During our years of testing reading materials we have found magazines of general circulation very consistent in reading level, and all below the reading-difficulty danger line. Pulp magazines (*True Confessions* and *Modern Romances* are typical) require sixth- to seventh-grade reading skill. Women's magazines, such as *Ladies' Home Journal,* average 10; *McCall's* and *Cosmopolitan* average 9 or 10; *Reader's Digest,* 10; *Time* and *Newsweek* regularly average 11. Issues of *Harper's* and the *Atlantic Monthly* average no higher than 11 or 12.

You may consider pulp magazines moronic, but you would be completely in error to conclude that all material testing 6 or 7 is for dull or relaxed minds. For this reading level includes a large portion of classics, both of the past and present, as well as the Bible.

The greater the person's experience and intelligence the more he is likely to get from a piece of writing. There may be concepts in *True Confessions* and other "confession" magazines that are not clear to sixth-graders (or were not when I went to school). Still the language can be read by them and they can get the fact-to-fact sense of it.

Consider the writing of James Thurber as a further illustration of this point. Although his language is very simple in structure, Thurber wrote with great sophistication. A child can read *The Secret Life of Walter Mitty* and get the sentence-to-sentence meaning of it. But he would probably miss overtones which have made the story a classic.

Or take this brief sample from another Thurber story, *Draft Board Nights.* He is speaking here of a draftee who tried to avoid service by swallowing a watch. The concepts of human relationships that lie behind the words are far more complex than the words themselves:

"This man seems to tick," I said to him. . . . A few minutes later, Dr. Blythe Ballomy got around to the man and listened, but he didn't blink an eye; his grim expression never changed. "You have swallowed a watch, my man," he said crisply. The draftee reddened in embarrassment and uncertainty. "On *purpose?*" he asked. "That I can't say," the doctor told him and went on.

Harper's and the *Atlantic Monthly* are read almost exclusively by persons who have the reading ability of college graduates. But even these "class" magazines are more readable than you might think. Our testers have never found an issue which averaged more than 12—the level of senior in high-school reading skill. No magazine of general circulation that depends on text alone averages higher and remains on the newsstands.

The facts about magazine difficulty show that readers do not choose to tax themselves to their fullest reading ability. And, indeed, there is little reason why they should. Nearly any subject can be discussed in prose that does not go beyond mid-high-school level in complexity. In *Harper's* and the *Atlantic Monthly*, for instance, many very difficult subjects are treated in articles that require no more than high-school-freshman reading skill. The authors understand their subjects well enough to be able to treat them simply. Furthermore, they have the good sense to use simple language and thus conserve the energy of the reader so he will be able to grapple with the complex ideas involved.

Some of these magazines have crept up in reading difficulty during the years since the first edition of this book in 1952, as we have discussed in the Preface. The change has been slight, however. While Henry Luce held a firm hand at *Time*, the magazine tested 10 rather than 11. And the great growth of the *Reader's Digest* was during the years that it averaged 8 or 9 rather than 10.

Some may say the increase in complexity is justified because the educational level of the general public has increased. In 1940 the average education level was about nine years of schooling. Now more than half of all Americans twenty-five years or older have had at least twelve years of schooling.

To me, this increase in reading difficulty seems rather a relaxation of standards. Professional writers, as well as those who have to write in other professions, tend to indulge themselves. We have observed, for example, that the writing of magazine staff members is usually more complex than articles and short stories bought from outside writers. Magazines that depend heavily on pictures tend to get away with more complex writing. For a period, *Life* was more complexly written than *Time*. More recently, *Life* has added many readable features to its opening sections. Writing as complex as Hugh Hefner's in *Playboy* is seldom found in a popular magazine. Some factor other than writing style has contributed to the wide sale of *Playboy*!

Always remember that these grade-level figures of the Fog Index indicate reading level, not intelligence level.

The reading difficulty of *Fortune* and the picture magazines is an interesting study. *Fortune*'s text is above the danger line of reading difficulty. Still it has been successful. Many buy it, leaf through, look at the pictures, but do not finish the articles.

Some years ago, we worked with the staff of *Look* and surveyed issues of the magazine for them for several years thereafter. The first test showed *Look* to have a reading difficulty of 10—the same average as *Time*. *Life*'s average was still higher. Both were aimed at a mass audience and had succeeded in building circulations numbering in the millions in comparatively short time. They did it with pictures, of course, and the experience of other magazines indicates that the relatively difficult text of the two magazines was a handicap that was overcome only by pictures. The writers of these magazines, relieved of the discipline of the reader's veto, wrote more complex prose than readers prefer. The readability surveys gave *Look* writers a means of gauging their writing and they soon succeeded in maintaining an average of 8 without sacrificing variety in style.

Newspapers likewise need special discipline to keep their news-writing geared to the public reading pace. With the aid of readability research they have made great headway during the last few years in shifting from double to single talk. Research of another kind has centered editors' attention on the problem. In Gallup-type readership surveys, thousands have told what news they read. Their answers dishearten an editor who pays good money for the latest from Rangoon, Oslo, and Sydney. The comics get far more attention than most front-page stories.

Here's a typical report:

On June 8, 1944—3 days after D-Day in Europe—more than 90 per cent of those who picked up the *Argus-Leader* in Sioux Falls, South Dakota, read one or more comic strips. Far fewer read of the fighting in Normandy. Only 78 per cent of the men and 54 per cent of the women read the leading front-page story on the battle that followed the landing.

These figures were gathered by the Continuing Study of Newspaper Reading set up the American Newspaper Publishers Association. The *Argus-Leader* had a circulation of about 50,000.

The Continuing Study has now been discontinued. Comparative measures of readership during the war in Vietnam are lacking. Some argue that Americans have increased interest in the important news of the day. And news-service writing has indeed improved. Meanwhile, studies show that television news continues to be written more simply, directly, and more conversationally.

Professional worriers have often used readership reports to argue we are morons with taste for little more than gossip columns and "Little Orphan Annie." But readability research tells a different story. It suggests that most national and international news goes unread through no fault of the reader. The trouble lies, rather, in the writing. Most of it is too complex to be either easy reading or good prose.

And why are the comics so readable? If you are interested in reaching an audience you will not be above learning from the comics even though you may consider them moronic. One of the most successful business and financial editors is Sylvia Porter who writes a column syndicated in many papers. She told a group of editors at the American Press Institute at Columbia University:

"I'm a comic fan just like other people. When I pick up a paper I glance at the front page and then turn straight to the comics. That's why I know most financial pages are too difficult reading to reach the broad audience they should."

There are two chief reasons why the comics are so readable and so widely read. In the first place, they are written in the *spoken* language. A similar quality (more grammatical than some comics, of course) in your own writing will help get it read. Also note that the comics deal out subject matter in short "takes," an idea or two at a time. Most newspaper writing and business writing crowds too much into each sentence and paragraph. Readers like periods and white space.

Despite the speed with which newspapers are produced, staffs trained in readability principles are able to hold most of their copy within the easy-reading range. The following chart shows the change of reading level in news articles written by the staff of the Louisville *Courier Journal*:

Grade Reading Level		2-Day Test, 1946	2-Day Test, 1950
(Each "1"	17	1111111111	1
stands for	16	111111	1
one news	15	111111	11
story.)	14	11	111
Danger	13	111111	11111
Line	12	11111111111	111111
	11	11111111	111111
Easy-read-	10	1111111	111111111111111
ing Range of	9	111111111	1111111111111111111
Average U.S.	8	111111111	1111111111111111
Adult	7	1111111	1111111111111111111111
	6	1	1111
	Mean	12.0	9.4

In the first test, articles above the danger line amounted to more than one out of three. Now only about one out of ten stories in the *Courier Journal* is above the danger line. I suppose some news stories always will be. There is, for instance, the matter of taste, as in the case of a Philadelphia paper. The day after the first survey and lectures, only one story tested on the 17 level. It started like this:

"The incidence of illegitimate births in Philadelphia has increased twofold during the last twelve-month period, according to the report of . . . , etc."

The city editor, Frederic Shapiro, wrote the following note to Walter Lister, managing editor:

"Sorry but we can't follow Gunning's suggestions on this one. The simple, direct story is: 'There are twice as many bastards in Philadelphia this year as last.' "

The most spectacular and most successful conquest of newspaper fog has been made by the *Wall Street Journal*, a paper devoted chiefly to business news. Today it has one of the most readable front pages in America. The paper discusses the most difficult subjects in the news—finance, taxes, business trends, economics, and politics. But it does so in English as simple and readable as articles in popular magazines that sell by the millions.

The *Wall Street Journal* was not always so readable. Some years ago its columns were written in the typical jargon of commerce and were as heavy going as the stodgiest news-papers. Bernard Kilgore was chiefly responsible for the change. He said, "Even a Harvard economist is glad to have his time saved by good, clear English."

When Kilgore was in the San Francisco office of the *Journal*, he was asked to write a series of articles clarifying tough problems of finance. He wrote them in letter form, be-ginning, "Dear George."

Kenneth Hogate, late head of the *Journal*, liked the approach and the clear, crisp explanations that followed. He brought young Kilgore East to write a column; then, in 1940, gave him full charge of the paper with orders to chase fog.

"Write for the expert," Kilgore told his staff, "but write so the nonexpert can understand."

Jargon was cleared from the columns of the *Journal* and presently such leads as this began to appear on news articles:

"The country store is combing the cockleburs from its hair."

Here is a simple concrete introduction to a story about the census:

"The big, once-every-ten-years count of the nation's people is turning out to be a tougher, slower job than the counters thought it would be."

Our organization worked with Kilgore and his staff to help the *Journal* increase its readability. Afterward our tests showed the paper scored a readability average of 11.

The *Wall Street Journal* circulation has passed the million mark. Before he retired at fifty-seven, Kilgore attributed "about half" of the *Journal's* circulation increase to the gain in readability. This record has knocked through the ropes the "special audience" argument of those who like to write complexly.

Another example of a publication that turned failure into success through improved readability is the *Scientific American*. In business for more than one hundred years, the publication's circulation shriveled. The magazine was on the brink of bankruptcy. Gerard Piel, who had been science editor of *Life*, took charge. Difficult scientific subjects began at once to be handled in direct, craftsmanlike writing. The magazine was soon in the black and became an outstanding success.

Business and industry could learn much about reaching an audience with the written word from the columns of the *Wall Street Journal*. But the lesson is learned very slowly. Businesses, for instance, buy advertising space in the *Journal* at considerable expense. Then, at the side of readable news copy which averages 10, they will place advertising which is hard reading for college graduates—and expect it to compete. Here is a 58-word sentence from an ad in the *Journal* (where sentences average less than 20):

"Ever since 1921, when A ———— established complete District Organizations at Los Angeles, Oakland, and Seattle, Eastern firms in need of new West Coast facilities have saved time, money, and complications through the 2-Way Contact by the A ———— office on the West Coast nearest to their building site and the A ———— office nearest to their headquarters in the East."

People don't read prose of such complexity unless they have to. And they don't *have* to read ads—particularly when there is news in the neighboring columns that is within easy-reading range.

To sum up, then, what do people read?

Tests of best-selling books and popular magazines show that readers resist prose which requires more than high-school reading skill.

This is no condemnation of readers. For any material can be treated within this easy-reading range. This statement is buttressed by the fact that nearly every successful professional writer of this century has used a literary style with an average complexity within this range of 6 to 12.

On the other hand, much written material issued by business, industry, and newspapers continues to be above the danger line of reading difficulty. There is no good reason for this. If writers in these fields followed readability principles they could avoid unnecessary complexity in writing and the waste that it causes.

Readability Yardsticks

Readability yardsticks were unknown outside a limited group of educators in 1944 when we began our work with newspapers and business firms. Although some formulas were already more than 10 years old, all were too complicated and too hard for practical use.

Our aim was to develop one that:

One: would be easy to use

Two: would give reliable measurement

Three: would center a writer's attention on those factors that cause readers most difficulty.

This chapter describes such a yardstick, shows how to use it to test your own writing, and gives the background of its development.

But first a warning. Like all good inventions, readability yardsticks can cause harm in misuse. They are handy statistical tools to measure complexity in prose. They are useful to determine whether writing is gauged to its audience. *But they are not formulas for writing.* Anyone who sets out to pattern his writing to the few factors of a formula alone may find that he is turning out dull, standardized writing that fails to attract readers.

Writing remains an art governed by many principles. By no means can all factors that create interest and affect clarity be measured objectively. In our work we have always distinguished between readability *analysis* and readability *testing*. Testing consists of scoring the difficulty of prose by means of formulas. It deals with style factors that can be measured with no difference of opinion among testers. These factors are counted and weighed in a formula to figure grade levels with which you have already become familiar in earlier chapters.

Analysis combines testing with judgment on principles that cannot be measured by a yardstick. Judgment, to be worth much, must be based on training and experience. The Ten Principles that follow this chapter contain our boiled-down experience of work with thousands of writers. The best path toward good written communication is first to absorb the *principles* of clear and readable writing. After you have written, a *formula* is useful to check the complexity of your writing. The *yardstick* will tell you if you have geared your words to your intended audience.

Let us examine some factors of writing style that lend themselves to measurement and thus can be used in a yardstick. Anyone who has given the matter a few moments' thought will be able to guess some of the factors of writing style that affect reading difficulty. The long sentence is generally associated with hard reading. And it is obvious that the meaning of a passage will elude a reader if he is unfamiliar with its words. During your earliest trips to a library you perhaps chose books with a generous portion of quotation marks. You had already learned that dialogue tends to make easier and more interesting reading. And, in school, if you had a good English teacher, you also learned the importance of using active verbs to keep your writing lively.

The aim of readability research has been to single out those factors of writing style that can be measured, and to take the added, important step of finding out *to what degree* each affects reading difficulty.

To put it in other words: It has long been general knowledge that long sentences tend to make reading hard. But readability research has given us an answer to the question, "How long can sentences be on the average before they discourage or derail the reader?"

Readability research has given answers to a number of other questions such as these:

> How rich a mixture of long, complex, hard, or abstract words will readers tolerate?
>
> What percentages of active verbs, concrete words, words referring to people are found in writing that has proved its acceptance with large audiences?
>
> And, most important of all—at what level of sentence and word complexity do readers begin to balk? What, in other words, is the danger line of reading difficulty?

In 1935, in *What Makes a Book Readable,* William S. Gray and Bernice Leary of Chicago University examined the readability work done up until that time and extended it. They singled out 64 factors of writing style that could be objectively counted and which were suspected of having an effect on reading difficulty.

They tested 44 of these with a group of adults and found 20 had important relationship to reading ease. This extensive examination covered such minor items as the number of words beginning with "i." It was found that the more there are, the harder a piece of reading is apt to be. On the other hand, words beginning with "w," "h," and "b" occurred with comparative frequency in easy materials.

Despite such industry Gray and Leary failed to cover some factors that have proved since to be the best keys to reading difficulty. They ignored verbs. They gave up trying to measure abstraction objectively, and they also failed to develop a hard-word factor that was both a good index and easy to count.

The factors weighted by Gray and Leary break down into two categories (1) those that deal with sentence length and the relationships within sentences and (2) those that relate to word load.

Most important among the first are:

Average sentence length in words
Average sentence length in syllables
Number of sentences per paragraph
Number of simple sentences
Number of prepositional phrases

Most important as measures of word load were:

Number of easy words
Number of words not known to 90 per cent
of sixth-grade pupils
Percentage of different words
Percentage of words of more than one syllable
Percentage of monosyllables

Unfortunately, *What Makes a Book Readable* is not a readable book. It is long on scientific data, but short on art. The authors did not put their discoveries to work. As a result the information they gathered was little used for the next decade.

Our firm has found a number of additional devices helpful in testing writing and in guiding writers. They are discussed in detail in the Ten Principles that follow. Of those factors that can be counted objectively we have found the following seven most helpful:

Average sentence length in words
Percentage of simple sentences
Percentage of strong verb forms
Portion of familiar words
Portion of abstract words
Percentage of personal references
Percentage of long words

In an appendix you will find the Gettysburg Address analyzed for these seven.

The Winnetka formula, the Lorge formula, and several Gray-Leary yardsticks were the chief ones developed in the 1930s as testing methods. They called for the counting of from three to five factors, and charts and long equations were needed for scoring. To test a passage took considerably more time than to compose it in the first place. As a result they were not widely used.

Two later yardsticks, the Flesch formula and the Dale-Chall formula, showed that two-factor measurements based on sentence length and word load were equally reliable and far easier to use. Both these yardsticks are widely used today.

Of the two the Dale-Chall is easier to apply but it has the drawback of being based on a word list. Its word-load factor consists of a count of words outside Dr. Edgar Dale's list of 3,000 known to 80 per cent of fourth-graders (see Appendix). There is no suggestion that one limit himself to this list, but writers often leap to this conclusion and as a result resist the formula.

The first formula developed by Rudolf Flesch was based on three factors—sentence length, a count of references to people, and a count of prefixes and suffixes as a measure of word load. Although the formula was a good one, few seemed able to identify prefixes and suffixes with certainty. As a result Flesch shifted to the counting of *all* syllables. This made the testing far more tedious. Furthermore, it served less well to center a writer's attention on the true cause of difficulty—the long words of several syllables.

It is, however, possible to take advantage of readability research without smothering writing in arithmetic. Only two factors need be checked—the average sentence length plus a hard-word factor that can be counted as rapidly as you can skim a page.

The portion of words of three syllables or more is, we have

found, the best key to word load. Word length is closely related to both familiarity and to abstraction. Among the 1,000 words E. L. Thorndike, the noted educator, found to be used most often, only 36 are of more than two syllables. In Dale's list of 3,000 most familiar words, only one out of 25 is of more than three syllables. On the other hand, among words beyond the 20,000 most often used, two out of every three are of three syllables or more.

Let us turn to popular magazines to see how much complexity, in terms of these two factors, the general reader will put up with.

Tests over the years show that the average sentence length in successful pulp magazines has been kept between 12 and 15 words. The *Reader's Digest* average is consistently between 14 and 17, and that of *Time* 17 to 19. Our count of three-syllable words shows the following averages for the same publications: *True Confessions*, 3 per cent; *Reader's Digest*, 8 to 9 per cent; *Time*, 9 to 10 per cent.

Less regular tests of *Harper's*, the *Atlantic Monthly*, *Newsweek*, *Ladies' Home Journal*, *The Saturday Evening Post*, and *McCall's* indicate that these magazines also remain on constant levels of style complexity week after week, month after month, and year after year.

None has scored a sentence average of more than 22 words or a hard-word count of more than 12 per cent.

Don't make the mistake of confusing constant level of reading ease with sameness of writing style. Thousands of different writers have contributed to these magazines. Articles and stories reflect the personal style of each. There is great variety of word choice and sentence length. But the *average* sentence length and the general percentage of hard words remains nearly the same issue after issue of each publication mentioned above.

Each of these magazines is carefully edited and each depends chiefly upon text to attract readers. Each issue represents an editor's guess about the reading abilities and tastes of the public. The millions who buy the magazines are evidence that the guesses are good ones.

Here is a rough comparison of the circulation of magazines in the various groups together with averages for sentence length, percentages of hard words, and the Fog Index:

Group	Approximate Total Circulation	Average Sentence Length	Per Cent Hard Words	Total	Fog Index
Class	Less than 1 million	20	10	30	12
News	About 5 million	18	10	28	11
Reader's Digest	17 million	16	9	25	10
Slicks	More than 10 million	16	7	23	9
Pulps	About 20 million	15	4	19	7

The Fog Index checks closely with school-grade levels of reading difficulty. The link between the two is the McCall-Crabbs *Standard Test Lessons in Reading*. These have been given millions of students throughout the country. A student is asked to read a passage, then answer questions based on it to determine how well he has comprehended.

In reading the passages under test conditions, the student is giving them his full attention. The averages below are for those passages for which members of the grades, listed to the left, could give nine out of ten correct answers:

School Grade	Average Sentence Length	Per Cent Hard Words	Total
12	20	9	29
10	18	6	24
8	15	5	20
6	14	3	17

Compare the averages and school grades in this chart with the averages and Fog Index in the magazine chart. You will see that totals of the two factors have a regular and rather simple relationship to the grade levels. Multiplying the total of the two factors by .4 gives a close approximation of the grade levels and Fog Index. It is near enough to be satisfactory for practical use.

To find the Fog Index of a passage, then, take these three simple steps:

One: Jot down the number of words in successive sentences. If the piece is long, you may wish to take several samples of 100 words, spaced evenly through it. If you do, stop the sentence count with the sentence which ends nearest the 100-word total. Divide the total number of words in the passage by the number of sentences. This gives the average sentence length of the passage.

Two: Count the number of words of three syllables or more per 100 words. Don't count the words (1) that are proper names, (2) that are combinations of short easy words (like "bookkeeper" and "manpower"), (3) that are verb forms made three syllables by adding *-ed* or *-es* (like "created" or "trespasses"). This gives you the percentage of hard words in the passage.

Three: To get the Fog Index, total the two factors just counted and multiply by .4.

Let us apply this yardstick to a few sentences from *The Summing Up* by W. Somerset Maugham:

> I have never had much patience with the writers who claim from the reader an effort to *understand* their meaning. You have only to go to the great *philosophers* to see that it is *possible* to express with *lucidity* the most subtle *reflections*. You may find it *difficult* to *understand* the thought of Hume, and if you have no *philosophical* train-

ing its *implications* will doubtless escape you; but no one with any *education* at all can fail to *understand exactly* what the meaning of each sentence is. Few people have written English with more grace than Berkeley. There are two sorts of *obscurity* you will find in writers. One is due to *negligence* and the other to *willfulness.*

The number of words in the sentences of this passage is as follows: 20—23—11—13—20—10—11—10. (Note that the third sentence is actually three complete thoughts linked by a comma, in one instance, and a semicolon in the other. These should be counted as separate sentences.) The total number of words in the passage is 118. This figure divided by 8 (the number of sentences) gives the average sentence length —14.5 words.

The words of three syllables or more are italicized in the above passage. There are 15 of them, or 12.7 per cent.

Adding the average sentence length and percentage of polysyllables gives 27.2. And this multiplied by .4 results in the Fog Index of 10.9, about the level of *Harper's.*

Use this yardstick often as a quick check to see if your writing is in step with other writing that has proved easy to read and understand. If your copy tests 13 or more, you are beyond the danger line of reading difficulty. You are writing on the college level of complexity and your reader is likely to find it heavy going even though he is paying close attention. Copy with a Fog Index of 13 or more runs the danger of being ignored or misunderstood.

Use the yardstick as a guide after you have written, but not as a pattern before you write. Good writing must be alive; don't kill it with system.

No one can say for sure what writing will succeed. However, it is clear, in view of the work of successful writers, that anyone who writes with a Fog Index of more than 12 is putting his communication under a handicap and a needless handicap at that. For almost anything can be written within the easy-reading range.

The following table compares the Fog Index with reading levels by grade and by magazine.

	Fog Index	Reading Level By Grade	By Magazine
	17	College graduate	
	16	" senior	(No popular
	15	" junior	magazine
	14	" sophomore	this difficult.)
Danger Line	13	" freshman	
	12	High-school senior	*Atlantic Monthly* and *Harper's*
	11	" junior	*Time* and *Newsweek*
	10	" sophomore	*Reader's Digest*
Easy-	9	" freshman	*Saturday Evening Post*
reading	8	Eighth grade	*Ladies' Home Journal*
Range	7	Seventh "	*True Confessions* and *Modern Romances*
	6	Sixth "	Comics

Use the Fog Index as a check to see if your own writing is in step with that which has proved easy to read and understand. Remember that the writing you find in popular magazines is being tested every month or every week. Magazines have to be readable to sell and they have to sell in order to remain in business. Much of the writing done in business, in government, in laboratories, and in schools keeps on coming out whether it is readable or not. Some warning system is advisable to keep it from getting out of hand.

Also, the Fog Index can serve to soothe your conscience. Most of us have a pile of material we have laid aside to read later. We feel guilty for not getting at it. Usually a Fog Index check will show that this laid-aside matter is more complexly written than it should be or need be.

The Fog Index is of particular use in helping others. Teachers find it useful to objectify criticism. Or a supervisor in business often finds it difficult to criticize the writing of someone under him. The Fog Index, however, substitutes measurement for opinion.

Two experiences illustrate this point:

In working with a research group, one man submitted as a sample of his writing the laboratory "Manual for Records and Reports." He was the author. The manual contained good thought. I learned things from it. But the writing was heavy.

"Everyone in the laboratory should read this manual," I told him in our interview.

"Yes, they should but they don't. All the directions for writing letters, memos, and reports are in there, but they call me on the phone instead of reading the manual."

"I'm not surprised," I told him. "Are you aware that you are writing sentences half again as long as those in *Harper's,* the *Atlantic Monthly*, or the *Scientific American*?"

No one can take offense at such criticism. It is simply data, rather alarming data. This conversation opened the door for improvement. This man was quite capable in the use of the language. He had a good vocabulary and he could put a long sentence together without the thoughts running off the track. But he had never had to submit to the discipline of profes- sional writing craftsmanship. He had never had to sell his writing. Once confronted by the facts, he listened to a dis- cussion of principles of clear writing and put them to use.

Here is another example of how measurement drove home the point: The central character is a brilliant and successful surgeon. Since college days he had hoped to become a novelist also. He wrote almost daily after long hours at the hospital. At length he composed several hundred pages—the makings of a novel. A publisher offered him a contract, but kept asking for revisions.

One night he read me pages of it. "It is brilliant and beautiful, doctor," I told him. "But you will never get it published in that form. The mixture is too rich."

He was puzzled at my meaning. I asked, "Who is your favorite author?"

"Somerset Maugham." (Maugham, you may recall, set out to be a doctor.)

"I want you to make this experiment," I told him. "Take any page of Maugham and count the average sentence length and the number of long words. Then take any page of your material and make the same count. Call me tomorrow and let me know what you find out."

The next day he reported his sentences and word choice were far, far more complex than those used by Maugham. It was a complete surprise to him. But he reformed. Today he has four successful novels and several TV plays to his credit.

For your everyday writing, however, we can give you a substitute for the Fog Index.

When you write, most of your attention must be on *what* you are saying rather than *how* you are saying it. No one should do writing by arithmetic.

As you write, there are three simple things to do to take care of the *how* of your writing.

First, say to yourself "To whom am I writing? and what would I say?"

No one could pretend that he could write well if he didn't know *to whom* he was writing and *what* he wanted to say. No professional writer writes until he has given thought to these questions. Of course, a magazine writer doesn't know all who will read an article he writes for a magazine, but he does think of individuals he knows who, he hopes, will read the article, and thinks in terms of addressing them. Most of the errors of those writing in business would be cleared up if they earnestly answered those two questions.

Second, notice the number of lines you write. A typewritten line averages 10 to 12 words. If you write a normal script, the same is true of handwriting. By the time you have written two lines you have written about 20 words. If you haven't completed a sentence, worry about it. This does not mean that you should never write a three- or a four-line sentence. *It is not the consciously written long sentence that causes trouble, it is the unconsciously written long one.* If you *have* written a long sentence and are watching the number of lines, then you have a signal to drop in a short one or two to vary the sentence pattern and lower the average length.

Third, *question every long word you are tempted to use.* Make each pass through a sieve. Many will go through. There is room for the necessary long word if you get rid of those that are unnecessary. If you are one chemist writing to another chemist, "stoichiometrically" will go through the sieve. It is an awkward word to pronounce and to spell, but it takes the place of many short words if you are talking to one who knows chemistry. Through questioning the long word, however, you will find that many are not needed. Suppose you are tempted to write, "A disposition toward the encouragement of the exercise of clarity in composition has prompted publication and distribution of this volume." Pull up short. Instead, write something like this: "The aim of this book is to help you write clearly."

If you follow these three guides, the Fog Index will be likely to take care of itself.

Psychologists continue to search for more refined readability formulas. They look for new factors that may influence reading difficulty. They work out interesting methods of testing reading difficulty, such as the Cloze test. In this method, blanks are substituted for every fifth word. Then the readability of the material is judged on the accuracy with which a reader can substitute words for the blanks.

One professional writer who has done most interesting work in readability (or perhaps we should say hearability) is Dr. Irving Fang. For years he wrote television news reports and he became concerned about the complexity of much news writing.

He developed an Easy-Listening Formula (ELF), a gauge of listening comprehension. IBM underwrote his research fellowship and Dr. Fang put computers to work on counting words, sentence length, and half a dozen other factors of writing style.

His ELF is a simple device: "In any sentence, count each syllable above one per word." He found that Walter Cronkite and Huntley-Brinkley scripts have an easy-listening score of below 12. The *Christian Science Monitor*, the most readable newspaper he tested, also averaged below 12.

Possibly the warning system could be simplified still further. We already have a bell on the typewriter to signal the end of the line. If you type through three rings without ending a sentence, beware. Then, perhaps some one can devise another warning signal that will flash a red light whenever one writes a multisyllable word.

All the investigation by professors is for the good. But those of us who are professional writers well know that there are limitations to the measurement of readability. What is needed is a simple warning system. No formula will guarantee that you write well. Nonsense written simply is still nonsense. Furthermore, if you get caught writing simply, you have failed. The writing craftsman is one who obeys a severe discipline of simplicity. But he also introduces much variety of sentence length, sentence structure, and vocabulary into his writing. As a result the simplicity, though there, is not conspicuous. Writers need some easy way of keeping the desire to elaborate under control. Most professional writers know this.

You can't make rules about good writing, and you will not find rules in this book. Rules are substitutes for thought.

What you will find in this book are *principles*—guides to be applied with thought. I invite you to build the Ten Principles that follow into your own writing style for your own success and for clearer communication generally.

PART TWO

Ten Principles of Clear Writing

Principle One

Keep Sentences Short

"Why write short sentences? Great writers—Proust, Dickens, Thomas Wolfe—are known for their long ones. Why do you keep preaching these rules to us? Shakespeare never paid attention to rules."

This outburst came from a Washington writer. It was directed at an executive of a business publishing house. He had been trying to persuade writers for his numerous trade magazines to write with the simplicity which magazine readers prefer.

He had no trouble making a reply.

"You aren't Shakespeare and you aren't Thomas Wolfe," he wrote to the Washington man. "You are writing for engineers, bus company operators, and retail merchants—not for the ages.

"P.S. I admire the brisk, short-sentence style of your note. It was written with feeling. Such writing is the best and almost always employs the short sentence."

This reply was a good one, but it omits a telling argument: None of the writers mentioned by the Washington man used long sentences *on the average*. And it is the *average* sentence length that is an important criterion of readability.

Sentences *must* vary in length and in structure if the reader is to be saved from boredom. There should be *some* long sentences, but they should be balanced with short ones. Every good writer maintains such a balance although readers rarely notice it. The effort required in reading the long ones imbeds those in the memory. Short sentences are usually so easy to read that no one notes their structure.

Consider the prose of Thomas Wolfe. No American writer of this century has a wider reputation for writing long sentences. A typical Wolfian sentence will roll along like this (he is speaking of American optimism):

> This is the peculiar quality of the American soul, and it contributes largely to the strange enigma of our life, which is so incredibly mixed of harshness and of tenderness, of innocence and of crime, of loneliness and of good fellowship, of desolation and of exultant hope, of terror and of courage, of nameless fear and of soaring conviction, of brutal, empty, naked, bleak, corrosive ugliness, and of beauty so lovely and so overwhelming that the tongue is stopped by it, and the language for it has not yet been uttered.

A total of 91 words. Still the average of all sentences on the same page of *You Can't Go Home Again* is only 22 words. The pattern of their sentence length goes this way: 6—44—10—2—1—3—18—8—2—2—60—91—12—2—67.

We set our testers counting Wolfe's sentences at a time when a client in the newspaper field had asked us to analyze the writing of Thomas Stokes, the columnist. We found that Stoke's sentence length increased greatly between 1944 and 1949. Stokes did some of the best political writing to come out of the 1944 national convention. Then his sentence average was 20 words. But a sampling of his columns in 1949 showed that his average had climbed to 28 words. (The *Atlantic Monthly* average is 22 words.)

Stokes was an individualist and a Southerner. Thomas Wolfe was also an individualist and a Southerner. It was easy to point out to Stokes that Wolfe, who has a reputation for long sentences, has fewer readers than he deserves. But the testers supplied a much more pointed argument as they completed their counts on Wolfe's novels. Each showed a sentence average of less than 20 words!

I know of no author addressing a general audience today who averages much more than 20 words per sentence and still succeeds in getting published.

Sentences of the past, however, were much longer. Dr. L. A. Sherman was the first to spend much effort counting sentences. Working at the University of Nebraska in the 1890s he determined such prose averages as these for English writers: Milton, 60.80 words per sentence; Spenser, 49.82; Defoe, 68; Thomas More, 52; Dryden, 45.26.

Dr. Sherman maintained that, ever since the beginnings of English prose, sentences have been growing shorter. His figures show that from Elizabethan times to the turn of the twentieth century the average shrinkage in length of the literary sentence was from one-half to two-thirds. In the 1890s the average was about 20 words. Our counts show that it has now decreased still further.

Judging from Dr. Sherman's averages, today's business sentence, with an average of about 26 words, is geared to the early 1800s. It is 150 years behind the times and about ten words longer than material which gets itself widely read today. And by the same measure much legal prose is 300 years behind the times.

Averages are averages. It appears from our own investigation that in *all* ages there have been practical men with something to say who wrote comparatively simply. For instance, Dr. Sherman had difficulty cataloguing Francis Bacon. He was writing "modern" short sentences 350 years ago. This sampling averages 20 words per sentence:

> I cannot call riches better than the baggage of virtue. The
> Roman word is better, "impedimenta." For as the baggage
> is to an army so riches is to virtue. It cannot be spared nor
> left behind, but it hindreth the march; yea, and the care
> of it sometimes loseth or disturbeth the victory. Of great
> riches there is no real use, except it be in the distribution;
> the rest is but conceit. So saith Solomon, "Where much is,
> there are many to consume it; and what hath the owner but
> the sight of it with his eyes?"

Bacon's general average was 28 words per sentence, less
than half that of Milton, who did most of his writing during
the 50 years after Bacon died.

Here is Captain John Smith, man of action, describing in
1612 the "Naturall Inhabitants of Virginia." The following
passage, with a sentence average of 16 words per sentence, is
a fair sample of the piece:

> For fishing and hunting and warres they use much their
> bows and arrowes. They bring their bowes to the forme of
> ours by the scraping of a shell. Their arrowes are made,
> some of straight young sprigs which they head with bone
> some 2 or 3 inches long. These they use to shoot at squir-
> rels on trees. An other sort of arrowes they use made of
> reeds. These are peeced with wood, headed with splinters
> of christall or some sharpe stone, the spurres of a Turkey,
> or the bill of some bird. For his knife he hath the splinter
> of a reed to cut his feathers in forme. With this knife also,
> he will joint a Deare or any beast, shape his shooes, buskins,
> mantels, &c.

Walker Stone, as editor of the Scripps-Howard Newspaper
Alliance, once asked us to check the readability of Thomas
Paine, one of his favorites. We found that in general Paine's
writing tested above the danger line of reading difficulty. But
the strong passages, the ones for which we remember Paine,
are in simple direct prose. Take this passage, perhaps his best

known, from the opening of *The American Crisis*. (It tests 7th-grade reading level.)

> These are the times that try men's souls: The summer soldier and the sunshine patriot will in this crisis, shrink from service of his country; but he that stands it now, deserves the love and thanks of man and woman. Tyranny, like hell, is not easily conquered; yet we have this consolation with us, that the harder the conflict, the more glorious the triumph. What we obtain too cheap, we esteem too lightly;—'Tis dearness only that gives everything its value. Heaven knows how to put a proper price upon its goods; and it would be strange indeed, if so celestial an article as freedom should not be highly rated.

Bacon, Smith, Paine were men more interested in communicating facts and ideas than in *self*-expression. Naturally the two go hand in hand, for it is impossible to wrap an idea or fact in language without leaving your mark on it. But emphasis on self in expression accounts for a deal of the fog in poetry, music, painting, and business letters. Self-expression has its place (see Principle Ten). But when it gets in the way of the daily commerce of information it contributes to chaos. If you wish to get facts and ideas across, do as Bacon, Smith, and Paine have done in these passages: *shift the focus of attention from yourself to the readers*. Such a shift encourages short sentences, the kind normally used in face-to-face conversation.

The previous chapter drew a line between "principle" and "rule." It is important to keep this distinction in mind when applying "Keep sentences short." For many have followed this line of thought: Since nearly all reading material that wins a large audience has an average sentence length of less than 20 words, why not make a rule—"Keep your sentences under 20 words"?

Just this has happened in a number of offices. Early in my

consulting work I spoke before the American Society of Newspaper Editors in Washington, and although nearly every newspaper office in the country has been touched by readability training since, the idea was brand-new to nearly all editors at that time.

Several managing editors went home from that meeting and put signs on their staff bulletin boards: "No more sentences over 20 words." The talk these men had heard dealt generously with "principle," *average* sentence length," and "variety." But they missed them all. Communication is, indeed, difficult.

Others who have absorbed a modicum of readability research have made the mistake of latching upon *rules* as easy guarantees for clear writing. The *principle* of the short sentence *is* an important guide to clear writing, but it must be balanced against other principles of equal importance.

Any writer with the spark of life in him should react violently to a ceiling placed on sentence length. A quick way to upset such a rule is to start writing sentences like this:

"Ontogeny recapitulates phylogeny."

That is a short sentence—only three words. If short sentences are readable that one should be crystal clear. But of course, short sentences alone are not enough. Long sentences, in fact, are not even the *chief* cause of fog in writing. Fuzzy words are the greatest block to clarity. Some sentences can be very long without derailing the reader. Here, for example, is a sentence from *A Farewell to Arms* by Ernest Hemingway, leader of the modern school of simple, direct writing:

> There were troops on this road and motor trucks and mules with mountain guns and as we went down, keeping to the side, I could see the river far down below, the line of ties and rails running along it, the old bridge where the railroad crossed to the other side and across under the hill

beyond the river, the broken houses of the little town that was to be taken.

That sentence has 71 words. Still it is far clearer than the 3-word one above. Hemingway chooses words that are concrete and specific. One after another they flash pictures in your mind depending upon your experience with trucks, mountains, roads, rivers, rails, bridges, guns, broken houses, Italy, and war.

The three words of the short sentence are, on the other hand, highly abstract words of scientific shorthand. Each stands for several others that come closer to being picturable. In layman's language the sentence means something like this:

"As a plant or animal develops from a single cell to its full-grown state, it takes forms similar to those which have occurred during the evolution of its species." The idea is often stated more simply: "The growth of the individual repeats the history of the species."

Such shorthand is often justified. An engineer may say, "The ore can be beneficiated by flotation." This means, "The useful part of the ore can be divided from the waste material by means of a washing process which will float the good ore away from the waste." If the engineer is certain that "beneficiated" and "flotation" are familiar to members of his audience and mean the same to them as they do to him, he will be safe in using these words. But if there is doubt about the audience's understanding of the terms, the long way around will probably be the shortcut in the end.

In a recent book, a roundup of opinion about what makes the universe and us tick, one expert wrote this:

"We move denotively from alerted sense-perception, which is an elementary kind of knowledge, to conceptually located notables. But there must still be relevant evidential sense-data, though the relation is now very complicated."

Adam MacAdams, a book reviewer for the Dallas *Morning News*, became disgusted with such jargon, which would be fuzzy to nearly all readers. He tried a translation in one-syllable words:

"To name a thing and know it, the first step is to see it with our eyes, taste it with our tongue, feel it with our hands and so on. We first know it by sense through the nerves of sense. Then these nerves of eye, nose, ear, and hand, as the case may be, wake up our brains and we come to know the thing in our head and give it a name. True, it is a bit hard to keep up with just how we do all this, but it is clear that the eye to see and the ear to hear and the like, do have and must have a part in it."

Mr. MacAdams's version requires more words than the original. But they are worth the space, if the idea itself was worth statement in the first place.

When we began surveying publications and business writing we fully expected many sentences to expand as they were put into clearer English. Quite the opposite has proved true. In less than one instance out of twenty have we found it necessary to use more words to express a complicated idea more simply.

The reason is simple: The chief disease of our everyday language is not obscure words but *fat*. In nearly all our revisions for clarity, sentences grow shorter because unnecessary complexity is omitted.

Here is a sample sentence from a business report:

"Applications from four departments for financial assistance in development of training programs were voted approval by the board of directors."

Take off the fat and you have this:

"The directors granted four departments money for training programs."

Nine words do the work of 20. Seventeen syllables do the work of 39.

And here is a typical padded sentence from a newspaper:

"Newly elected officers of the Wigwam Lodge, 118, Mohawks, were officially put into office last night during installation exercises at the 16th annual banquet of the organization."

Sheared of unnecessary complexity, this becomes:

"New officers were installed at the 16th annual banquet of Wigwam Lodge, 118, Mohawks, last night."

Sixteen words do the work of 27.

The measurement of reading difficulty rests on two factors —words and the relationships between them. This chapter about short sentences has had considerable to say about word choice because lack of skill in selecting words often makes sentences longer than they should be or need be. However, the main reason why sentence length is a good measure of reading difficulty is that it measures relationships. The longer sentences are, the more words; the more words, the more relationships between them—and, consequently, the more effort for the reader.

There is one type of long sentence, however, in which relationships are so simple they give the reader little difficulty. Here is an example from a book for children, *Stuart Little*, by E. B. White. The sentence contains 107 words:

> In the loveliest town of all, where the houses were white and high and the elm trees were green and higher than the houses, where the front yards were wide and pleasant and the back yards were bushy and worth finding out about, where the streets sloped down to the stream and the stream flowed quietly under the bridge, where the lawns ended in orchards and the orchards ended in fields and the fields ended in pastures and the pastures climbed the hill and disappeared over the top toward the wonderful wide sky, in

> this loveliest of all towns Stuart stopped to get a drink of sarsaparilla.

For years Mr. White contributed to the "Talk of the Town" section of *The New Yorker*. He is one of the outstanding masters of English in America today. He is also an intelligent and sensitive person eager to reach his audience—either young or old. He would not have put this extremely long sentence in a child's book if it were not easy reading. And why is the sentence easy reading? Well, partly because the words are concrete and picturable, as they were in the Hemingway sentence already quoted. But so long a sentence would still be unreadable if the relationships between the words were not of the simplest nature. You will note that the description of the town is almost entirely a series of "where" clauses. It is a *list,* and in a list the units have similar value. Each bears about the same relationship to another and to the rest of the sentence. In testing readability we usually skip long sentences that are lists because most of them are easy reading.

The relationships within long sentences are usually more complicated. Marcel Proust enjoyed writing sentences like this:

> For with that eccentricity of the Guermantes, who, instead of conforming to the ways of society, used to modify them to suit their own personal habits (habits not, they thought, social, and deserving in consequence the abasement before them of that thing of no value, society—thus it was that Mme. de Marsantes had no regular "day," but was at home to her friends every morning between ten o'clock and noon), the Baron, reserving those hours for reading, hunting for old curiosities and so forth, paid calls only between four and six in the afternoon.

Respect is due a writer who can play out a long sentence like this and keep all relationships in order. This talent, however, was probably overemphasized in the schooling of most of us. We look back with awe upon certain authors we studied (and probably haven't returned to since).

If you are tempted to write sentences that would diagram like a floor plan of the Pentagon, take this advice: *Do not inflict such sentences on others until after you have written at least two successful books.* By that time you may have had enough practice to be able to sound a dozen notes in the same sentence and keep them all in harmony. Or, what is more probable, you will have overcome, by that time, the desire to show off in rhetoric.

In business some of the most complicated sentences appear in announcements sent employees about pension and insurance plans. See how long it takes you to straighten out the relationship of this 137-word sentence:

"As to such personnel who are within the scope of the 1932 Annuity Plan or who are eligible to equivalent benefits as outlined in the resolution adopted by Consolidated Company, (California) on July 24, 1944, and who have had no interruption in service since Dec. 31, 1933, the Annuities and Benefits Committee appointed under the 1932 Annuity Plan is authorized to grant outside the terms of any other annuity program of this company, such immediate or deferred annuities as may be necessary to accord the same recognition to service with the Consolidated (New York) group of companies as is accorded service with the Consolidated (California) group of companies, except that service with the Consolidated (New York) group of companies prior to the date of acquisition shall be credited on a 'continuous active service' basis."

It would be a rare employee who would be clear about this after half a dozen readings. A first step would be to break up the marathon sentence and reduce the complex relationships. The words ending "Dec. 31, 1933," could be placed in one sentence. The remainder could be broken into two sentences at the comma before "except." That would help, but the three remaining sentences would still be long and complex in relationships.

In actual practice an employee confronted with a sentence like this calls the pension office and asks, "What is this all about?" The member of the pension department, with a thorough understanding of the situation, is able to explain. How does he do it? He divides the explanation into small bites and gives the questioner one or two facts at a time. He shortens sentences and reduces relationships. In talking directly to people all of us long ago found this to be necessary.

As Chet Shaw, once editor of *Newsweek*, said, "Use periods. They take no more room than commas and less room than 'which's.' "

The pension sentence above shows a strong legal influence. Lawyers have an odd idea that it is safer to put all ideas in one sentence. Legal mazes result. In patent descriptions they reach the height of absurdity. Here is an example from the *Official Gazette* of the Patent Office. We'll let you in on a secret. The passage describes a zipper.

> A garment fastening device for the upper edge portion of a garment whereby smoothness and freedom from wrinkles are substantially attained, comprising the combination of a nether garment having an elongated substantially vertical opening and an attached belt forming the upper edge of said garment, said belt being peripherally effectively of greater extent than such garment and terminating at each end in free tabs arranged for overlapping relations in closing said opening, said opening being delineated in part at least by flexible flaps formed of the material of the garment each extending vertically from the lower end of the opening to termination vertically above and close to the lower edge of said belt peripherally spaced from the tab ends, two slide fastener parts including stringers seamed respectively inwardly of and behind the respec-

tive flaps and of a length such as to extend from the bottom of said opening upwardly across the upper terminations of the respective flaps to termination vertically below the upper edge of said belt and peripherally spaced from the respective tab ends, a locking slide for said parts arranged when in locked relation to be disposed vertically between the upper terminations of the flaps and the upper edge of the belt and transversely between the overlapping tabs, said belt and slide fastener parts so arranged that when the latter are locked the tabs conceal the locking element and adjacent portions of the slide fastener parts above the lower edge of the belt while the flaps conceal the slide fastener parts from a point just inside of the lower edge of the belt to the bottom of the opening, while the entire tensile strain of the belt is taken by said locked slide fasteners in the peripheral line of the belt.

With such sentences as these a lawyer can build a secure future. By writing sentences that only he can understand, he succeeds in being retained in order to interpret them later.

So much for monsters. Let us look at a more common variety of business prose. Here is a typical piece of copy from an accounting department. The item appeared in printed form. It was distributed to thousands of busy persons—average readers, whose thorough understanding of the passage was of great importance to the company. The message contains two sentences that average 54 words in length. Its Fog Index is 17 plus:

Account or "code" numbers are designated for each controlling account, for purposes of identification and reference, and both the titles of the accounts and the relative code numbers should be used in the official books of accounts. In cases where an affiliated company now has in use an effective code number plan and it will not be expedient, for its own purposes, to adopt the code numbers designated herein, it is recommended that on the general ledger sheets, which should bear the account titles set forth in the accompanying chart, there be recorded the relative code numbers under both the affiliated company's plan and the plan herein outlined.

This passage requires about a half minute's reading time for the average person. And its complexity is such that it would require a rereading from most of us. The following revision saves one word out of three and brings the reading level down to that of popular magazines. Changes like this can save a company thousands of dollars that are now lost in wasted time and in the mistakes that often result from misunderstanding:

"Each controlling account has a code number for use in official books, along with the account title. An affiliated company may have a code number plan which, for purposes of its own, it may not wish to drop. If so, it is recommended that ledger sheets with account titles found in the accompanying chart bear both the code number noted under the affiliated company's plan and the one suggested here."

To summarize: What are some practical methods of keeping sentences short?

First, bear in mind that any long sentence can be broken up. And often you can save words by doing so.

When we did the first readability survey years ago for the United Press we found nearly all bulletins sent out over their wires were knit into single sentences. This would be typical:

"General Dwight D. Eisenhower's Allied battle team broke the Albert Canal line today and closed on Liège in advances that carried to within 25 miles of the German frontier at three points along the 200-mile assault front as the Germans stiffened along the whole front before the Siegfried Line and the Rhine."

I asked those in charge of United Press news writing why bulletins were always written in one sentence and it was explained that this was for condensation. It was somewhat of a surprise to the U.P. when it was shown that 50-word bulletins could usually be broken into two or three sentences simply by cutting out connectives. The resulting bulletins were shorter by several words.

The bulletin above, for instance, could have been written in three sentences, thus:

"General Dwight D. Eisenhower's Allied battle team broke the Albert Canal line today. Advances closing on Liège carried within 25 miles of the German frontier at three points along the 200-mile assault front. Meanwhile the Germans stiffened along the whole front before the Siegfried Line and the Rhine."

This not only makes relationships easier for the reader, it also saves three words.

Occasionally the force of writing is improved by breaking a compound sentence in two so that the second sentence begins with "and" or "but." Should this strike you as a novelty, reread Genesis. The majority of its verses begin with one or the other of these two words.

Aside from breaking up long sentences, be sure that each word in every sentence carries its weight. Throw out words that are not needed, and where one word will do the work of two or three, use that. Avoid using words that don't say anything and avoid saying the same thing twice as a research engineer did in this sentence:

"Experiments initiated to determine when corrosion began showed that the metal corroded upon contact with the saline solution."

All he needed to say was:

"Experiments showed the metal started to corrode when it touched the saline solution."

We have already mentioned, at the end of the chapter on Readability Yardsticks, an easy way to control sentence length: Simply notice the number of lines you write. A type-written line, or a line in average handwriting, averages 10 or 12 words. Vary the length of sentences, but worry a little about those that run more than two lines.

Those who dictate to a stenographer can use the same method of checking sentence length when the typed copy is laid before them. Centering attention on sentence length for a few days is usually enough to cure the marathon-sentence habit.

Principle Two

Prefer the Simple to the Complex

Mark Twain, a complex man who knew how to write simply, supplies the texts for this chapter.

In a letter to a young friend Twain wrote:

"I notice that you use plain, simple language, short words, and brief sentences. That is the way to write English. It is the modern way and the best way. Stick to it."

Another time he put the same idea less solemnly:

"I never write 'metropolis' for seven cents when I can get the same price for 'city.' "

A third statement should be balanced against these—for it is equally important. Twain also wrote:

"The difference between the right word and the almost right is the difference between lightning and the lightning bug."

To sum up: If the *right* word is a big word go ahead and use it. But if a shorter word does the job, use that.

Note that in stating Principle Two we use the word "prefer." The principle does not outlaw the use of a complex form. You need *both* simple and complex forms for clear expression. At times the complex form is best. But, if in *your* preferences, you use as good judgment as Mark Twain and other successful writers, you will give the simple forms more than an even break.

The "prefer," by the way, is borrowed from H. W. Fowler, an Englishman whose good sense and good humor are reflected in *Modern English Usage*, a helpful book to keep beside your dictionary. Fowler, together with his brother, wrote another book, *The King's English*. It begins with this boiled-down advice:

> Anyone who wishes to become a good writer should endeavor, before he allows himself to be tempted by the more showy qualities, to be direct, simple, brief, vigorous, and lucid.
>
> This general principle may be translated into practical rules in the domain of vocabulary as follows:
> Prefer the familiar word to the far-fetched.
> Prefer the concrete word to the abstract.
> Prefer the single word to the circumlocution.
> Prefer the short word to the long.
> Prefer the Saxon word to the Romance.

Great teachers of English have always preached simplicity. But no one has made the sermon more concise than this.

Of all principles discussed in this book, the warning against complexity is the one most violated. Nearly anyone facing either a sheet of blank paper or a stenographer with poised pencil begins to put on airs. The youngster with literary ambitions cannot resist the gingerbread of four-syllable words. The businessman dictates three words where one would do. He mats his sentences with participles and subjunctives he would never use over a long-distance phone, or in talking face-to-face.

Without excusing this complexity we can understand why it occurs. We are all up to our chins in details. Unsorted facts multiply like fleas in August and are even more difficult to keep under thumb. Each day brings a thousand new concepts, objects, processes, and materials. Meanwhile names grow longer—radiological warfare, psychosomatic medicine, beneficiation, xerography, deescalation, pseudohallucinogens. We are supposed to know them all. As if names for the new were not enough, longer names are found also for the old. What was a hairdresser yesterday is a cosmetologist today.

The faster the world moves the more complicated it becomes. And, it is likely to burst like a skyrocket one day—if we don't use our heads.

So it is good to be reminded from time to time what the head is for. The purpose of the head and its mysterious contents is to draw order from chaos—to draw the simple from the complex.

The universe is complex. Knowledge of it is complex. Language is complex (and headed for more complexity). But the struggle of the individual human mind must be in the other direction. Its reason for being is to find the law and pattern that underlie the complexity. You may call this "meaning" if you like.

If you wish to inform another of facts and ideas, put your mind to the hard work of ordering them. Bring them into focus. Resist the mischief of making what you have to say even more complex in the telling.

Distillation of the complex into the simple can be seen in the work of a scientist. We know the names Newton, Darwin, Pasteur, Einstein because these men drew simple truths from the multiplicity that surrounds us. Thus the complex relations of movement and energy in the middle of matter itself settles down to the simple formula: $E = Mc^2$.

The craft of the poets has a similar goal. Many of the moderns are up Fog Alley at the moment. Temporarily, let us hope, for a tablet of thought such as this can make more point than a whole novel:

"Fortune, men say, doth give too much to many,
But yet she never gave enough to any."

Because that reduces a wealth of detail to simple statement, it is as fresh as when John Harington wrote it in about 1600.

If you attend professional meetings you know which men are most likely to speak clearly. Is it those who know most or those who know least? You have heard the engineers, doctors, or teachers on the lower rungs of their profession. They read papers burdened with heavy words and complicated language. The aim is to be impressive. But the effect is soporific. Then the man at the top of the profession speaks. The ideas he has to communicate are probably more complicated than those that have been delivered before him. But his talk has the clarity of logic and the simplicity of one who knows what he is saying.

While working with the staff of the *Wall Street Journal*, I asked Sidney Self how he managed to write so clearly of scientific discoveries.

"I go to the man at the top," he answered. "The head research engineer can always put the matter simply. Usually it is a waste of time to talk to the laboratory helpers. They are lost in details."

Simplicity is widely praised but narrowly practiced. Directness, thrift in words, brevity—everyone speaks well of them. No one boasts that he is windy and wordy. It would be as rare as finding a politician who advertised himself as reactionary. In our world today almost everyone wants to be known as a "progressive." And there is no sure measure for that term.

But there is a measure for fog found in writing—the readability yardstick. It is a particularly useful tool because so much complex writing is produced by those who believe themselves to be writing simply.

Some have no idea that they have the bad habit of stringing syllables together like beads. They consistently write "utilization" when they could just as well write "use." They write "modification" again and again when the short word "change" would do. "Initial," "optimum," and similar words are overworked while simple, crisp words like "first" and "best" are neglected.

We found a typical example of this blindness to complexity in working with hundreds of engineers at a large research organization. In nearly all reports certain long words were overworked—"encounter," "demonstrate," "objective." Time and again I asked authors of the reports why they did not prefer shorter synonyms such as "meet," "show," and "aim."

The typical reply was, "I prefer short words, but now and then you have to use longer ones—as a change." But counting showed that "encounter," "demonstrate," and "objective" outnumbered their shorter substitutes ten to one.

Unconscious use of complexity is hard to overcome. Roots of the fault are sunk deep in habit and custom.

Maury Maverick of Texas gave one interesting explanation for complex writing. Maverick, you will recall, invented the term "gobbledygook" to describe the language of Washington.

His theory was that bureaucrats, snug in their jobs, used fog to avoid action. Through circumlocution and abstraction they managed to put themselves on record without causing anything to happen. There are many persons in the top and lower drawers of bureaus both in government and business who have a distaste for the commotion caused by events taking place. They prefer a peace which doesn't shake the status quo. Better to approach the problem indirectly. If you follow Washington prose you know what I mean.

You know, for instance, that a bureau never "works." Nothing so simple. A bureau busies itself "maintaining operations." And rarely is this done by means one can lay a finger on. A bureau maintains operations through its "facilities." The facilities, in turn, are not simply "used"; they are "utilized to their maximum potential."

Each bureau worker must "follow established methods of procedure." But if he fails to do so he is not fired. He may be in danger, however, for "his immediate superior will use his broad discretionary powers to initiate dismissal action."

Gobbledygook crops up in other fields aside from public office. It is the language of caution and do-nothing. The language of leadership is something sharply different. Words that make us act must be sharp and clear. They must hit so close home that they sting or jolt us into action.

We expect our schools to promote and protect democracy. We depend upon them to stave off the divide-and-conquer tactics of dictators.

A leader among schoolmen might say:

"Schools must fight race hatred. They can do it by teaching respect for all cultures and by bringing to light what is at the root of one group's dislike for another."

But here is the way this idea was actually stated in a booklet prepared by a national committee of teachers of the social sciences:

> Racist thinking and scapegoating, the fomenting of divided loyalties, the accepting of stereotypes about supposed hereditary superiorities of groups, are consonant neither with our democratic way of life nor with the scientific findings of our anthropologists and psychologists. As part of a

societal attack on the economic and psychological roots of intergroup hostility, intercultural education in the schools can make a contribution.

What was the object of the committee, do you judge? To get things done, or to put itself safely on record, at the same time being careful to disturb no one?

For expression and variety, compound and complex sentences are needed. But too much of the writing of daily commerce and journalism is made up almost entirely of such sentences. Writing that succeeds, on the other hand, has a generous mixture of simple direct sentences. In popular material which is easy reading about half the sentences are simple in form.

Here is a simple sentence:

"Records at Washington, D.C., show an increase of three degrees in the mean annual temperatures during the last hundred years."

Here is an example of a complex one that is not too hard reading:

"In your car, after the spark ignites the vaporized gasoline, it takes the 200th part of a second for the flame front to cross the combustion chambers and either burn the fuel evenly or cause a knock."

Here is one from a corporation report in which complexity is likely to throw the reader:

"Disequilibrium may be said to exist when there is a large and persistent deficit in the combined current and normal capital accounts resulting in abnormally large short term capital flows so that a high level of economic activity in the country proves to be incompatible with equilibrium in the balance of payments in the absence of exchange controls."

So long as a writer obeys Principle One and keeps his sentences short, the complexity of sentences will give little trouble, for it is the long ones that are complicated. Furthermore, the breaking up of sentences has a valuable by-product. As one writes shorter sentences he usually writes shorter words also.

This is not surprising. As you make an effort to keep your sentences short you tend to become more conversational. And when you are conversational you avoid long, bundlesome words.

This linkage of short words and short sentences is the reason the short-sentence principle is stated first. However, if *one* factor of fog is to be singled out as most important, that factor is word choice.

The day-to-day language of commerce and journalism suffers more from many-syllabled words of fuzzy meaning than it does from long sentences. The average sentence of business writing is only about 50 per cent longer, on the average, than writing which sells in best-selling books and magazines. But the load of long words is often four or five times as great.

The mixtures of words of three syllables or more in best-sellers is comparatively lean. Here are a few averages:

Best-seller	Percentage
Gone with the Wind	4.96
Oliver Twist	5.97
Ben-Hur	5.69
Ivanhoe	6.86

Much of the business writing that comes to our office for testing is weighed down with from 20 to 30 per cent of polysyllables—most of which are unnecessary. At the left below is but one sentence from a committee report which had 25 per cent of words of three syllables or more. The version to the right says the same thing and is completely free of verbal clinkers:

Fog Index 17 plus
25% POLYSYLLABLES

If management continues to defer maintenance operations through failure to supply sufficient funds to make repairs as they naturally become necessary from time to time, the operating efficiency of the plant will be considerably lowered and, as a direct result, major construction tasks will then become imperative.

Fog Index 7
0% POLYSYLLABLES

If those in charge fail to provide a *little* money from time to time for repairs, the plant will become run down. At length it will cost a *lot* of money to put it in shape.

Jargons of professions and business are saturated with complex words, and once a person gets the jargon habit it holds him fast like a chronic disease.

An engineer in the grip of this malady wrote repeatedly of the "*unavailability* of crude rubber during the war." He was greatly relieved to have the one-syllable word "lack" offered him as a spare for the seven-syllable "unavailability."

Each time a writer in the critical stage of the jargon habit reaches for a word, he comes back with a long one. The editor of a business column who had it bad used to write sentences like this:

"The bureau has accumulated statistics regarding the number of new installations currently under construction."

Not one of those words is unfamiliar. But many of them are long, dull, tired, and dim in outline. After the "cure" the same man wrote the same sentence like this:

"The bureau has gathered figures on the number of plants now being built."

He saved his readers eye fatigue with only 19 syllables instead of 32. And he saved himself trouble by hitting the typewriter only 71 times instead of 106.

Long, woolly words do to good prose what rolls of fat do

to a girl in a bathing suit. If you wish to keep your writing trim and attractive, keep your mixture of polysyllables lean. And how is it done? The method is simple: Question every word of three syllables or more that you are tempted to use. Ask yourself, "Is there a simpler word I can use?" "Can I recast my sentence in simpler form?" After thus grilling yourself you will leave a certain number of long words. But you can be fairly sure those will carry their weight. The long words that cause mischief are the ones that creep into your copy when your guard is down.

In the Appendix of this book is a new type of synonym list which suggests the short word for the long. Many long words are overworked and need a rest. Try to give short ones more than an even break.

Principle Three

Prefer the Familiar Word

This chapter deals with word choice. It is presented as answers to the chief questions asked about vocabulary in our Clear Writing Seminars. The questions and answers follow:

How many words do I need?

Because this book talks of simplicity, there is danger some will take it as suggesting that writers be limited to words of one or two syllables. Straight off let us be clear about this.

How many words do you need? The answer is:

You need all the words you can master.

You can perhaps get along with 5,000. But if you aim to succeed in this complicated society you will be better off with 30,000.

You need a large vocabulary so that the precise word will be at hand when you require it. Men and women at the top in business and professions command more words than those under them.

Tests show that vocabulary size is linked closely with success and with intelligence. But this does not mean that it is intelligent to use a big word when a little one will do. The intelligent man (provided he has strength of character as well)

uses his large vocabulary only to give clear, exact meaning—
never to show off.

There was a time when a flow of polysyllables was effective
in influencing others. America was younger then. The yokel
element that could be hypnotized by long difficult words was
larger. But general education has had at least one good effect
in America. The person who showers big words on his listeners is now generally disregarded as a show-off or laughed at as
a clown.

A person who earnestly wishes to communicate facts and
ideas to others uses his big words sparingly. He does his best
to keep many thousands of words at his command. But he does
not make the mixture of big ones too rich. He does not let
them impede his meaning.

The short words are mostly concrete. They stand for places,
persons, objects, acts. The long words are more often abstract,
dealing with qualities of and relationships between concrete
terms. Long, abstract words often bundle together many concepts and, because of this, they are great timesavers—a shorthand of the mind. You need thousands of these complex abstract words. You need them to *think* with.

But thinking is only the first step in communication. Big
words help you organize your thought. But in putting your
message across you must relate your thoughts to the other
fellow's experience. The short, easy words that are familiar
to everyone do this job best.

If your reader doesn't understand the words you use, his
attention will go elsewhere. If he *mis*understands the words
you use, he may do what you least expect.

Yes, you need a large vocabulary, but to communicate
clearly you must discipline yourself in its use.

Aesop Glim, the advertising writer, puts it very well:

"Big men use little words; little men use big words."

How many English words are there?

The new *Webster's Unabridged Dictionary* has more than half a million entries. Still the dictionary by no means covers the language.

In the first place it cannot keep pace with it. There is a constant stream of technical terms, slang terms, and foreign words pouring into everyday speech.

Within recent years the word "creep," for instance, has been given two meanings you will find in only the newer dictionaries. In a slang sense a "creep" is an obnoxious person, the sort who would make your flesh crawl. To an aircraft designer "creep" is a property of a metal, the amount it will stretch when weight is hung on it.

Craftsmen and technicians are constantly making up terms to name new articles and operations. "Laser" and even "maser" are in the new dictionaries, but "fortran," constantly used by computer operators, hasn't yet made it. "Psychedelic," although it is in wide use and constantly bobs up in the newspapers, may not be in your dictionary unless yours is a new one.

New words like this come too fast for the dictionaries even though new editions come out quite often.

Then, aside from the new words, there are others centuries old to which standard dictionaries have closed their eyes. These are the vulgar and improper words you don't print publicly unless you are a top-flight novelist.

Eric Partridge lists such outlawed terms of the language in his *Dictionary of Slang and Unconventional English*. It has 50,000 entries.

Dictionaries have grown at an astonishing rate during the last one hundred years. This is only partly the result of new words coming into the language, for the diligence of the word hunters is constantly bringing to light old words of rare and special use.

Noah Webster put 70,000 words in his first dictionary in 1828. This was 12,000 more than Dr. Samuel Johnson had found for the American edition of his dictionary.

By 1864 *Webster's* had swelled to 114,000 words. By 1890 it contained 175,000 and by 1909 a total of 400,000. A peak of more than 600,000 entries was reached in the last revisions of the *Second Edition* of the *Webster's Unabridged*. But in the 1965 *Third Edition* of *Webster's New International Dictionary* the wordmen gave up trying to cover the entire language. Although it includes some 100,000 new words or new meanings, the volume has about 100,000 fewer total entries. Many old words included before were dropped.

The vast majority of these words you will not meet in a lifetime.

How large a vocabulary do I have?

Whether a person's vocabulary grows or shrinks after he leaves high school depends upon the extent of his reading. The fact that you have come this far in this book, shows you have a more than passing interest in reading, writing, and language. It would be safe to predict on this evidence alone that you have at least 20,000 words at your command.

By means of the list of 100 words below, you can make a rough check on your vocabulary size. There are about 20,000 words in the English language that are used more often than any word on this list, according to Edward L. Thorndike and Irving Lorge, authors of *The Teachers Word Book of 30,000 Words*. Their book is based on a count of 18,500,000 words from a wide variety of written materials. It is a helpful book to anyone who wishes to expand his vocabulary with those words that have proved most useful generally.

Words in the following list are a spaced sampling from 10,000 words which appear less often than once per 1,000,000 written words but more often than once per 5,000,000. In other words, this list is from the 10,000 words that come next in the frequency list after the 20,000 you are most likely to know.

Check the number you could define or use in a sentence. The table will help you judge the number of words you know:

abrasive	doubloon	maelstrom	sampan
aegis	éclat	marinade	scraggy
alleviation	emblematical	melodramatic	shaveling
anise	equivocation	metamorphic	shelly
archenemy	exorcise	milliard	shillelagh
attribution	fascia	modicum	simulation
bambino	flabbergast	mossback	snuffle
beechen	forgather	nabob	spheroid
besprent	fructification	necromancer	stethoscope
bigamous	gaby	nonpareil	subservience
binomial	genital	offing	surrogate
buckram	gondolier	oubliette	tabard
calender	grunter	padrone	tannery
carom	hansom	participator	therapy
chaffer	herbivorous	perforation	tocsin
cloister	hornbeam	pickaback	trefoil
cochineal	hypotheses	plumbago	tyro
collusive	inadmissible	pottle	unchartered
complainant	indubitable	prioress	urbane
constitutionality	internationalist	psychiatry	vesicle
cosine	jamb	quiescent	waggle
daguerreotype	kapok	rearrangement	well-disposed
demagnetize	laminate	reimburse	wimple
devourer	leukocyte	revocation	yachting
disembowel	lodgment	rotund	zodiacal

Use this table to estimate the number of words you know:

Words You Know in Above List	Your Probable Vocabulary
100	50,000 or more
90	40,000
80	30,000
70	25,000
60	20,000
50	15,000
40	12,000
30	10,000

Here's a dictionary game you can play to get a still better idea of the number of words you know. Open a small dictionary at random and skim down a column to see how many of the words are familiar.

Say you start with a paper-backed *Merriam-Webster Pocket Dictionary*. Here are the words from a column of the page in the exact middle of the book:

Pickax, pickerel, picket, picking, pickle, pickpocket, pickup, picnic, picot, pictorial, picture, picturesque, pie, piebald.

All these are generally known with the possible exceptions of "picot" and "piebald." If you happen to know something of sewing, "picot" will be familiar, and you will know "piebald" if you have interest in horses.

This small dictionary contains 25,000 entries, and the average person who spends a portion of his time reading and writing will know 80 per cent or more of them.

Next pick up a typical desk dictionary. *Funk & Wagnalls College Standard Dictionary* contains 145,000 entries. *Webster's New College Dictionary* has more than 125,000; the *Thorndike-Barnhart*, 80,000. You are likely to be surprised by the large portion of unfamiliar words.

One day I was discussing vocabulary size with a professor of education at a large state university. He has what is often described as a "photographic memory." He regularly quotes full pages that he has read long ago, indicating that nearly anything he has read with attention remains printed on his memory. An ideal subject for the dictionary test.

We looked first at the pocket dictionary, turning to a column in the A's. It began like this:

Ambassador, amber, ambergris, ambidextrous, ambient, ambiguous, ambition, ambitious, amble, ambrosia, ambulance.

Nothing unfamiliar there unless you forget that "ambient" means "surrounding" or "encircling."

And, of course, the professor knew them all. But when we looked into the desk dictionary of 100,000 words the result was quite different. The corresponding column in the bigger dictionary runs:

Ambiguous, ambit, ambitious, amble, amblyopia, ambo, amboyna, ambrosia, ambrosial, ambry.

The professor was not certain of "amblyopia," "ambo," "amboyna," or "ambry."

But he recovered on the next word, "ambsace."

"I know that one," he cried. "It's 'snake-eyes,' a double ace in dice. You will find it on page 8 of Mary Johnston's *To Have and to Hold*. The full sentence is: 'If I throw ambsace,' I said, with a smile for my own caprice, 'curse me if I do not take Rolfe's advice.'"

On other pages the professor with the enviable memory had about the same batting average. He knew only a little more than half the words of the 100,000 in the desk dictionary although he retains nearly all words he comes across in his wide reading.

How large is the average man's vocabulary?

There is a surprising difference among experts in estimating the vocabulary of the average man. Some have said he gets along with 2,000 words. Others say he uses as many as 20,000. The confusion centers on two questions:

One: What is a word? ("Part" is entered four times in the unabridged dictionary. Twenty-nine different meanings are given. How many of these should be counted as separate words in one's vocabulary?)

Two: When does a man know a word? (Is "vagaries" in your vocabulary when you recognize it, when you can define it accurately, or when you make common use of it in speech?)

For this discussion we will consider a "word" as a separate entry in the dictionary. And we will say that a person knows a word if he is able to use it correctly in a sentence.

On this basis the average high-school student knows in the neighborhood of 10,000 to 15,000 words. The routine conversation of average people rarely goes beyond the 3,000 most familiar words.

What words are most familiar?

The most familiar words are ten short ones: "the, of, and, to, a, in, that, it, is, I." They make up one-quarter of all that is written and spoken in English.

The 50 words most often used make up 50 per cent of written English.

The 1,000 most common words turn up 80 per cent of the time and the 10,000 words most often used account for 98 per cent of all that's written.

Thorndike, Lorge, and their helpers at Columbia University, whose word book we mentioned, have shown us what words are used most often in English. In general, the words used most frequently are also the most familiar. The exceptions are words that are used quite often in speech but appear rather rarely in the printed language, the basis of the Thorndike and Lorge count. The familiar word "ouch," for example, turns up only about once per 1,000,000 words in print.

Most writers who have had wide experience with people as well as with words are able to judge which words will be familiar to their readers. But if you have difficulty in this you should study the *Thorndike Century Senior Dictionary*. After the definition of a word an italic number from 1 to 20 appears. A "1" indicates the word is within the 1,000 most frequently used. A "10" shows the word to be within the 10,000-to-11,000 level in frequency of use, and so on.

Edgar Dale has made another approach to checking familiar words. He asked fourth-graders to mark words they recognized, then made up a list of 3,000 words familiar to 80 per cent of fourth-graders. Presumably this would be a basic vocabulary familiar to all adults. The Dale list is printed in the back of this book.

If you set yourself the task you can discuss nearly anything within the range of these 3,000 words. But such strict discipline is not necessary. According to the Dale-Chall formula, material that has as many as one out of five words from outside the 3,000 will still test easy reading if sentence average is kept under 20 words.

The very familiar words, within the first few thousand most frequently used, are the basic fabric of all writing. But to a great extent it is the words outside these few thousands that give writing flavor, personal style, and special meaning. How far should you go in mixing in the less familiar words? That leads to the next question.

What mixture of hard words is likely to tire, bore, or derail a reader?

This is a key question. If you can learn to use less familiar words only when you can make them count, if you can keep the mixture of them from getting too rich, you will have mastered a basic skill of effective writing.

Time, one of the most successful publishing ventures of this century, has a taste for unusual words. It surprises *Time* readers to find out that only about one word per hundred in the magazine is outside the 10,000 words most frequently used.

Occasionally *Time* goes beyond the 20,000 words most often used in print. Here are examples from the "National Affairs" section of one issue (you probably can define them all): motivated, coalition, irrevocably, pollsters, litterateur, roistered, bonanza, cesspool. An ad in the same issue used that long-time favorite of theater editors in reviewing a girly show—"callipygian." (If it isn't familiar, you may enjoy looking it up.)

Let's analyze the mixture of big and little words in the Gettysburg Address. In this concise and beautiful piece of prose Lincoln used a number of words more complex than necessary. A copyreader hipped on simplification might have blue-penciled Lincoln this way:

> *Eighty-seven* — Fourscore and seven years ago our fathers brought forth on this continent *here* a new nation, conceived in liberty, and
> *born*
> *pledged* dedicated to the proposition that all men *belief* are created equal.
> Now we are engaged in a great civil *fighting* war, testing whether that nation, or any nation so conceived and so dedicated, *such* *last.* can long endure. We are met on a great battlefield of that war. We have come to *set aside* dedicate a portion of that field as a final

Of course, no one with any feeling for the language would make such changes. Each word Lincoln used was perfect for his purpose. The address is within the easy-reading range with a Fog Index of 10. The mixture of big words is not so rich that it would stall the reader. There are only 7 per cent of polysyllables and only two words out of 267 ("detract" and "nobly") are outside the 10,000 most frequently used.

There are many authors today, however, who would please more readers if someone did blue-pencil their copy. Here is E. M. Pooley, an outstanding editor of the Southwest, calling down an author:

> There are two kinds of books that make me a bit sore at their authors. In one the writer picks up a strange word and uses it over and over again; in the other there is a great collection of obscure and unusual words which send the reader looking for a dictionary.
>
> I have just finished one of the latter type. Time after time there are phrases like these:
>
> "The veteran orators of the Senate . . . masters of the flatulent phrase whose baroque fulminations tried the mnemonic patience of generations of American school boys. . . ."
>
> "Archaic Jeffersonian conception of parochial sovereignty. . . ."

Mr. Pooley set down a long list of words from the book that annoyed him—words such as these: congeries, draconian, inchoate, nexus, supposititious.

Now all these are good words, ones which might prove useful in any informed person's vocabulary. Perhaps they were all so familiar to the author that he did not realize that they might puzzle others. But there is a good chance they do, for all these words are rare. Not one occurs so often as once in 1,000,000 printed words. "Draconian," "nexus," and "supposititious," according to the Thorndike and Lorge studies, are outside the 30,000 words most frequently used. And "congeries" and "inchoate" are only a little more familiar.

If you are tempted to use such words, it is wise at least to consider substitutes which are more familiar. Here are some ladders of familiarity for these words. The higher the word is on the ladder the more likely it is to be over the heads of readers. (The figures stand for the thousand-level of each word's occurrence in English. For example "false 2" shows that "false" is within the first two thousand words most frequently used.)

congeries	25	cruel	2	undeveloped	11
aggregation	14	nexus	over 30	incomplete	10
collection	3	junction	15	just begun	2
heap	2	connection	3	supposititious	
pile	2	bond	3	over	30
mass	2	link	3	fradulent	12
draconian	over 30	inchoate	25	spurious	12
barbaric	9	embryonic	19	counterfeit	8
harsh	4	incipient	16	false	2
severe	2				

Isn't the use of big words good showmanship?

Yes, the occasional use of a big word is good showmanship. A good glittering long word, even though it is unfamiliar, may be the making of a piece of writing.

John S. Knight, the newspaper publisher, began one of his weekly "Notebook" columns with this sentence:

"The freakishly feeble Voice of America is taking a frightful beating from members of congress who have just discovered what a *facinorous* project it really is."

You will find "facinorous" in your dictionary if it is a big one. But it is familiar to very few. However, from the way it is used, the word would be unlikely either to derail or annoy a reader. Here is a ladder of familiarity of its synonyms. (This time the numbers indicate the number of times the word turns up per million words.)

facinorous	*very rare*	sinful	4
iniquitous	*rare*	sinister	6
atrocious	2	vicious	9
villainous	2	vile	14
disgraceful	3	foul	27
scandalous	3	wicked	36

Did showmanship justify the use of the unfamiliar word? Knight, a good judge, says yes.

Here is a piece of showmanship in words that has stuck in my mind since boyhood. In the mid-twenties G. K. Chesterton, the rotund Englishman of letters, came to the United States. An editorial writer of the New York *World* wrote to praise and welcome him, but he ended his editorial with a stinger. He said Chesterton was one of the great writers of the day but "he too often mistook his own *borborygmus* for the rumblings of the universe."

"Borborygmus" is a little-used medical term that is listed only in the largest dictionaries. But the person who takes the trouble to look it up is repaid. It means "rumbling of the bowels." Any copyreader who would have removed that word from the editorial should have been fired.

John L. Lewis, always a great showman, often thundered forth with long and rather unfamiliar words. But he rarely made the mistake of getting his mixture too rich. In fact, the power of his prose rests more heavily on blunt simplicity than on fancy words. Consider this caustic letter he released to the press when William Green, then head of the AF of L, refused to pool union money to back a steel strike:

> Dear Mr. Green: You have justified my judgment. I did not think you would do anything. You didn't. You rarely do. Unfortunately you follow invariably your well-known policy of anxious inertia. You cry aloud for labor peace and labor security, but seldom do anything to achieve it.
>
> I note that you are going to Europe with nine of your

associate executives. While there, doubtless you will adjust the European situation. When you adjust it satisfactorily and return to your own country, I may write you again.

At the moment I am too busy to continue a fruitless discussion.

Shouldn't a writer use some unusual words in order to educate people?

This sort of high-mindedness is quite contagious among writers. Not for a moment would I care to discourage it. Education is my work, too. But let us not use benevolence to excuse pomposity.

Let us ask: How do you educate? Do you do it by *hoping* your reader will go to the dictionary? Or do you rather educate by making the meaning of a new word emerge through the use that is made of it?

Let us use Philip Wylie as an example. Wylie's bitter criticism of all aspects of our society is evidence of his eagerness to educate. Wylie also poses as despising simplicity in writing. In one of his columns he said, in part:

> Most American "authors" have gulped the dogma of a recent school which insists upon one literary quality alone: Simplicity.
>
> Never use a big word where a little one will do, says this school. Keep your sentences short. Cut your adjectives to the bone. If you must have modifiers, use adverbs. And verbs are "better" than nouns.

A fine example of simple, direct writing, don't you think? The entire column, by the way, had a Fog Index of 9. Wylie may condemn simple writing, but he is not so foolhardy as to use any other kind. He wants an audience.

In this column, however, Wylie, trying to make his point,

did use a number of unusual words. His opening sentence read: "The editor of this feuilleton asked me to give him a 'short piece.' . . ."

"Feuilleton" may not be in your dictionary. It is a French word meaning "leaflet" or "newspaper." But the word does not derail the reader in the way Wylie uses it. The reader may not know the precise shadings of the word, but he has a good idea of its meaning, for he has an example in his hand.

Later in the same column Wylie makes some concessions, still using big words. "A plethora of adjectives," he says, "is like too much sugar in the tomato soup." "Plethora" shows up about once in 3,000,000 printed words. It is barely within the list of 30,000 words most frequently used. Many would be puzzled by it if it stood alone, but they would get as good or better idea of its meaning from Wylie's sentence than they would by going to the dictionary.

So long as you use a big word with precision you can educate without befogging.

Try to develop a keen sense for the right word. President Franklin Roosevelt showed such skill when he edited his address to Congress just after Pearl Harbor. His opening sentence originally began: "Yesterday, Dec. 7, 1941, a date that will live in world history. . . ."

As you can see in the exhibit of his papers at Hyde Park, he crossed out "world history" and wrote in its place "infamy" —"a date that will live in infamy." The phrase lives along with those simple but perfect word patterns Winston Churchill forged during World War II.

Another piece of editing was less effective, in our opinion. When Edgar J. Goodspeed wrote his "American" translation of the New Testament, he changed "Jesus wept" to "Jesus shed tears."

A final word of warning: If you do have a taste for big words, be certain you know their meaning. One engineer was preparing a proposal for a military contract involving many millions of dollars. He wished to say that through *duplication* of parts much money could be saved. But he wrote, "The economies effected in this proposal are accomplished through *duplicity*." Had not the editor caught that error it could have caused scandal.

Don't big words save many little words?

Yes, a big word can often do the job of scores of little words. A draftsman speaks of "perspective." Many words and a few demonstrations, perhaps, would be necessary to make the term clear to one who had never heard it. "Organic" combines a whole body of relationships for modern architects, and a quite different body of relationships for scientists. "Physiognomic" says a bookful to certain sociologists and psychologists. For a stock manipulator a "Bombay straddle" holds within two words a multiplex of complicated detail.

Such words are the tools of thought. But they should be used with caution if you wish to communicate with another. You will not transfer your message to your reader unless he interprets the word in about the same way you do. And such highly abstract terms often have meanings that are vague or have entirely different meanings for different people.

Educators have a special term for words that fail in this way. They caution against COIK, words that are Clear Only If Known.

Tell a schoolboy that the Pilgrims landed 128 years after Columbus discovered America and the date will be clear to him *provided* he knows America was discovered in 1492.

A newspaper editor tells the cub reporter to take a picture to the morgue. The direction will be clear to the boy only if he knows that "morgue" is a newspaperman's word for reference files.

Many of the less familiar words are perfectly clear to you. But are they clear to the person you are writing or talking to? In using big words for short cuts, don't trip into the pitfall of COIK.

Clichés are familiar, should a writer use them or avoid them?

Clichés are phrases that get scuffed and worn for the same reason old shoes do—they have been useful and they are comfortable. It takes no effort to slip into the old phrase.

When you say "his face was as round as an apple" or "love is blind," you are transmitting an idea to your audience. But the words are not so keen-edged today as they were 600 years ago when Geoffrey Chaucer was using them.

It is next to impossible to write without using clichés. But your writing will lack force if the clichés are too numerous. Learn to recognize them, and try to resist them. Each time you are tempted to use one put it through this filter. "Can I think of another phrase that will say the same thing but will be so fresh and so expressive that it, in turn, might become a cliché?"

Think what a triumph of wit for the person who first said, "I can't get a word in edgewise." But today the phrase is so dulled by use that we no longer appreciate the invention in it.

It takes courage to say the old thing in a new way. Suppose you, rather than James Russell Lowell, had been the first to say, "What is so rare as a day in June?" If one cared to be dull he could insist these words make little sense. But Lowell chanced them and they proved so right the phrase is now common coin of language.

In the course of everyday writing many clichés will go through your filter because you will not be able to find substitutes for them. But so long as you keep the filter working your writing will improve. It is the *unconscious* use of clichés that makes so much everyday writing lifeless.

Never strain yourself trying to avoid the clear comfortable words familiar to everyone.

According to Aulus Gellius, Julius Caesar advised all writers:

"Tamquam scopulum sic fugias inauditum atque insolens verbum."

Or, in more familiar words:

"Avoid a strange and unfamiliar word as you would a dangerous reef."

Principle Four

Avoid Unnecessary Words

The greater part of all business and journalistic writing is watered down with words that do not count. They tire the reader and dull his attention. In surveys for corporations we find letters that can be cut in half and still say the same thing. Here is a short example. The revision shows nearly half the original to be useless padding:

90 WORDS

This is to inform you that we have your order of April 23rd for four 6.50-16 black 4-ply Acme tires for which we thank you.

We regret to advise you that we are out of this size and hereby wish to advise you that we are now producing this tire only in the 15-inch air-cushion type. However, we do have the size you ordered in our Samson tire. Please advise whether you wish us to ship your order in the Samson tire.

Awaiting your favorable advice, I remain,

44 WORDS

Thanks for your April 23 order for four 6.50/16 black 4-ply Acme tires.

We are now producing these tires only in the 15-inch air-cushion, and have no stock of Acmes in the size you ordered.

May we have your permission to substitute Samson tires?

The mock lawyer is responsible for many surplus words in everyday writing. A clerk is given the job of drawing up a rule, or a committeeman sets about drafting a resolution. Neither turns his main effort to clear statement. Object No. I is to wrap the words in the awesome thunder of a lawgiver.

As a result simple orders are often written in twice the words they need be. Here is an example:

38 WORDS	17 WORDS
It is the responsibility of each and every department head to properly arrange the affairs of his organization in such manner that each salaried employee, including himself, will receive the full vacation to which he is duly entitled.	Each department head must see that he and each salaried employee under him gets his full vacation.

Below to the left, is a committee's imitation of legal language. The statement to the right not only saves words, it would get more attention and more action:

47 WORDS 24% POLYSYLLABLES	32 WORDS 10% POLYSYLLABLES
The committee charged, "A critical housing shortage continues to exist in an ever increasing and aggravated form because of the disinclination of the housing industry to adapt modern methods of production, excessive and unnecessary middleman charges and markups, and failure to make maximum use of available labor."	The committee charges, "An already critical housing shortage is growing worse because 1) builders refuse to use modern methods or make full use of available labor, and 2) middlemen charge too much.

Lawyers themselves often make the mistake of using this pseudolegal language when only ordinary prose is called for. Here at the left is a paragraph from a speech made by a corporation attorney. He used three words for two and twice the number of polysyllables he needed, as the revision at the right shows:

77 WORDS 14% POLYSYLLABLES	52 WORDS 6% POLYSYLLABLES
In order to protect the Laird Meadows water reserve, and in order to obtain the right to mine lead ore from the Laird Meadows property if a further investigation disclosed existence of lead ore in commercial quantities, the Ore Company decided to ascertain the names and whereabouts of the persons owning the mineral rights in the Laird Meadows property and to endeavor to acquire from such persons the right to mine lead ore from that property.	The Ore Company wanted to protect the Laird Meadows water reserve and it also wanted the right to mine lead ore there, if this proved worth while. So it was important to find out who owned the mineral rights and try to get from them the right to mine lead ore on the property.

Those who use such high-sounding words purposely are completely misguided. Whatever may be gained in awe is more than lost through diminished attention and understanding.

For the most part, however, unnecessary words are included unconsciously. There are many wordy old phrases that grow on business prose like moss on a boulder.

Some pretend to lead the reader from one idea to another. They resemble (and deserve the same fate as) those long strings of beads that used to hang in parlor doorways. They merely entangle the person who is trying to make his way from one point to another, and they have no place in a jet-propelled age.

Among such fat old phrases are "in connection with," "with regard to," and "with reference to." You will find that you can usually cross them out and substitute some short word such as "on," or "about."

Watch out also for unnecessary expressions of time such as "prior to the start of" instead of "before," and "up to the present time," which can usually be dropped.

Accountants have a habit of using "in the sum of" or "a total of" before almost any figure they mention. They say "a check for the sum of $300" instead of "a check for $300." None I have talked with has been able to explain this or defend it.

After the worn-out links are removed in the following two short sentences, 20 words do the work of 38. Note the italicized words that disappear in the revision:

It has been customary in most foreign markets to loan *sums* of money to dealers *for the reconstruction of existing outlets. Up to the present* the *total* amount loaned *for this purpose* is in the millions of dollars.	In most foreign markets we have lent money to dealers to rebuild retail stores. These loans total millions of dollars.

In the next one, tossing out unnecessary phrases and dropping the mock-legal tone saves one-third of the wordage:

59 WORDS	38 WORDS
This department has been requested to assemble certain information which is needed in connection with an atmospheric pollution problem which might arise from operation of the plant which is proposed for the Coalton area. In connection with this an attempt has been made to secure certain data relative to codes and similar rules regulating atmospheric pollution in the community.	This department has been asked to check on the atmospheric pollution problem that may arise if we build the Coalton area plant. We have tried to find out what regulations the community has made to keep air clean.

Worn phrases are a familiar clutter in letters—particularly at the beginning. Often they can be cut out without leaving the slightest scar:

We wish to bring to your attention the fact that our invoice . . .	Please note that our invoice . . .
We take this opportunity to advise you that we are now producing . . .	We are now producing . . .
Reference is made to your letter of Nov. 10 in which you asked . . .	On Nov. 10 you asked us . . .

There is no need to tell the other fellow what he already knows. "We have received your letter. . . ." That's obvious. Otherwise you wouldn't be answering.

Now and then I find a writer who has developed the use of unnecessary words as if it were a writing skill. This is the type who believes in padding. He will argue that when his superior asks for a report he expects 10 pages regardless of whether there is that much to say. This nonsense that a busy man measures words by their volume rather than by their sense is deeply ingrained in some subordinates. They are the ones who usually remain subordinate.

Here is a small sample from an engineer's report. It shows the technique by which a fact is spread thin over more than twice the necessary space:

47 WORDS	19 WORDS
The results obtained from the test indicated that two months' aging of the rubber had no apparent effect on its elastic properties. There was no significant change in the results obtained in the torsion test on the original rubber and on the rubber after two months' aging.	The torsion test showed that two months' aging of the rubber had no apparent effect on its elastic properties.

There are other types of padding born of ignorance or lack of clear thought. When one writes that a new mine is "easily accessible" he is saying the same thing twice because "accessible" means "easy of access." If you write the "job will be done by means of an agency" you show an ignorance of the meaning of "agency." It *is* a "means of" doing a job. You have said the same thing twice.

My favorite among such examples of word ignorance is "one of the most unique," a phrase often found in the social news. Since "unique" means "the only one of its kind," the phrase would equal "one of the most only one of its kind." Unique, indeed.

One plant executive who was having trouble getting the men under him to combine several operations issued an order that they were to "act at once to get the operations *consolidated together in one unity*." That is saying the same thing repeatedly within five words. Even the plea of emphasis does not justify it.

The personnel man who wrote the paragraph to the left below said the same thing twice because he didn't get his thought clear before he began to dictate:

52 WORDS	34 WORDS
To be sure you have gotten a chance to see each employee's card at the time he is certified, I would advise each of you to initial on the same line as the supervisor with your initial, so that you can definitely know whether or not you have had the card.	Make sure you have seen each employee's card at the time he is certified. A good way to keep check on this is to add your initials on the same line as the supervisor's.

Some have a habit of padding with "the." It is a short word and takes little room. But its constant repetition annoys a reader who is aware that "the," though a useful word when needed, is otherwise a nuisance.

Here is a single sentence from a school announcement. It contains one-third more words than needed, many of them excess "the's":

30 WORDS	20 WORDS
It is hoped that the parents of the children who attend the Macon school will insist that the children keep all of the appointments that will be given to them.	It is hoped parents of children who attend Macon school will insist that their children keep all appointments given them.

Newspaper writers are constanly reminded to avoid unnecessary words. The deskmen with their big soft pencils apply constant pressure for conciseness. In these days of costly newsprint and momentous events, space is always short.

On the other hand, newspapers are produced at high speed, and hasty thought often leads to poor organization and unnecessary words.

Here is a brief story from a metropolitan paper. In revising it from a very high fog level to an easy-reading level the word saving is 25 per cent.

Fog Index 16 104 WORDS	*Fog Index 10* 71 WORDS
The Veterans Administration yesterday outlined a new ruling for the handling of veterans' compensation applications for service-connected tuberculosis which have been rejected in the past.	Veterans who became 10 per cent disabled from tuberculosis within three years after their discharge can now claim aid as if their disease began in the service, the Veterans Administration states.
Under Public Law 573 which became effective June 23, a veteran who acquired at least a 10 per cent disability from tubercu-	This was not so before June 23 when Public Law 573 went into effect.

Fog Index 16
104 WORDS

Fog Index 10
71 WORDS

losis within three years after he was discharged can now file an application for compensation on the presumption that the disability had its origin while the veteran was in the service.

The new law applies to World War II veterans and to Spanish-American War veterans. World War I veterans were granted a comparable presumptive period several years ago.

The law applies to veterans of World War II and of the Spanish-American War. World War I veterans were granted the same aid several years ago.

We have preached to newspaper writers that the way to make haste is to take time to think first. One minute spent organizing a mass of details will save several minutes in its writing. Furthermore a few minutes spent in going over copy and correcting it will also pay off. The writer is usually in a better position to cut unneeded details from his own copy than is the copyreader to whom he hands it.

The same suggestions apply to those who write business letters. However, I have sympathy with busy executives who must dictate scores of letters each day. They have said to me, "I can't take the time to work over what I write and make it good concise English." The sense of such argument has added weight because so many dictated letters go to only one reader. Is the time of one reader more valuable than that of the writer? Should the writer spend an extra minute in clearing his thought or revising his language in order to save a minute for the one receiving the letter?

Let the busy executive consider these points in making his decision:

One: Every minute spent clarifying the language of the

letter at hand will help you write future letters more clearly on the first try.

Two: A clear, concise letter does more than simply aid the reader to understanding. It gives a good impression of *you* as well.

When a message is to be mimeographed or printed no reason is good enough to excuse anything but the most concise English possible. Every minute spent in revision at the sending end may save minutes by the hundreds at the receiving end.

Here, for instance, is a single sentence printed in accounting manuals of a large company. This is an instruction that goes to many hundreds of bookkeepers all over the world. What is said in 41 words could be said much clearer in 28:

41 WORDS	28 WORDS
When changes in manuals are noted that do not involve the substitution of sheets, it is suggested that the number of the bulletin authorizing such changes be noted on the sheet affected and that all bulletins be filed for reference purposes.	When a change in a manual does not require a new sheet, note the bulletin number describing the change on the sheet affected. Always file bulletins for reference.

Padding is so ingrained in some office workers that they use excess words even when their attention is presumably centered on conciseness. For instance, I have some fine examples of needless complexity from memos circulated for Clear Writing Clinics. Here is such an announcement—a 66-word sentence with 30 per cent excess words:

66 WORDS ONE SENTENCE	45 WORDS THREE SENTENCES
Furthering the executive committee's recent authorization of making arrangements with Mr. Robert Gunning, who will con-	The executive committee recently authorized Robert Gunning to hold two clinics aimed at making written materials of the company

66 WORDS   ONE SENTENCE

duct two clinics with the purpose of simplifying and making more readable written material in the company, Mr. W. requests that samples of all written material, typical of that prepared by each department, be forwarded to him by Monday in order that it can be given to Mr. Gunning for analysis.

45 WORDS   THREE SENTENCES

more readable. Mr. W. asks that samples of typical writing from each department be sent him by Monday. He will forward them to Gunning for analysis.

False courtesy causes many unneeded words. For fear of being abrupt, we bow and scrape in writing. But it is not courtesy to waste the other person's time with excess. Nor is it likely that on the written page, any amount of verbal maneuvering will cover up the import of your words. Your best tactic is to depend upon a direct, frank, and friendly tone.

On a hotel desk I saw this sign:

"In order to substantiate our desire to accommodate our guests we would appreciate your cooperation to anticipate your credit requirements before departure."

I asked what it meant and the clerk said:

"Please let us know in advance if you want us to cash a check as you leave."

I would rather they said that in the first place.

You are acquainted with the sort of palaver as is shown at the left below. The version at the right is more courteous and more convincing:

24 WORDS

We solicit any recommendations that you wish to make and you may be assured that any such recommendations will be given our careful consideration.

10 WORDS

Please give us your suggestions. We shall consider them carefully.

Suppose you owe one hundred dollars to a firm you deal with regularly. Since you are going to get a bill of some kind, which of the following would you prefer?

53 WORDS 18% POLYSYLLABLES
Reference to our ledger indicates that the January account of $100 is still outstanding. Since the billing is overdue we shall appreciate your remittance to close it at your earliest convenience, or if you do not have a record of it, please let us hear from you so that duplicates may be furnished.

31 WORDS 6% POLYSYLLABLES
The $100 you owe us from January is overdue, and we would appreciate receiving it. If you lack a copy of the billing we shall be glad to send you one.

True courtesy is largely a matter of 1) getting the other person's point of view and 2) considering his feelings. These two are as important to effective communication as they are to good manners.

After we had worked with the staff of a steel company, a letter written by one of the salesmen bounced back to the office of the president of the company. It had been sent to a man who wished to buy a prefabricated swimming pool.

The salesman's letter read in full:

> Dear Sir:
>   We don't make swimming pools and we don't intend to.
>   Yours,

The writer of that letter obeyed the principle of conciseness, but he broke the higher principle of friendly courtesy into small pieces. He could have observed all principles of both courtesy and readability by writing simply:

> Dear Sir:
>   I am sorry but we do not make swimming pools and do not plan to. A sheet-metal firm in your own community might be able to help you.

Suppose you were a workman in a plant where there had been some layoffs. Which of the following announcements would be most reassuring? The one on the left was issued by a personnel office. Our suggested revision is at the right:

43 WORDS   18% POLYSYLLABLES

Curtailments, some of which have already taken place, involve workers with little senority and may be of short duration. The layoffs in one department were largely seasonal retrenchment and in another they resulted when production returned to normal after filling a big order.

35 WORDS   8% POLYSYLLABLES

Recent layoffs affect only workers newest on the job and may not last long. In one department they were seasonal. In another they came when production returned to normal after a big order was filled.

Or take this piece of advice on thrift. Does the version to the right lose any touch of courtesy in delivering its message more directly?

33 WORDS   20% POLYSYLLABLES

Careful thought should be given to the desirability of being in attendance at the convention and the value accruing to the company from such attendance before asking us for approval of the expenditure.

18 WORDS   11% POLYSYLLABLES

Before you ask for convention expenses, think carefully whether the trip will be of value to the company.

Economy in the use of words is the mark of craftsmanship, as it is in any line. The good designer aims toward simplicity. Each part must have its function. No engineer would design an unneeded part into a machine. Ornate language may have had its place in the past when crowds went to hear orators for entertainment as they now go to movies. But language intended to inform needs simple, beautiful streamlining, like that of an airplane. Can you imagine an airplane designed with the curlicues of baroque style?

English is perhaps the best language for the exercise of economy in words. Otto Jespersen, a Dane and one of the world's greatest philologists, speaks of the "businesslike shortness" of English.

English, more than any other Western language, has lost the complexities of noun and verb endings. This resulted during those centuries after 1066 when English was the language of home and street, a spoken language. Norman French or Latin was used in the schools and the courts.

In English, the position of a word in a sentence determines whether it is a verb, noun, adjective, or other part of speech. Consider the varied functions of "stop" in these groups of words:

Stop!   Stop sign.   Bus stop.   When did the clock stop?

This flexibility is a great aid in writing to make every word count.

Perhaps you have noticed instructions written in various languages. Those telling how to leave a transoceanic plane if it lands on water are an example. The French, Spanish, German, and Italian versions all run longer than the English.

Someone in the French-speaking section of Canada handed me these two versions of instructions that he found in a washroom.

> "Voulez-vous, s'il vous plaît, faire opérir
> l'eau sous les pressions dans cette closette
> d'eau après chaque besoin."

The English version was:

> "Please flush."

To summarize: How does a writer get rid of the unnecessary word habit? The remedy is simple enough, but stout resolution is required to apply it.

Before you write or dictate—ask yourself, "What am I trying to say?" The clearer your idea the fewer unneeded words will drift into your writing.

After you have written—go over your copy with a pencil. Question every word. Cut out each one that is not absolutely necessary to your meaning. Try to recast sentences to make them more concise.

If you dictate, go over carbons as often as possible. What you learn in copyreading today's carbons will help you dictate better letters tomorrow.

Every minute of close attention you spend going over your own copy will pay rich dividends. There is no better road toward a clear, brisk writing style.

Principle Five

Put Action in Your Verbs

"The fullback *hits* the line." That sentence has an active verb. "The line *is hit* by the fullback." In that sentence the verb is passive. The electricity has gone from it. The snap of action is no longer there.

The same idea translated into typical business jargon goes something like this: "The hitting of the line is an activity engaged in by the player acting in the capacity of fullback."

Here the act is completely smothered, being submerged in participles and other words derived from verbs. Such academic tone you might expect from a scholar out of touch with life. But it is discouraging (and disturbing) to find men of action using such prose.

In both the great writing of the past and the successful writing of the present, strong verbs account for an average of about one word out of ten. But we find many samples of business writing and many newspaper articles that have no strong, active verbs at all. The two paragraphs that follow, for example, originated with businessmen and were passed along to the public by one of the larger newspapers of western Pennsylvania:

"Resumption of operations at all mines is expected Monday as a result of action taken by the Coal Producers Association at its regular meeting last night rescinding a previous decision against operating the coal mines under any contract extension providing for retroactive pay in any wage terms negotiated.

"The decision has been rescinded as a result of the recent trade ruling giving coal producers and dealers the right to 'open-bill' consumers, thus enabling them to receive later the difference between the current cost of coal and the new price yet to be established."

There is not an active verb in the two paragraphs. Restore action to the verbs and the piece becomes clearer and more readable:

"Members of the Coal Producers Association decided at their regular meeting last night to open all mines Monday. The operators thus reversed an earlier vote to hold up work until new wage terms are set. They had not wished to reopen the mines so long as they might have to pay retroactive wages.

"But a new trade ruling has opened the way to operation. Coal producers and dealers may now 'open-bill' customers. In other words, they may charge customers the present price of coal, then send bills later covering the price increase when it is granted."

Strong-flavored, active verbs give writing bounce and hold a reader's attention. They play an important part in the lively style that has made *Time* a success. In the following example a *Time* writer faced the difficult problem of writing something fresh about New York, which has been discussed in millions upon millions of words. He succeeds through good use of verbs:

> Once it was just an island between two rivers, with a bedrock which *defied* digging. But it had a magnificent, deep-water harbor and a river which *led* to the hinterland. Slowly its farms *turned into* city blocks, its mud streets *grew* cobblestones, its docks *stuck* fingers into the sea. First

its sewers, then its wires, and finally its trains *went* underground. The higher its buildings *rose,* the deeper *went* their foundations. Its bowels *became* a vast catacomb *laced* with the ganglia of communication. It was an aggressive organism; it *touched* everything within reach, *attached* itself to everything it *touched.*

In 1918 and 1919 when Woodrow Wilson was campaigning for the League of Nations, William Bayard Hale, a leading newspaperman of the day, wrote a criticism of the President that consists entirely of an analysis of his prose style. It is a thin but devastating volume called *The Story of a Style.*

President Wilson failed to put his message across to the American people. He died broken and disappointed and the world drifted into a succession of wars. There are a multitude of reasons for this. But Hale's study of Wilson's writing is extremely interesting in view of the President's conspicuous failure to influence people.

The first fault Hale found with the President's style was a poverty of strong verbs. He cited some samples of Wilson's writing which depended almost entirely upon forms of the verb "to be" that merely link and do not record action. Hale also showed Wilson's adjectives outnumbered his verbs. Then for comparison he checked Carlyle, Macaulay, Stevenson, Poe, Shakespeare, Scott, Dickens, Hardy, Shaw, Mark Twain, Stendhal, and Maeterlinck. These writers averaged, per hundred words, 13 strong verbs and 4.5 adjectives—about three to one.

Many have written in praise of the verb, but Hale's eulogy from *The Story of a Style* is one of the best:

It is with a true instinct that language calls the part of speech which represents action, "the verb"—*the* word. The task of speech is to predicate, not to paint. The advance of thought is just so swift as verbs carry it. Adjectives qualify, describe, limit. They are a brake, a drag, on the wheel—often necessary in order that advance may be kept in the right track—but not near so often necessary as they are commonly and lazily deemed to be. They are popular, because easy; they eke out effortless poverty of idea. The man who has something to tell has little need, little time, for them; he snaps out his tale in words of action. The thought that pants for deliverance bursts out in verbs. A very little study will show that the world's great storytellers and thinkers have generally written in action-words, not quality-words; some by instinct, some on principle (as Stevenson, for one, confesses) eschewing mention of all but most necessary attributes. The artist in language suspects an approaching adjective as he would suspect a possible rogue at the door.

You, no doubt, have heard outcries against the adjective before. And you have also learned that the adjective is not all rogue. Even Hale in his short piece deploring them is obliged to use more than a dozen.

But the warning against adjectives is important to those who write speeches or who wish to write for newspapers and magazines. A simple principle of psychology lies behind the advantage verbs hold over adjectives. It is this: Readers and listeners prefer fact to opinion.

Concrete, picturable verbs and nouns reflect facts and events as directly as it is possible for language to do so. Adjectives and adverbs, on the other hand, always smell of opinion. You may report that a woman is "extremely attractive." That's opinion. More convincing evidence of her charm would be the fact that she had the lead in a hit musical comedy and had married a Rockefeller.

The best fiction writers tell the reader what a character does rather than describing him. Thus the reader gets a clearer impression because he judges for himself. He gets the story through verbs rather than adjectives.

This I'm-from-Missouri attitude of readers and listeners relates to the smallest details. It is better communication to report that "the assailant sprang into the room" than to say he "came into the room quickly" or "came in with a quick jump." The first is not only more colorful writing, it is also more free of the odor of opinion.

In the writing of daily commerce, plagues of adjectives are less of a problem than the cold-blooded murder of the verbs themselves. The verb force, the very juice of the sentence, is squeezed out with passives and through the use of gerunds and participles which mummify verbs in the form of nouns and adjectives.

The passive verb has, of course, its special uses. If you are writing a football rule book, rather than giving an eyewitness report of a game, you put down, "The whistle is blown by the referee," instead of, "The referee blows the whistle." The emphasis here is on the agent rather than the action. The first version indicates that the refree and no one else blows the whistle. However, today in industry we find more and more that even procedures and instructions are written in the active tense. In the Playscript approach (and variations of it) developed by Leslie Matthies of Tulsa, Oklahoma, instructions and procedure are set forth in terms of "who does what."

The passive is also needed for variety, so essential to all good writing. The normal sentence, however, contains an active verb. The passive is dull reading in comparison.

The best way to show this is through examples. Here are sentences gleaned from material that has passed through our office. They are work of writers who have fallen into the passive-verb habit. In each instance the active form would have made more lively reading:

> PASSIVE: Unsatisfactory results in the coating department *have been reduced* through use of a new wash.
> ACTIVE: A new wash *has reduced* unsatisfactory results in the coating department.

PASSIVE: Present design methods *are predicated on the assumption* that one-piece windshields *are preferred* by the public.

ACTIVE: At present designers *assume* the public *prefers* one-piece windshields.

PASSIVE: When an application of wax *is made* to this surface a brilliance *is imparted* to it.

ACTIVE: Waxing this surface *brightens* it.

Active verbs not only bring sentences to life, they shorten them as well. The examples already given show how verb trouble breeds unnecessary-word trouble.

Strong verbs are dynamic and on the move. They should go hand in hand with a healthy business. But typical business prose, aside from being overloaded with passives, packs verb force into cocoons of gerunds and participles and throws it into hibernation.

It is not necessary to be able to identify gerunds and participles in order to spot this fault of writing. Once you learn where to look for them, the symptoms of the disease are as obvious as measles on a small boy's face. In the following announcement sent to a newspaper by a public-relations man, the signs of the smothered-verb disease stick out in italic type:

"Allan R_____, secretary, called public atten*tion* Friday to the resump*tion* of opera*tions* by the State Tax League. The deci*sion* of the league in favor of incorpora*tion* was noted in the announce*ment*. Enroll*ment* of members is expected to be encouraged through elimina*tion* of individual financial responsibility result*ing* from incorpora*tion*. In deal*ing* with future legisla*tion* aboli*tion* of the state sales tax will be the inten*tion* of the league, Mr. R_____ said."

Note the word endings that point out smothered verbs. The chief culprits are *-ion, -tion, -ing,* and *-ment,* and all these show up in the above paragraph. Also keep watch on the endings *-ant, -ent, -ance, -ence, -ancy,* and *-ency.*

Most of these endings come from Latin and are means of changing verbs into nouns and adjectives. This is a highly useful device, for it is often a means of saving words. But these endings, like all good devices of communication, including radio and television, can either be used *well* to inform and entertain or they can be used *poorly* so that they confuse and annoy.

The above announcement about the tax league becomes much clearer when purged of the "measly" word endings. As they disappear, action is restored to the verbs:

"The State Tax League is operating once more, Secretary Allan R———— announced Friday. The league has decided to incorporate, he said, and more members are expected to enroll, since that move relieves them of individual financial responsibility. The league intends to back future bills to do away with the state sales tax, R———— said."

Now let us see how these endings can be put to good use. Here is a statement that is clear but it is wordy and in rather childish form:

"The company made an offer to settle the strike and the union refused the offer and the management of the company was annoyed."

By making good use of those endings that change verbs into other parts of speech we can state the same idea in less than half the words:

"Refusal of its proposed strike settlement annoyed the company management."

That's better than the original as a piece of clear communication. In business parlance, however, the endings often expand and deaden a sentence instead of making it shorter and clearer. Thus this same idea becomes:

"Rejec*tion* by the union of the proposi*tion* of settle*ment* advanced by the management of the company was a subject of annoy*ance* to the latter."

Note that the sentence has a bad case of "measles."

In smothering verb force, a Latin ending usually has, as an accomplice, a weak verb. Forms of "to make," "to be," and "to have" are the most frequent partners in sabotaging strong verbs. Also watch out for "seem," "occur," "become," "takes place," "was noted." Thus "apply" is submerged in "make application." Here are some others:

substitute	make substitution
intend	have intention
impose	become an imposition

From industrial and periodical copy come the following examples of smothered verbs:

SMOTHERED: An improvement in quality has been made.
ACTIVE: Quality has improved.

SMOTHERED: A sharp decrease in profits was noted.
ACTIVE: Profits decreased sharply.

SMOTHERED: Arrival of the delegates occurred at 12:15.
ACTIVE: The delegates arrived at 12:15.

SMOTHERED: Increases in sales of 10 per cent were obtained in July.
ACTIVE: Sales increased 10 per cent in July.

SMOTHERED: Evaporation of the liquid takes place.
ACTIVE: The liquid evaporates.

SMOTHERED: Acquisition of coal by the barge company could be most readily accomplished in Kentucky.
ACTIVE: The barge company could acquire coal most readily in Kentucky.

SMOTHERED: The store is dependent upon our aid for its operation.
ACTIVE: A store operates only through our aid.

SMOTHERED: When application of pressure is employed by the operator release of the pin is accomplished.

ACTIVE: When the operator applies pressure the pin releases.

Simple carelessness and bad habits sacrifice much verb force. But false attitudes of caution and modesty are also to blame. Many men are gripped by fear of the record whenever they face a task of writing. Let us look at an example:

Suppose the executive committee of a company has for some months been discussing an incentive plan. At length the head of the company calls for memos from each vice-president. Since the vice-president in charge of operations recommended the plan in the first place, he can reply directly:

"I believe we should adopt the incentive plan. Once our employees understand it, they will favor it."

That reply shows self-confidence, decision, directness—all qualities that go with executive ability. Every verb in the statement is active.

But such simplicity is as rare as a decrease in tax rates. The memo is more likely to read this way:

"The conclusions drawn from exhaustive study are to the effect that it seems advisable under present circumstances to initiate adoption of the incentive plan. If a presentation of the full facts of the plan is duly made to the employees, our considered opinion is to the effect that their approval will be forthcoming."

Such verbiage closely resembles the dun-colored fuzz with which nature covers the timid animals of the woods. Notice that the strong verbs of the original statement have retreated into words with -*ion* and other endings. Only weak verbs remain; "is," "seems," and "is made" (in a figurative sense).

And "I" has disappeared completely. Since the memo will be signed, this isn't much of a dodge. Perhaps the vice-president is genuinely shy and wishes to keep in the background.

This trait, however, did not appear in conference. The fact is he pounded the table and declared, "I this" and "I that" in favor of the plan.

No, the blunt truth is that the vice-president in charge of operations has been gripped with *fear of the record*. When it came to putting what he believed on paper, he began to pussyfoot. Now if the incentive plan succeeds his record will be clear, of course. And if it should fail, he has left himself a number of loopholes:

"Under the present circumstances"—perhaps circumstances changed between the time of the memo and the time the plan went into effect. Then the "conclusions" were only "to the effect that." That doesn't say "for sure," does it? Besides "presentation" may not have been made of the "full" facts. Or, even if the *full* facts were given, they may not have been presented "duly."

I have observed many corporation executives at work and have noted this: Because buck passing is almost as common a misdemeanor as overeating or lustful thoughts, it is widely understood—and excused. But I have never noted that it was respected.

In fact, I know one executive who has a studied technique of admitting *occasionally* that he was wrong. He believes it adds to his status. He confided to me:

"You know and I know so many men who make constant mistakes but can always explain them away. I have noticed that when someone confesses an error, I immediately conclude, 'This man must be right most of the time. Otherwise he could not afford to admit he is wrong this time.' I try to be direct and when I've been wrong I admit it. And it has proved a good policy."

This executive, by the way, has little verb trouble.

I leave the argument about caution to your judgment. There are, of course, excellent reasons for protective writing.

But when prose is made foggy to shield oneself, it usually protects no one. Others see through it too quickly.

Overcautious, foggy writing can be a handicap to both personal success and the success of your business. The smothering of verbs quickly becomes a habit and confuses communication when there is no question of either modesty or caution.

Scientists and engineers, who are so numerous in the management of industry today, are the source of much passive writing. They have been told in school or early on the job to avoid the first person. Usually they can't quite put their finger on the source of the advice. "There is a certain unwritten something" that forbids it, one engineer said. This vagueness is understandable because much feeling against "I" and "we" results from overcaution and pussyfooting.

"It is recommended that . . ." someone writes in a report. Two weeks later the lid blows off. "Who the devil recommended that?" No one is quite sure.

The subject of personal pronouns arises in this chapter because use of them is the easiest way to keep verbs active. This is plain from daily conversation. Try to carry on an oral discussion in the third person passive. Such an exercise will give many a clue as to why engineers hate writing. They are trying to do it in a quite unnatural manner.

Any informational report should be objective, of course. But objectivity is not a matter of grammar; it is a matter of integrity. You can lie in the third person passive just as readily as in the first person active.

In the armed services also there is a strong feeling that the third person, and the passive verbs that go with it, are required. Quite the contrary is true. For example, here is an excerpt from *Army Pamphlet 1–10*, "Improve Your Writing":

> When you prepare official correspondence to be signed by someone other than the commander, you properly should avoid the use of *I*. But you gain nothing by using the im-

personal *it is* in place of *we* or *this headquarters*. In correspondence in which you speak for yourself, you should refer to yourself as *I*. The self-conscious use of *the writer, this officer*, and *the undersigned* is not dictated by any regulation or valid custom of the service.

In the four chapters preceding this the emphasis has been on "don't." *Don't* let your sentences run too long. *Don't* use too many complex or unfamiliar words. *Don't* use unnecessary words. The aim has been to get you to tear faulty structure from your writing.

This chapter begins the remodeling. Principle Five and those that follow emphasize "do." In the first place, *do* use strong verbs, preferably active.

In phrasing your resolution say, "I intend to write clearly," rather than, "Clarity in composition is my intention."

Principle Six

Write Like You Talk

For years the Bureau of Naval Weapons was rated in Washington as one of the most staid, the most reserved, the most "bureaucratic" of bureaus. But government bureaus are made up of human beings, and, particularly at the top, they know how critical it is that humans communicate clearly. Consider this statement from an October 1962 Bulletin of the Bureau of Naval Weapons:

> Our biggest problem in communications is that you're there and we're here! We'd have no problem if we could all get together and talk whenever we wanted to. But we can't do that so we have to resort to writing to "talk" to each other.
>
> At best, writing is a poor substitute for talking. But the closer our writing comes to conversation, the better our exchange of ideas will be. And when you think how 99% of the Bureau's business is conducted by the written word you realize how important it is to write as simply, clearly, and directly as you can. We have a job to do, and we have an obligation to be intelligible to each other.
>
> Clear writing doesn't just happen; it takes practice to say exactly what you mean in the fewest possible words. But

119

you owe it to your readers to make the effort. Dust off your copies of "Plain Letters"* and review the techniques of direct, plain letter writing. (We might even do the same!) You know the Navy heartily endorses *every single word* of this pamphlet—even the use of "you" and "we" and "please," as revolutionary as they may seem. Nowhere in official Navy literature will you find that these simple words are anything but desirable. So when you write to us, don't hesitate to say "you" and refer to yourself as "we." You don't need to tell us that you are "the station" and we are "the Bureau." The shorter word is always the better one. It's easier to read and sounds more natural than the longer one.

Oh, we know what your first reaction to this is: "Look who's talking about direct, conversational correspondence!" But just because we bureaucrats have always been accused of gobbledygook doesn't mean that we couldn't change with the right encouragement. "Talk" to us in your letters. Who knows? We may even "talk" back!

When you catch yourself writing a vague or complex phrase or sentence, ask yourself:

"How would I *say* that? If the reader were sitting across the desk how would I say it to him? What would I tell him if he were on the other end of a long-distance wire?"

Usually this will bring to you a simple, direct way of writing what you want to get across. Of course, you can't write exactly what you might say. For one thing, most of us talk rather untidy English. We repeat ourselves—thinking out loud—seeking the best way to frame our thoughts in words. Still, a brushed-up spoken version is usually far easier reading than a formal written version.

Whenever you write remember that the written word is no

---

* A records management Handbook issued by the General Services Administration of the Federal Government.

more than a substitute for the spoken word. This should keep you from "freezing up."

Work with thousands of writers has convinced me that "write like you talk" is most helpful advice to anyone wishing to write clearly. But I must tell you at the begining that it is controversial.

In the first place some grammarians insist the statement is bad English. They say it should read "Write *as* you talk." I continue to use "like" for three reasons.

One: Good writers for centuries have used "like" as a conjunction whenever they felt like it.

Two: "Write *as* you talk" would violate the principle in the statement of it. The great majority who speak English use "like" as a conjunction in their conversation.

Three: The use of "as" gives the sentence two possible meanings, and there is no principle of grammar more basic than to avoid ambiguity.

The other objection to the statement was expressed well by the managing editor of one of Ohio's leading newspapers when we were working with his staff.

"I like that idea, 'Write like you talk,' " he said. "I like it so well I am going to stick it right up there by the clock where everyone will see it.

"But," he added, "when you talk to Josephine, she's on the society staff, go light on that point. That's her trouble now. She *does* write like she talks."

It is most certainly true that the flow of some conversation when placed unedited upon paper looks bad. Anyone who has studied a transcript of court testimony, for instance, knows it is often difficult to get its meaning. At points the words seem utter confusion because they are divorced from the gestures, facial expressions, and tones of voice that helped them communicate when spoken.

Josephine of the society staff had not developed very far in either her oral or written style of composition. She was still in the "and-a" stage. You can observe this best in children. A seven-year-old will say:

"Aunt Mary came and she took us downtown and we went to the store and I saw a big doll and I want you to get it for me for Christmas."

These ideas are in the simplest possible arrangement—a chronological series. Some adults never get beyond this. On our party line in the country I hear:

"So I came home and I didn't know what to get for dinner and I looked in the cupboard and I decided to make some pudding."

The way you use language in either speech or writing is, of course, very closely related to your thought process. If you improve one, you improve the other. As a person matures, his vocabulary grows and he develops the use of new relationships between words.

After the "and-a" stage, a child will learn to use contrast. "But" appears in his speech. Then his consciousness of time relationships grow with "when," "before," "then," "after," "until," and the like. An understanding of cause and effect produces clauses tagged with "since," "for," "because," "although," and "if."

There is an interesting parallel between this speech development of a child and the growth of English prose. Some of the first samples of written English have a marked "and-a" tendency. Here is a sample, the climax of the battle between King Arthur and Sir Mordred (from Sir Thomas Malory's *Morte d'Arthur*):

> Then the king gat his spear in both his hands, and ran toward Sir Mordred crying: Traitor, now is thy death day come. And when Sir Mordred heard Sir Arthur, he ran until him with his sword drawn in his hand. And there King Arthur smote Sir Mordred under the shield, with a foin

of his spear, throughout the body more than a fathom. And when Sir Mordred felt that he had his death wound he thrust himself with the might that he had up to the bur of King Arthur's spear. And right so he smote his father Arthur, with his sword holden in both his hands, on the side of the head, that the sword pierced the helmet and the brain pan, and therewithal Sir Mordred fell stark dead to the earth; and the noble Arthur fell in a swoon to the earth, and there he swooned ofttimes. And Sir Lucan the Butler and Sir Belvidere ofttimes heave him up. And so weakly they led him betwixt them both, to a little chapel not far from the seaside. And when the king was there he thought him well eased. . . .

Apparently these early writers had little skill in subordinating one idea to another on the written page. At the same time they felt a compulsion to link strings of ideas together in a way which only the least skilled speakers do in talking.

English poetry in those days was never so tangled. In the early days poetry seems to have been the more "natural" way of writing.

Prose, meanwhile, through the Romantic period of the nineteenth century, produced a multitude of highly decorated sentences. Every possibility of relationship within a sentence seems to have been explored, but even so, prose sentences in this period were much shorter than they were in the earliest days of English. From the beginning, English prose has been coming closer and closer to the conciseness and concreteness of the best spoken communication.

Garrulous, unorganized speech of the "and-a" type usually has little to do with communication. It is self-soothing flow poured out by persons who, in constant fear of loneliness, must keep wigwagging the outside world.

Speech for the purpose of communication, on the other hand, has always practiced economy as a matter of necessity.

To get action from the other fellow, attention must be focused on the audience. There is no time to indulge the self. This fact burns with clarity as you look into a listener's eyes. Their movements remind you of the fickleness of human attention and compel you to get to the point if you are to succeed in influencing him. The honor of even a portion of his attention spurs you to speak directly in order to hold him.

The practical nature of communication is far more apparent in face-to-face conversation. When one writes, the electric nature of the direct contact with life is lacking. One is alone with his thoughts and can drift into indulging his own peculiarities. But the presence of a hearer is usually enough to dispel such whims of verbiage.

Writing is never under the heavy discipline that bears down on oral speech. Writing, as we have said, is a substitute. In business, if the written word fails, you can telephone the other person or go see him. If the supposedly careful writing of lawyers fails, they can go argue the matter out in court.

In literature one can delve within himself, giving little thought to readers, and, surprisingly often, some avant-garde critic will see in the fog a "higher form" of communication.

But when face-to-face conversation fails because of vagueness or self-adoration, the failure is so painfully embarrassing that all involved learn a lesson.

Ever since you first cried for a bottle of milk you have been gathering experience in vocal communication. You have found out what sort works and what sort fails.

Every day of your life, without giving it thought, you are testing communication. You talk to another, you watch his eyes, you are alert for the signs of his moving on. His expression tells, if his tongue does not, when he is following you and when he misunderstands. You have learned that your words must be direct and picturable or he will walk away from you. Even if he must pay you the respect of staying, you can sense his attention "walking away" from any vagueness that shadows your words.

More than this, in conversation he will *tell* you what he does not understand and will ask questions that will direct your explanations.

This education that we have all had in oral communication has been so long and so decisive that it is almost impossible to find a person who talks as complexly as he writes. The tendency toward simplicity in speech is automatic—because of years of daily experience.

In comparison, writing, the substitute for talking, is quite foreign. In the first place, few of us have a serious experience of writing before we reach high school.

And the high-school teacher gave most of us the idea that writing is some rather mystic, special thing, encouraging us to write on the "flowery" side. Her intent wasn't bad. She was trying to teach how marvelously varied and flexible the language is. She wanted us to learn more words and new ways to build sentences. We all need those skills, but too many of us left school thinking of communication by the written word as an unnatural act.

Meanwhile, in relaxed fashion, nearly all are able to use the spoken word to good effect. No one gets far without being able to do so.

Now what I am suggesting to you is this:

Tap that great reservoir of experience you have from communicating with the spoken word. Put it to work to make your writing clearer. When you start to write or dictate, don't turn on some special lingo or jargon. Use simple, direct English —the same kind you use when you are talking face-to-face. Your letters and other writing will be clearer as a result. And they will be more effective because the tone will show they are the work of a human being.

Let this principle be no excuse for slovenliness. Quite the

contrary. That same reservoir of experience tells you that disorder in oral, as well as in written words, causes your audience to drift away.

Time and again in working with writers I have seen them draw clear statement from fog by shifting from the written to the spoken language. After a Readability Clinic for a Middle Western utility company, a young man from the personnel department laid before me a piece of copy. It began like this:

"The Company's Employee Retirement Plan has been amended to permit each participating employee to share his annuities with certain contingent annuitants."

"What does all this mean?" I asked him.

He relaxed: "Well, it's very important. You see we have had a retirement plan around here for a long time and the people like it. But some have felt that a wife or child should be able to share a pension if the employee himself died. We have fixed it now so they can do this. And I have to get this message over to them."

"You mean these 'contingent annuitants' are people?"

"Yes, as I said, the wives and children can share in the pensions now."

"But when you write about it why do you put down 'contingent annuitants'?"

"Well, that's what the insurance men call them. I thought I should put it in."

"Are you writing this for the insurance people?"

The young man got the point and was able to write his piece more conversationally. He started it this way:

"From now on, if you wish, you can assure your wife or child a pension after your death. You can do this through the Company's Employee Retirement Pension Plan by choosing one of two new types of pension plans. . . ."

From our work with newspapers comes the example of Leonard. He was a reporter of several years' experience and better than most in collecting facts, but he had trouble shaping them into a lively story.

One of his pieces started like this:

"Commissioners of Franklin County are considering the adoption of a safety campaign inaugurated last month in Cuyahoga County where constables have been urged to stop cars and demand to see the licenses of the drivers.

"Drivers who are caught without their licenses are taken before justices of peace and fined and are not allowed to drive their cars away until they obtain a license. . . ."

As the story was written it probably would have been buried in the back pages. It lacked the spark of good communication.

After I had read the story in copy, I said to him, "Leonard, I don't have a driver's license."

"You better look out," he cried.

Confronted by some one who would be affected by what he had to tell, he burst forth with the news. On the framework of his oral telling of the news he rewrote the story:

"If you have no driver's license—watch out.

"Constables in all townships may be lying in wait for you next week.

"Franklin County commissioners said today they are considering following the example of Cuyahoga authorities. In that county last week constables arrested 105 drivers. They were fined by justices of peace and were not allowed to drive their cars until they obtained licenses."

The temptations to become lofty when writing are particularly strong for those who write of literature, art, and music. The able music critic of one paper came up after a readability lecture.

"What you said was of great interest to me," he said, "because if there is one thing I wish to do, it is to spread an interest in good music in this town."

"How is R——— doing here?" I asked him, mentioning

the name of one of the nation's leading conductors who had just taken over the symphony orchestra of the city.

"Wonderfully," the music critic replied. "He's tops. I think he is the best in the country. Stubborn, though. Last year, for instance, some of us wanted him to program Cadman's 'Appalachian Suite.' It would have been a good idea. Cadman was a local boy, you know. But would he do it? No. Stubborn."

I mentioned to the music critic that his oral style was considerably more direct and simple in structure than the columns he wrote for the paper.

"Well," he said, defending himself, "the problem of communication becomes much more complicted when one must obey the dictates of procrustean—" He paused for a moment, just long enough for me to nod that I happened to know the word.

He ignored my nod, "You know what I mean—principles that demand you cut a story off so it fits."

The music critic's explanation is typical of what we do in conversation. We rarely give the hearer credit for a grain of information. Even though he saw me nod that I understood the word "procrustean" he ignored this and went ahead to explain it—with gestures—his two hands chopping down a few inches apart.

He did this because (like the rest of us) he has had years of bitter experience of the difficulty of oral communication.

Reaction to vocal communication is constant. In comparison, response to the writing in a newspaper or publication is rare. A writer has little means of checking whether his work is being read and understood. He hopes. Still he usually makes less effort to be simple and direct than he would if trying to communicate orally.

In making a speech to 50 people a man will put great energy into gesture, inflection of voice, and facial expression. These can be extremely helpful in getting meaning across. The same man will scratch off an announcement to an equal number of people without half the attention to his choice of words. In the written announcement he lacks the aids of gesture and expression. In addition, those who would be listening to his speech would probably not gather the courage to walk out on him. But a reader is quite different from a listener. All a reader need do is shift his eyes and you have lost him.

More effort is needed to communicate by the written word than by the oral. And that effort should go into thought and organization. Much talking is in fact organization in process. We say, "I'd like to talk this over before I put it down." W. L. George makes this sharp observation:

"Very few of us ever attempt to discover what the other man thinks. We talk so as to assert to him what *we* think; this helps us to discover what we really think."

This sort of exercise is permissible in conversation but a reader expects you to have your facts organized before writing them down. Sylvia Porter, who writes a column in which she does a good job of making the facts of business and economics understandable to laymen, has a simple rule for organizing her material. "I see to it that I understand it myself," she says.

The writer of a letter, a report, a speech, or a newspaper or magazine article has a responsibility to the reader which goes beyond merely setting down the facts. The writer should organize those facts so that their *implications* are clear to the reader. A man who orders a chair doesn't expect you to deliver a load of lumber. Details are the bricks of a piece of writing but they must be laid up in such a way that the reader will not be left with the burden of organizing them.

In the broadest sense, there are two methods of organizing a mass of detail in written form. And your experience in oral communication will cue you when to use each. One is the narrative form and the other the inverted pyramid.

In high-school English classes we hear about the first. You may recall seeing the teacher draw a diagram like this:

She said most stories, novels, and plays followed that pattern—starting off with statements of fact and descriptions of events that gradually built up to a climax. After this peak, events quickly dropped off to a close.

This is the method of organization you use in telling a funny story. You lay in the background, create the atmosphere, and build up to the point or tag line. This is the dramatic way to organize. It has suspense. It gives you a chance to stir emotions.

I have run across men in business who thought this was the way to write reports: Feed out details gradually, "create suspense," save the big news to the last. But this is a poor way to organize a piece of writing that is chiefly information. The long pull to a climax may be quite effective in a speech or in a story told to influence or persuade your listeners or to illustrate a point. However, when your chief aim is to hand on information, the inverted pyramid form is best. Tell the most important item you have first, then fill in with the other details, more or less in the order of their importance. In diagram an inverted pyramid looks like this:

In this type of organization you tell the reader the most important fact first and let details follow. At each step you prepare the reader's mind for the details you are about to tell him. Surprise may be an important factor in the facts themselves but you do not use the form of your writing to surprise him. You tell him in general what you are going to tell him, then give the details. There is a great advantage to this method if your aim is passing along information. No matter at what point the reader stops he will have some of the meat of your report.

Newspapers have had long experience in organizing articles of fact. Whatever their faults, they have brought the inverted pyramid form to high development. It is discussed further in the chapter on The Fog in Your Newspaper.

The key to all clear writing is clear thinking, and clear thinking is just another way of saying good organization. *Any message must be carefully organized before it can be either spoken well or written well.*

Speech can often go astray because we are under pressure either from lack of time, lack of wit, or fear of going on record. Here is the way a member of a President's Cabinet replied on a TV discussion of public power. He was asked whether he was on record as favoring a Missouri Valley Authority similar to TVA. He said:

> "Well, what I have said, that I am in favor of an Authority to develop the valley. Now, there are so many variations of that kind of an authority and you can get into an argument with most anybody about the different kinds and I first want to see them go ahead and be doing the things that obviously have to be done in any event—be doing those now without wasting and losing time and if you do that then your coordinated authority, when it is finally established in whatever form that Congress and the people decide they want, will be an easier job at least to accomplish what is needed to be accomplished."

We are in favor of persons writing like they talk, *provided they have something to say, and wish to put it on the record clearly.* The individual voice that comes through in what we read helps hold attention. The best writing is never just like talk, but it seems to be. Ernest Hemingway, critics often said, succeeded in putting true speech on paper. But it was never precisely like the spoken word.

Certainly there is the human voice in almost any sentence written by a highly successful writer. Often the very first passages of a book set this conversational link between writer and reader. I pick up random books of two American authors who have won Nobel prizes. Ernest Hemingway's *A Moveable Feast* begins talking about the weather:

> Then there was the bad weather. It would come in one day when the fall was over. We would have to shut the windows in the night against the rain and the cold wind would strip the leaves from the trees in the place Contrescarpe.

John Steinbeck's *Travels with Charley* begins:

> When I was very young and the urge to be someplace else was on me, I was assured by mature people that maturity would cure this itch. When years described me as mature, the remedy prescribed was middle age. In middle age I was assured that greater age would calm my fever and now that I am fifty-eight perhaps senility will do the job. Nothing has worked. Four hoarse blasts of a ship's whistle still raise the hair on my neck and set my feet to tapping. The sound of a jet, an engine warming up, even the clopping of shod hooves on pavement brings on the ancient shudder, the dry mouth and vacant eye, the hot palms and the churn of stomach high up under the rib cage. In other words, I don't improve; in further words, once a bum always a bum. I fear the disease is incurable. I set this matter down not to instruct others but to inform myself.

Probably the greatest American novel, Mark Twain's *Huckleberry Finn*, begins:

> You don't know about me without you have read a book by the name of *The Adventures of Tom Sawyer*, but that

ain't no matter. That book was made by Mr. Mark Twain, and he told the truth, mainly. There was things which he stretched, but mainly he told the truth. That is nothing. I never seen anybody but lied one time or another, without it was Aunt Polly, or the widow, or maybe Mary.

In working out the complex relationship between the written and spoken word be careful of what you may write within quotation marks. Some writers display a tin ear for the natural cadences of speech when they set down words others are supposed to have said.

In years of working with newspapers I have collected a number of striking examples such as these words printed in the European edition of the New York *Herald Tribune*:

" 'It was an open, olive-drab, Ford-make jeep, French registration number 5958 RPI, motor number 206,720,' Miss Dietrich said with a catch in her voice."

I class these as "Curley Harper quotes" in honor of a comic-page hero. Curley has now disappeared and would be forgotten except for his dialogue, the most stilted ever to reach public print. Curley was a cub reporter. The strip would show him rushing into the Mayor's office:

"Good morning, Mr. Mayor. My editor, Mr. Haynes, has sent me to get a scoop story for the *Morning Courier*. If you will give me a statement of what you think of the murder that has just been committed I will be most grateful to you."

Artificiality in quotes is quite irritating to most people and may destroy the impact of your message if you let it creep into your copy.

Presidents serve as interesting examples of the relation of the written and spoken word. President Eisenhower had particular difficulty speaking in well-cast sentences. They had to be closely edited to look good on paper. President Kennedy, on the other hand, was a highly skilled word-smith even under the rapid-fire questions of a press conference. What he said usually required little change to make it satisfy the stricter discipline of the written word.

The New York Times reported of President Johnson:

> In the urgency of his desire to get his message across, the President last week twice did what he seldom does these days. He tossed away his prepared text.
>
> What came out was vintage campaign Johnson—rostrum-thumping, colorful, colloquial, direct and compelling.
>
> Whether his audiences agreed with him or not, the President kept them awake. This was in marked contrast to some of Mr. Johnson's performances with prepared texts, which almost seem calculated to set his listeners nodding. . . .
>
> The President may discover what many White House observers have long felt—that the authentic Lyndon Johnson, a forceful man of strong convictions, may appeal more to more people than the Johnson image projected by aides who labor so hard to get the grammar right in prepared texts.

And to end this chapter, here is a quotation from an article by Edward E. Leech, who was a great reporter and for many years editor of the Pittsburgh *Press*. It is an interesting story of the comparative power of conversational and formal prose. This was written in April 1948, months before Harry Truman faced Thomas Dewey in election. (Also keep in mind that Mr. Leech, both before and after this piece, opposed the Truman Administration.)

> Two entirely different Harry Trumans spoke before a banquet of the American Society of Newspaper Editors.
>
> The first of them read to a national radio audience a dry and unmoving speech in the faltering and unimpressive manner which has come to be regarded as typical of Mr. Truman. For 15 minutes he inflicted on the banquet guests and the unseen audience something which had been writ-

ten by somebody who thought it was what he ought to say.

And then, with the broadcast ended, this man laid aside his manuscript with obvious relief. And for half an hour a very human, earnest, good-natured and intensely sincere gentleman who looked like Mr. Truman delivered a moving address.

Surely it couldn't be the President. With neither manuscript nor notes, he was speaking so easily. There were little flashes of wit aimed at both the editors and himself. There was emphasis and deep earnestness in his words. No halting or fumbling. And, above all, such warmth as could not fail to win admiration.

It is a fiction, at best, to believe that anybody can speak to a big audience in a completely confidential manner. But politics is so cautious that it clings to the make-believe.

Sometime—and soon—President Truman should break through that caution, get away from his ghost writers, and reveal himself to the people. If he would speak to them from the heart, as he did the other night to that limited audience, it would cheer and hearten millions. It would cause them to feel that this man is honestly and deeply trying to preserve peace. That he is prayerfully and in great humility trying to do what is best both for humanity and America. That he is tolerant and well-disposed toward others. And that he has no selfish ambitions to dominate either this country or the world.

In short, if the President could break through the barrier around him, the people would get a glimpse of an intelligent, but somewhat average, American citizen trying to do his level best in the toughest job on earth.

And, incidentally, the Democrats would have a real candidate.

The Democrats did, indeed. While Truman was opposed by the written word in nearly all newspapers, his talk from the back of trains was influencing voters. His election was one of the biggest surprises in American presidential history.

Principle Seven

Use Terms Your Reader Can Picture

One difficulty with long words is that so many are abstract. The short, simple words—for the most part—stand for things you can see and touch. A far larger portion of the long words soar into the blue and stand for concepts that can't be pointed out. It is much harder to say just what they *do* mean.

In English classes we used to talk about abstract and concrete nouns. But it is not easy to draw a line between the two. The fact is that all terms, even proper nouns that name a person or place, have some quality of the abstract.

No word you use will deliver to your hearer exactly the impression that it leaves with you. It is safer to rely on the simple, concrete words which are easy to picture. But even these are tricky.

Consider the word "dog." It is one of the first words a child learns. It is a "concrete" noun in the ordinary use of the term. Everyone "understands" it. Still "dog" has different shades of meaning for each of us. You may have a great dane or a dachshund. The word "dog" creates a very different picture in your mind from the one in mine. I own a collie.

There are others who have been bitten by dogs, who raise them for sale, or breed them as fighters. There are dog trainers, dogcatchers, dog lovers, and vivisectionists. For each the associations that cling to the word are very different for— and this is a point that must be very clear—meaning isn't *in the word*; it is in the head of the person who uses it or hears it.

You have no doubt sat through pointless arguments as I did one evening. A young man was attacking New York. "A cheap, degraded, tawdry place," he called it. He was saying he preferred to live in the country, in the Middle West, "the true heart of America where there is still hope and respect for the land."

He was talking to an older woman who assured him that New York was something quite different. She would prefer to live in New York she said, "because it is the very center of all that is good in American life.

"It has," she said, "the best in music, the best literary minds. In New York we have the best hope of seeing, someday, a mature America."

They were both discussing "New York," but they were not talking about the same thing. Each was talking about *his own* experience of New York. The young man had lived in New York for several years. His experience had centered in the entertainment and night-club district. He had found it exciting but unsubstantial.

The woman, on the other hand, was a musician of talent and fine intellect. Her experience of the city included friendships with many of the leading musicians and writers of the day.

The word "New York" in its full meaning is a package of infinite experience. It means something different to each person in the world, depending on how much or how little he knows of it. Let us go further and consider such proper names as Rover, a particular collie dog, and Joe Doe, a particular resident of New York. Even these can't be pinned down.

Rover today is man's best friend and tomorrow is a vicious beast who bites the milkman. Joe Doe may have lent you money when you were in great need, but he overcharged me when I rented an apartment from him. You and I will not agree on just what "Joe Doe" represents.

Less picturable words are open to even more widely different meanings to different people. Look what the Russians have done with the word "democracy."

If you don't mind causing confusion ask each of the guests around the table at a dinner party to give the meaning of "love," "honor," "truth," or "fidelity." This can be as dangerous as playing with firearms, but if you do get answers, they will be neither simple nor uniform.

The meaning of any word you use spreads very wide through the experience of many people. And there is where you must look for it rather than in the dictionary. The dictionary is a help, of course. What it does give is the details of meaning upon which nearly everyone agrees. This is the patch where the various meanings known to millions of people overlap. For example, *Webster's Unabridged* says:

> New York—(City) cml. center of the U.S. & largest city of W hemisphere, SE N.Y. state at mouth of Hudson riv. lat. 40°42.7′ N. lon. 74°00.1′ W.

> dog—A carnivorous mammal (*Canis familiaris*) of the family Canidae, kept in a domesticated state by man since prehistoric times; in a wider sense, any member of the family Canidae (which see).

This latter is, of course, only the first meaning of "dog." There are 10 other primary meanings and 10 submeanings for "dog," as a noun, ranging from "the jaws of a lathe chuck" to "ostentatious style" (put on dog).

You can amuse yourself by looking up words like "truth" in a big dictionary. The definitions are longer, but they say less that you can lay a finger on.

In writing to inform, the aim, as we have said before, is to get the audience (1) to read, (2) to understand, and (3) to accept what you have written. "Accept" can be broken down still further into "believe, remember, act upon."

An understanding of "meaning" and the process of abstraction is basic to each of these steps. This chapter deals with the first two and the following chapter with the question of acceptance.

Picturable words are excellent bait to catch readers and hold them. A typical story is told of Arthur Brisbane, one of the most able communicators of recent times. When he was an editor for Hearst a new writer brought Brisbane an editorial headed "Hygienics and Dietetics in Ancient Times."

As he read it he was surprised to find that it made a highly interesting comparison between modern and ancient health and living standards. But with that title, he told the writer, no one but a few professors would read it. He crossed out the headline and wrote in words the reader could picture:

PITY POOR MOSES—HE HAD NO BATHTUB

"Now everybody will read your editorial," said Brisbane.

If you wish the reader to understand your message and to do so quickly—shy away from abstract terms.

The difficulty is that when one becomes very familiar with an abstract term he is in danger of forgetting that it may bring only a fuzzy, or sometimes a positively misleading, picture to the mind of the reader.

"Contingent annuitants" may have a concrete meaning to a person who deals with pensions and insurance, but few others will know that it stands for wives and children who may share in benefits.

In working for an oil company with international subsidiaries, I came across a letter aimed at discouraging new employees from taking their families abroad because of "unsuitable conditions." When asked to describe these "conditions," the writer did so in quite vivid terms: "no plumbing, few roads, sweltering climate." These words would have made a far more persuasive letter. They are picturable and easier to understand.

Those who work in the railroad industry have fallen into a habit of overusing the word "facility." When a traffic manager writes "the lake facility," a massive structure is pictured in *his* mind, but not in the mind of a reader who hasn't seen it. The correct picture would flash into any reader's mind more quickly if the traffic manager used the word "dock." Railroaders use the dustbin abstraction "facility" over and over when such words as "tracks," "roundhouse," and "yard" would communicate their meaning more clearly.

Search your own writing for fuzzy words. "Conditions," "situation," "facilities," "inadequacies" are typical examples. See if you can substitute for such foggy generalities, terms that come into focus with definite pictures.

The words which stand for things we can know by the senses are the safest for communication because the experience you and your reader have had with them has a larger area of overlap. When the movies first began, a most successful idiom of the new medium was the custard pie. These mushy missiles communicated not only to the eye, they awakened sensations of taste, touch, smell, and squashy sound as well.

Psychologists have shown that one sense in action often supports another. William James tells of an experiment by Urbantschitsch, "The hue of patches of color so distant as not to be recognized was, immediately, in his patients, perceived when a tuning fork was sounded close to the ear. Letters too far off to be read could be read when the tuning fork was heard."

Anyone working closely within an area of knowledge picks up its special terms because they are handy to think with. But in shifting from thinking to communication, place yourself in the position of the reader. If he is an outsider you must try to remember how little you knew before you picked up the special knowledge you know now. Failure to do this accounts for much foggy writing in newspapers. After a few months of "covering" the city hall, courthouse, or the Bureau of Standards, a reporter will start using terms which he didn't understand clearly himself a few months before. But now the abstractions have become so familiar to him that they seem concrete.

In an article about candidates who were expected to enter a city election, a Texas reporter wrote, "Raising the mayor's salary will also have political significance." For a reader "political significance" is an empty phrase until filled. The filling was in the reporter's mind but he left it out of the story. When asked what the phrase meant he said, "Raising the mayor's salary will bring more candidates into the race."

Another reporter trying to obey readability principles wrote this concise leading sentence, "The city's bonded indebtedness will be frozen after July 1."

Although short, the sentence is foggy. "Bonded indebtedness" had become a concrete term to this writer, who had covered the city hall for years. But for the public he should have used terms closer to the experience of most of us, for example: "After July 1 the city will be unable to borrow more money through sale of bonds.

Even the banker would understand that more quickly.

A farm editor wrote of "emergency facilities for wheat storage" and throughout his article failed to make the term more concrete. It turned out the wheat was being stored in airplane hangars. Imagine how "picturably" the newsreels could have told that story.

The translation from abstract to concrete for the purpose of understanding is important for good communication to the "insider" as well as the "outsider." The insider may be fully acquainted with the special uses of words within a company, an industry, or profession. The concrete words such as the special terms of the oil fields, "boom," "bit," "roughneck," give little trouble. But more general terms often fog communication even within the limited group which uses them regularly.

For example, an engineer wrote in a report that an alloy was "not fabricable." This is a general term that could mean many things. When he was advised to shift to more picturable terms, he wrote, "The alloy cracks when it is cold-rolled." This is a more particular and much clearer message for the engineers with whom he works.

A school principal who wants the PTA to buy a "slippery slide" and a "teeter-totter" for the playground will get further if he appeals in these concrete terms than if he asks for "recreational equipment."

At a luncheon meeting I heard a social worker speak on juvenile delinquency. He had a fine voice and a good vocabulary. The Rotarians seemed to be listening with attention.

But I put the talk down as failure. The Rotarians were given to understand that the problem was serious. This was bolstered by generalizations and supported by statistics, but the problem remained as remote as a food shortage in India.

The social worker was eager for the Rotarians to help young people of the community and keep them from getting into trouble. But he never brought the problem home to his listeners nor was he concrete as to what they could do about it. Here is a sample of his abstract language:

"Unless due regard is given the development of the child, the result will be irresponsibility, moral laxness, and inability to cope with the complexities of life."

Like the rest of the speech, that has a learned ring to it. But reduced to everyday language the message is not startling.

Everyone knows well enough that *Children brought up with out care are likely to become bums, crooks, or nitwits.*

That version puts the message in concrete terms rather than abstract ones but in so doing it also reveals the poverty of the idea. To have done a job of communication, the social worker would have had to go much further in picturing the problem. For instance, he might have said this:

"Gentlemen, I had a boy in my office this morning. His name was Tom and I want to tell you about him. Tom is in trouble. Last week he broke into a drugstore and smashed the cash register. He didn't get much—only fourteen dollars. But, then, he wasn't looking for much. He said all he wanted was some money to go to shows and wrestling matches.

"I've looked into Tom's case. His father's dead and his mother works to support Tom and three other children. I want to tell you how Tom was dressed, what he had for breakfast, and how he spends his time after school. . . ."

The social worker might have gone further in picturable terms and tied Tom's troubles directly into their own lives. He could have said:

"We are sending Tom away for a while now. But there are hundreds like him in this city. They need your help before they get into trouble. They need more playgrounds and more gymnasiums in community centers. They need men like you as friends they can talk to.

"And if something isn't done, a boy like Tom will be in your neighborhood some night soon aiming to steal and ready for violence."

Talk like that would have brought forth volunteers. It might even have wrung money from the treasury.

Thousands of speeches and editorials on juvenile delinquency have been wasted because they were pitched in terms too high up the ladder of abstraction. The social worker spoke to the Rotarians from the top rung of this one:

JUVENILE DELINQUENTS
BAD BOYS
TOM, DICK, AND JOE

The speaker had had much experience with boys in trouble. He could have come down to solid earth and told his story in picturable terms. Instead he stayed in the clouds atop the ladder of abstraction.

This is a mistake that great communicators never make. Aesop's *Fables* have lived for thousands of years because he turned lessons about greed, envy, anger, and other abstractions into picturable stories. Jesus spoke in parables.

Clear communication is always chancy when the terms used are well up the ladder of abstraction. It is safer to stay on the lower rungs, using the words that can be sensed through sight, touch, tastes, and smell. And when you do climb up the ladder of abstraction make quite sure you can come down quickly without missing a step when anyone asks, "What do you mean?" or, "How do you know?"

If you can do this you will not have lost your way with words. You may be speaking in general terms or in terms inferred from observable facts, but your meaning will be clear to you, at least.

The social worker, the engineer, and the news writers we have been discussing were all on upper rungs of the abstraction. They were not writing or speaking as clearly as they might have. But they were still straight in their own minds as to what they were talking about. Their abstraction was largely unconscious, but it was not irresponsible.

The most dangerous sort of abstraction floats on the top of a ladder which has no bottom. Very few are entirely free from this. We glibly use terms that have only a vague connection, if any, with observable facts. I have seen this happen with some of the best newspaper reporters in the country, men who are trained to seek and recognize the concrete.

A particularly able reporter handed me a story for testing when we were working with the staff of a Cincinnati paper. It concerned hospital insurance and included the sentence, "The rates are set by actuarial principles."

"That's a readable story, Mike," I told the reporter. "But what are 'actuarial principles'?"

"Oh, you know," he responded. This is the usual reply of one who has been caught on a limb of abstraction.

"No," I told him, "it's not very clear to me."

"You know," he persisted, " 'actuarial principles' are what insurance people use. . . ."

"To set rates. That goes round in a circle."

"I guess I don't know much about it." Mike smiled sheepishly. But he immediately set about finding out. He called the hospital-insurance people. They were not eager to give information. But after some persuasion and digging they backed "actuarial principles" down the abstraction ladder for us. Next day Mike had an excellent story telling the public in concrete terms what they wanted to know about their hospital-insurance rates.

Often news of public importance is hidden in the vagueness of an abstract term.

James Marlow, long a Washington columnist, considered it a duty to shoot down as many as he could of the abstractions that soar over Washington. It took several days to nail down the meaning of the simple term "handicapped person" used constantly by the Social Security Administration.

"What is a 'handicapped person'?" he asked at that office.

"You are a 'handicapped person,' " he was told.

"Me? Why?"

"You wear glasses."

"You mean you are going to give me money?"

"Oh, no."

"Then who are the 'handicapped persons' who can expect benefits?"

Marlow finally got a concrete story. "I think the session not only gave me a column," he told a session of the American Press Institute, "but also clarified thinking in the social security office."

Vast bitterness and violence has generated at the top of this ladder of abstraction:

CORPORATION PROFITS
MONEY WE EARNED AFTER TAXES
SIX CENTS ON THE DOLLAR

"Corporation Profits" is highly charged. When the term is mentioned many shareholders, on the one hand, and employees, on the other, tend to feel cheated.

Claude Robinson of Opinion Research Corporation made a survey several years ago among industrial workers. Their average guess as to what profits they thought companies made during the war was 30 per cent. The average guess for peacetime was 25 per cent. The workers questioned estimated a fair profit at 10 per cent.

Most companies make less than any of these figures. For better understanding, their communication about profits should be pitched at the lower levels of the abstraction ladder. Here are two other ladders of abstraction that have "fightin' words" at the top:

Socialistic Agitators	Malefactors of Great Wealth
Labor Bosses	Privileged Few
Union Executives	Corporation Executives
Phil, John, Walter	Ben, Henry, Frank

The pictures that come to mind when the terms at the top of these ladders are mentioned are the drawings made by cartoonists. But the better one knows the men who lead industry and labor the less likely he is to use, or become emotional about, the abstractions at the top of these ladders.

Below, to the left, is an example of the customary abstraction of business language taken from a corporation memo. The rewrite to the right is in more picturable, clearer terms.

ABSTRACT	PICTURABLE
Experts accused the city transit company of inefficient management and high operating costs due to poor scheduling, excess of manpower in the maintenance department, and purchase of buses beyond actual needs.	Experts said the city transit company was wasting money by (1) having buses at the wrong places at the wrong times, (2) hiring too many men for upkeep, (3) buying too many buses.

All of us are more likely to use picturable terms in speech than in writing. Recently I was working with a magazine staff. A woman writer produced this sentence:

"In industrial communities the chief motivation for the purchase of curtains is practicality."

I asked what that meant. In the spoken word her abstract statement became quite picturable. She said:

"In factory towns housewives buy curtains that wash well."

This single sentence illustrates most of the principles that we have so far discussed.

"Industrial communities" is far up the ladder of abstraction. But "factory town" is closer to earth. You can see a factory town—and smell it. The written sentence is little related to human experience. The spoken version introduces a human being as subject, the housewife. In the spoken version the force of the verb is smothered in "motivation for the purchase of." This became an active verb "buy" as the writer spoke. And that foggy abstraction "practicality" in the oral version becomes "wash well." The spoken sentence, you will also note, is considerably shorter.

Principle Eight

Tie In with Your Reader's Experience

This chapter, like the one before it, deals with meaning. But it moves to a distinctly different level. It is one thing to say that your reader *understands* what you have written, and quite another to be able to say that he *accepts* it.

Picturable words attract attention and hold it. They are a great help in getting the reader to take those first steps: (1) to read, and (2) to understand. But the third step goes beyond words. To find out what makes a reader *believe, remember,* and *act upon* what you write, you must study people rather than words themselves.

Words can be empty of meaning or they can mean the opposite of what they are intended to, when considered in relation to a background. And the background a reader brings to your words comes solely from his own experience. You can affect it only indirectly.

Much communication fails because writers ignore the beliefs of their readers, ignore how they came by them and how firmly they hold them. Millions of dollars are wasted each year in institutional advertising, for instance, because those who pay out the money are not aware of, or simply are im-

patient with, the preconceptions of those they hope to influence.

Some of the important research of recent years in
perception is the work of Professor Hoyt L. Sherman of Ohio
State University. Although a member of the Fine Arts Department, he has worked with aviators, dentists, advertising
men, and television staffs, helping them to see better with their
eyes and with their brains. For a time he even helped coach
the Ohio State football team. He showed backs how to see
faster and surer in spotting pass receivers and oncoming
tacklers. He broadened that age-old sports advice, "Keep
your eye on the ball."

"Certainly," says Professor Sherman, "keep your eye on
the ball. But in doing that don't fail to keep your *attention*
on the whole field."

Professor Sherman adapts a classic psychological demon-
stration to show what Gestalt psychology calls the relation of
"figure" to "ground." The subject sits in a pitch-dark room.
A point of light (figure) is flashed on. Although it is stationary it *appears* to move. No observer is able to keep the
light from seeming to wander. But the moment another light
is thrown on the subject, say on the end of his nose, the first
one becomes stationary. The figure now has a ground and takes
a position in relation to that ground.

We perceive words in much the same way. A statement cut
off from context is a "figure" that simply floats about. There
must be another point of reference, a "ground" to give it
stability and meaning. And you can't count on the reader's
going farther than the end of his nose to construct that ground.

For the reader the "ground" always comes from his past
experience. He judges your words and gives them meaning
on the basis of that experience. And he looks between and
around the words for side-signals and often gives these more
meaning than he does the words themselves. The tone of a

piece or the manner in which it is printed may serve as a side-signal. There are many of them. We shall have examples presently.

You may know your reader. You may have done business with him or he may know the company or organization you represent. If so, you have had a part in building his past experience. Furthermore you may help him recall certain parts of his experience that will persuade him to accept your meaning.

But you can never supply his "ground" for your "figure." To have your meaning accepted you must understand his ground thoroughly and project your figure on it and in harmony with it.

The story of a friend of mine who came home from engineering school for the holidays illustrates how absurd a figure can be when it gets out of harmony with ground. My friend's aunt told him he must be in the annual church Christmas pageant. He insisted that this year he would not. He would be glad to handle the lights.

"We have someone for the lights," his aunt told him. "You simply must be in the pageant. I'll make it easy for you. You won't have to rehearse. You won't have to learn lines. Just go to the costumer's and get a pilgrim's costume and the night of the pageant you can come late and walk on and read your lines from a scroll."

The student went to the costumer's and got his buckled shoes, gray suit, tall gray hat, and blunderbuss. He arrived just in time to receive his scroll and walk on. And there, before the Virgin, the Child, and the manger, and with the star of Bethlehem shining above, he unrolled the scroll and read with the rising inflection of a shocked and startled man:

"Here come I a pilgrim from—*Far Arabia!*"

My friend had brought *his* figure to the audience without giving thought to *their* ground. Much industrial advertising and promotion is as thoughtlessly produced and equally out of harmony. The words of the printed material may mean what they are supposed to mean to those who write the words and pay for them. But because of a different background of experience readers get an entirely different meaning from the same words.

An experiment conducted by *Fortune* showed how much more important ground can be than figure in a piece of printed matter. Here's the magazine's account:

> A cartoon chart of "The Four Goals of Labor" was clipped from a CIO newspaper and photostated. A new legend, however, was attached to the bottom: "From June 3 National Association of Manufacturers Newsletter." Twenty CIO members were then shown the ad and asked if they thought it was a fair presentation of labor's goals. Four grudgingly said it was and two couldn't make up their minds. The remaining fourteen damned it as "patronizing," "loaded," "paternalistic," "makes me want to spit."*

Probably no one, and almost certainly no adult American, takes words to mean just what they say unless they are surrounded by other signs which allow their acceptance. Anyone interested in the problem should study films Allen Funt prepared for his *Candid Camera* show on television. In one, an excellent lesson in the relation of words to their setting, Funt takes over a photographer's shop on the upper floors of a New York building. A keen, friendly gentleman of about fifty drops in for some pictures. He is a missionary just returned from an overseas post.

Funt, posing as the keeper of the shop, expresses interest in this work and asks questions about the natives and what is

* Copyrighted, *Fortune*. From "Is Anybody Listening?" by William H. Whyte, Jr. September, 1950.

being done for them. While the two are talking Funt's assistant enters. In a routine voice, as if he were asking for another can of developer, he announces the building is on fire. The firemen are in the street below, he says, and flames are spreading.

The missionary hears all this. He looks at Funt and, since there is no show of alarm, he immediately returns to conversation about his mission.

Dick, the assistant, returns twice more with bulletins about the fire. Finally he comes in putting on his coat. The front stairs are blocked by flames, he announces quietly. When Funt and his customer leave they had better take the back way.

For the first time the missionary shows concern, but he still looks to Funt for the sign that will give Dick's words the meaning that will set them all running for their lives. When Funt finally says that perhaps they should go, the missionary springs for the door and then the hoax is revealed.

This example is interesting because it once more shows the overwhelming importance of ground—the experience of the listener or reader. The missionary had very little immediate evidence to form his ground for Dick's words. Funt was almost as much a stranger to him as Dick. Still the missionary rejected Dick's words and looked to Funt for judgment. He did so for two reasons.

In the first place the side-signs of danger were not present. The scene did not fit the missionary's preconceptions of how a fire is announced. None of the stereotypes were there. Anyone who has been in a fire, or who has done no more than read the comics, knows what these are. Sirens sound and bells clang. There are shouts of *"Fire!"* and the smell of smoke. Everyone is excited, even the strong, tense character who orders, "Don't get excited. File to the nearest exit. Walk; don't run."

But even more instructive is the trust the missionary placed in Funt. Here he was, very far from the land he called home, and in the presence of two strangers. But one of the strangers during a few short moments, had been interested in him and what he was doing. As a consequence the missionary automatically assumed that here was a friend—a friend who would not allow him to perish in a burning building. He took his meaning from the reaction of the new friend rather than from the words of another who had paid him no heed.

No one who writes, I suppose, is wholly unaware of the need to tie in with his reader's experience. Still, very many failures in communication, I have found, can be chalked up to violation of this principle. The failure can be said to take one of two forms:

One: Failure to examine the reader's experience thoroughly enough with the result that some side-sign is overlooked and upsets the intended meaning.

Two: Failure to understand that the reaction the reader makes to your words is part of his basic mechanism of survival and will be based on sensation rather than reason. A writer often becomes impatient or stubborn when a reader fails to accept what is logical (to the writer). The only path is one of patience. If a message is truly logical there will be a way to relate the writer's figure to the reader's ground so that it will at length be accepted.

The reader's personal experience is not only the sole means he *will* use, it is the sole means he *can* use to give your words meaning.

Clinging to any printed page are side-signs that may speak louder than the words of the immediate message. An unknown firm can gain stature by placing a large ad in a well-known publication. Quality of stationery or the name on a letterhead may give a reader definite meaning. A collection letter on the stationery of an attorney may get action where the same letter on a grocer's letterhead failed.

Side-signs change from day to day. Every public-relations man is alert to timing. He knows that a news release about a price increase will mean one thing to the public the day after a wage increase and something else the day after an appeal from the President to check inflation.

Particularly important is the tone of a message, and the Fog Index can be useful here. Let us consider two examples of announcements made by companies during labor trouble.

During one of the most costly strikes of recent history, one company published a series of expensive newspaper advertisements. Since each ad contained nearly a thousand words, there is room here for only a sample. A single sentence, however, will give you an idea of the style:

"Notwithstanding the importance of reestablishing employment and resuming production at the earliest possible moment, the above reasons have made it impossible for the company to participate in the proceedings of the board under the procedures as now established, and it has therefore withdrawn from the hearings."

The ad as a whole had a Fog Index of 13 (above the difficulty rating of the *Atlantic Monthly*). Very few newspaper readers would have labored through it. The aim of the ads was to win favor with the general public. But it was not written in language familiar to the public. Most of it had a strong legal flavor.

In any strike a company hopes to influence the members of a union man's family. If the wife of a striker had managed to struggle through one of these long ads, the side-sign of the tone would have been enough to alter the meaning: "They don't speak my language. Ed must be right."

In contrast, consider this small sample of prose prepared by one of the most able public-relations men in the country. The strike in this instance never occurred. The men accepted the company's offer and did not walk out:

NOW WHAT'S IT ALL ABOUT THIS TIME?

The company has made a proposal that would make its employees among *the highest paid in this industry.*

But the union leaders demand more—always more.

You'll agree—any fair-minded person will agree—that the company's proposal is reasonable and just.

Let's see—

The company has proposed:

—an increase of 12 cents over the board an hour for everyone

—a reduction in scheduled hours of work from 44 hours a week to 40

—pay for 7 holidays with double time for those who work on these holidays.

Note that this is a hard-hitting piece. This chapter says, "Consider the reader's point of view." But don't take that to mean, "Go over to his way of thinking." Your *figure* should be as personal as his *ground.* If you write in his language and tie your facts into his experience, you have a good chance of his accepting them. The announcement above has a Fog Index of 7—easy reading for nearly anyone.

The author of this piece goes to great length to get the workmen's point of view. For instance, when a strike threatened in a West Coast plant he was dissatisfied with reports he received from the offices there. He traveled across the continent, and, in workman's clothes, sat, fishing, for several days on the docks. He found out from other fishermen what was wrong at the plant. They were minor items such as too short time for personal relief and poor food in the restaurant. Nothing had been said about these matters in the union's demands. But when these items were remedied the unrest disappeared.

Judge for yourself the side-effects of the following two pieces of prose. They are excerpts from employee handbooks and both deal with the same subject. The one to the left was written before we worked with the writers of that company. The second was prepared by a writer following readability principles. The Fog Index shows the piece to the right is much easier reading. However, the improvement in tone is as important as the improvement in ease of reading. The piece to the right is written with the reader in mind and is related to his point of view:

Fog Index 17	*Fog Index 6*
Separation Classifications	If We Part

As the separation of personnel is bound to be necessary in any business, the company has established certain policies and practices to assure that such separations are made on an equitable basis and only after full and complete consideration of the individual case, as follows:

When an individual leaves the employ of the company it may be due to one of a variety of causes such as voluntary resignation, misconduct, unsatisfactory service, the curtailment of discontinuance of operations, etc. Some of these causes are within the control of the employee; others are not. It therefore becomes desirable to establish separation classifications based on the causes of the separation so that the employee's equities may be adequately considered. These classifications are emphasized in detail in the Appendix on pages 12 and 13.

We want you to like us. We want you to fit in. We want you to belong. But if the day does come when we must part company, we want you to understand your rights and privileges.

Before you consider *resigning* for any reason, talk with your department head. There are many opportunities with this company. You may miss a good one if you leave us. If you do resign, we'd appreciate your giving us at least two weeks' notice.

It's an unpleasant task, but sometimes for the good of an employee, his fellow workers, and the company we must discharge or dismiss one of the men or women who work for us . . . etc.

The side-effects a piece of writing may produce have roots deeper than the immediate tone. They trace to the reader's knowledge of the behavior, up to that time, of the source of the words. No person, institution, or company can say one thing and do the opposite without destroying faith in what is said in the future. The sensitivity of Americans to this practice is indicated by the number of colorful terms used to describe words that do not jibe with action. "Boloney" is one of the more polite.

Officials in both government and business often tend toward complex and formal language because they fear the word-twister. Statements are couched in semilegal terms with the idea they can only be taken to say what they are meant to mean. Such practice is usually misguided. Announcements with a high Fog Index are excellent grist for the word-twister. Straightforward English that can be easily read and understood by everyone is the safer course.

What I have been saying emphasizes that human beings are self-centered and intent on their own purposes. This is not startling news. Anyone will agree. But it is easy to hold a view without giving it full application. Much failure in writing results from a lack of understanding of how self-centered readers are. The writers, you see, are too self-centered themselves to notice the quality in others.

Consider, for instance, how self-centeredness underlies an important difference between real life and fiction. Successful fiction is full of villains. But if one sets out to find a villain in real life the problem is less simple. You have your list of villains, no doubt, and the other fellow has his, but seldom do any two lists agree. The better one knows a man the less likely he is to list him a villain. And I doubt that anyone puts himself on the list.

Some years ago when a large state penitentiary was my newspaper beat, I often talked with the men in "death row." I found no villains there—by their own estimates. Most of the condemned men admitted certain acts (shooting policemen, for example). Some would even admit that such acts were crimes. But I never ran across one who did not feel that he was justified in what he had done. Hitler, of course, had a similar point of view.

But a writer who spins stories in which all men are well-meaning finds his wares hard to sell. A struggle between good and evil has long been the mainspring of storytelling. It is difficult to construct a story without an embodiment of evil. And the reason for this goes back once more to the self-centeredness of human beings.

We prefer to read about people who are more wicked or worse off than we are. Al Capp, who draws "Li'l Abner," declares humor has the same basis. He says humor is usually a picture of misfortune and we laugh at those less fortunate than we are because it makes us feel good.

In his *How to Write a Novel*, Manuel Komroff points out that readers will accept any amount of misfortune in a story, with little explanation. On the other hand, if a character has a single piece of good fortune there must be a careful build-up or the reader will not accept it.

Note how strongly you project your own purposes or welfare into each reading experience. When you read an editorial, in the back of your mind are the questions: What is he trying to get me to do? What is he trying to sell me? What is in it for him?

There is no reason to despise this attitude of self-centeredness. It is part of the mechanism of survival. Even suspicion is healthy so long as it is not carried to extremes.

Charlie, who cooked for a group of us on a camp trip, was one who carried suspicion too far. We found Charlie easy to get along with, but on the first Saturday night Charlie went to the neighboring village and ended up in jail for striking a stranger. When we went to bail him out, he explained:

"This fellow came down the street. I could see he was going to hit me. So I hit him first."

On the second and third Saturday nights Charlie started

fights on the same basis. After a drink or two Charlie thought not only that everyone's attention was on him but that "they" were after him, as well. For Charlie *believing* was *seeing*.

Charlie's suspicion bordered on paranoia. Not many readers are so far gone. But they all have a little of it. Charlie's plight is quite depressing when one reviews international affairs of recent years and notes the deadly parallel.

The good teacher constantly makes use of analogy. In fact, the measure of a teacher rests on his ability to link the new fact or idea with some experience the pupil has already had. An engineer friend of mine once demonstrated this. He had come to my home with his three small children. While he and I played tennis, his children and mine froze popsicles in the refrigerator. As we were having a cooling drink, his nine-year-old spoke up, "Daddy, how does a gas refrigerator work?"

At this point many would say, "Run along and play." But my friend was a good father and a good teacher.

"Do you have some rubbing alcohol in the house?" he asked me. I nodded. "Get me some and some cotton," he said.

When I returned, he had half-a-dozen children circled around him. "Stick out your hands," he told them, demonstrating with his own fist, back of hand up.

He dabbed alcohol on hands all around. "Now blow," he instructed, then asked, "What happened?"

"It got cold," was the answering chorus. The engineer was halfway home with his lesson. He had found a way to tie in with the experience of even the youngest. Even the five-year-old ended up with a better understanding of the gas refrigerator which is still a mystery to his mother.

Let us briefly summarize in five points this principle and the last, both of which deal with abstraction and meaning.

One: Words are not fixed. They vary in meaning from person to person, the meaning depending upon the experience of that person and the pictures the words recall to mind.

Two: Highly abstract terms are often very useful for thinking but they are tricky in communication because they are open to such wide interpretation. It is safer to stay on the lower rungs of the ladders of abstraction so you can quickly demonstrate when someone asks, "What do you mean?" or "How do you know?" Above all, be sure that the abstract terms you use in either thought or communication are tied to facts. Don't be caught on the upper rungs of ladders of abstraction which have no bottom.

Three: In trying to persuade the reader to accept your words, remember that the meaning he gives them will be determined entirely by his past experience and purposes.

Here are a few quotes from Dr. Adelbert Ames, Jr., then head of Institute of Associated Research, Hanover, New Hampshire, which is devoted to research in visual sensation and human behavior. Dr. Ames's work links closely with that of Professor Sherman, whom we mentioned at the opening of this chapter. And at Dartmouth College and Ohio State and Princeton Universities there are visual centers where the public can witness laboratory demonstrations based on Dr. Ames's work. He says:

> Although the human organism in its behavior acts as the result of stimuli, these stimuli have in themselves no meaning. The significances that are related to them in consciousness—and are experienced by the organism as sensations—are derived entirely from the organism's prior experience, personal or inherited.
>
> This point of view is contrary to the prevailing lay and scientific belief that what is in consciousness has its origin either in whole or in part in the immediate externality or in the stimulus pattern.
>
> Meaning is significance which is determined by the organism's prior purposeful action. . . . The function of sensation is to establish between the evolving organism and the ever-changing environment a relationship on the basis

of which the organism may effectively carry out its purpose. . . . The function of sensation is to disclose alternate possible courses of action. It is the purpose of the organism in the "now" that determines which course will be followed.

Or to paraphrase, we see what we, from experience, *expect* to see; and we attend what we believe is useful to us—at this moment. Many others, over the years, including possibly Aristotle, have said much the same. The difficulty: few listen.

These principles of Dr. Ames are open to very wide application over the whole field of human behavior. But, here we are rather far up the ladder of abstraction. Let us back down quickly to see how all this can be applied to a practical problem of day-to-day business communication.

One of the largest corporations of the nation used to send out a form letter as follows:

"Kindly favor us with a reply to our Delinquent Invoice Request dated ———, a copy of which is herewith attached for your ready reference.

"It is imperative that we have an early reply to this communication."

This message is framed in the language, and from the point of view, of the accounting department. It is a follow-up letter and the company found it was often tossed aside without answer like those that preceded it.

In order to get action, the following revision was framed from the point of view of the person who was to receive the letter:

"We may owe you money. But we can't pay you until you send us a bill. The attached form will help you make out the invoice. Please send it to us at once."

Four: To get your words read, understood, and accepted you must have a very clear understanding of your own purposes and of the purposes of the reader. If these purposes differ you have two courses for winning acceptance of your message. You must either change your reader's purpose, or you must show him that though your purposes differ in part, they have, at the same time, much in common.

A short-story writer can write fantasy and convince the reader he should accept it by making plain the promise of an exciting story.

In writing a business letter you can persuade the other fellow to help you if you show, with particulars, how he can help himself at the same time.

I hope that you will write clearer, more effective English. So in this book I try to persuade you to do so by telling you how many more readers you will gain and how much your skill of clear writing is needed in business and journalism.

Five: The last point is perhaps most important. In writing don't get lost in details. "Keep your eye on the field as well as on the ball." Otherwise you will overlook some side-signal that will destroy or undermine the meaning of your words for the reader.

M. H. Williams, editor in Worchester, Massachusetts, had a favorite saying: "It isn't enough to write so you will be understood. You have to write so you can't be misunderstood."

Principle Nine

Make Full Use of Variety

The very complicated matter of clear communication involves, after all, but three factors: (1) the audience, (2) language, (3) you.

This book has paid particular attention to the audience, pointing out that most writing that fails does so because the writer is ignorant of the reader's tastes, abilities, purposes, and mental processes.

And, as all books about writing must, this one has spent many pages suggesting how words of the language can be made to serve you best.

This chapter turns to you. It deals with the development of your personal writing style. What you are, as well as what you know, shows up in your writing. There is no such thing as an "impersonal" style unless you choose to define it as one that shows the writer is not interested.

The richer your experience, the wider your knowledge, the deeper your feeling—the better your writing will be, provided you are able to transmit these values into words. *The style of your writing will grow as you grow*. You can help it present you to the world as you wish to be presented by becoming versed in the variety of the language.

There are interesting psychological reasons why variety is so important in writing.

In the first place you will rarely find in the realm of words "the reproducible experiment." No one can be sure that last year's advertising slogan will work next year. And certainly the speech that was such a success a month ago will have to be revised this month. If the audience is to be the same as last month's, the speech will have to be entirely different.

This fact, that the right way to put a particular message into words is always changing, is annoying to most people. The easiest way to run a business is to set up rules and patterns that work and then to move on to the next problem. The easiest way to do a job is to do it like someone else did it, and not undergo the effort of thinking whether the job could be done better. Most people at work worship the reproducible experiment. And well they might, for it has done wonders in the laboratory, the shop, and the office.

An engineer working in Sweden melts three metals together and produces a new alloy that will stand up under the terrific heat of jet engines. An engineer in America can follow the record of the Swedish experiment, take the same steps, and come up with the same result.

Much that man has built can be credited to the use of the reproducible experiment. It is an extremely handy device in any institution. Once the step-by-step pattern of a job is developed it is relatively simple to train others to do it. They learn by imitation. The old employee "breaks in" the new man.

In the same way each generation begins, not at the start, but where the other left off. Thus the human race, as well as nations and corporations, keep on growing even though individuals die off.

It follows that your ability to learn by imitation is one of the most valuable skills you have for serving an employer or your community. There are many patterns proved by use. The quicker you learn them and fit into them, the more useful you will be to a going concern. This applies to spelling and to the multiplication table. It goes also for the basic methods of accounting and touch typewriting and for the laws of libel. Mathematics, the rules of spelling, the law, and the most efficient manner of working a mechanical device are all comparatively fixed.

But writing—that's a different matter. Words are never fixed like numbers or machines. Some administrators and efficiency experts would perhaps be happy at the discovery of *the* way to write, *the* advertising campaign that is sure to pay off, or *the* simple explanation that everyone is sure to understand. But you can rest assured you will not see such discoveries. Before they come the human race will have turned to stone.

You cannot be satisfied with imitation and do any job of writing well. You must be able to create as well as imitate. You must be able to size up each new situation, see how it is different, and fit the different words to it that do the job best. To do this you need a wide knowledge of the flexibility and variety of the language.

Now and then certain combinations of simple words will grow in power as they are read or heard and repeated by more and more people. Slogans, proverbs and some lines of poetry are typical examples. To work their way into the language they must fit the tongue well and usually they must have a twist that entertains the wit: "A stitch in time saves nine." "Something there is that doesn't love a wall." "Good to the last drop."

To wear well and grow with repetition a slogan or proverb must be of such a nature that people can pump meaning into it. It can be, on the one hand, highly abstract so that each man can find his own meaning in it. The motto of the French Republic—"Liberty, Equality, Fraternity"—is an example. Or, on the other hand, the words may be very concrete but open to broad figurative interpretation. "Birds of a feather flock together," for example.

If you can frame an idea in words so apt that others will repeat them you have done a good job of communication. But this job of creation is sharply different from composing with the clichés and phrases borrowed from others. When you try to express *your* message in combinations of words created by others, communication is weakened. Catchwords intended to inspire, if they are right, grow in power with repetition. But with the common stream of words intended merely to pass along facts and ideas, the principle is different. The power of such words tends to deteriorate upon repetition.

No one likes to receive a form letter. He has an imbedded distaste for such stereotypes, sensing that they cannot be perfectly fitted to either the occasion or the person. Still, form letters are a necessity in a big company. Most companies go to a great effort to disguise a form letter and have copies of it typed individually on mechanical typewriters. But even so, the text goes out of date rapidly. Few will hold up more than a year.

In the human mind there is constant tension between the desire for security and the desire for adventure. On the one hand, we like things that don't change. On the other hand, we can't stand them if they stay the same. Most of us will settle for fixation in the laws of, say, physics and morality. But in day-to-day life we want change and action. This certainly applies to what we read.

When words are brought together to carry a message, they acquire something they did not have separately. Their message may be compared with a charge of static electricity. Come in contact with the group of words and the spark of meaning jumps. Thereafter the words will have lost something of their power for you. Once you have absorbed the message, that particular pattern of words will be for you a sucked orange skin. To make the same message have a spark for you again, words will have to be brought together in a fresh way.

The deterioration of meaning can be observed even in single words that are repeated over and over. The evolution of "soon" contains a wry comment on human nature. Originally the word meant "at once," "without delay, immediately." But that meaning is now obsolete. Today "soon" means "before long." "Directly" is undergoing the same decay. In common speech "I'll do it directly" means "I'll do it when I get around to it." What may "at once" mean in another century?

How does one go about getting the variety into his writing that will make it interesting and give it his personal touch? There are many mechanical devices of prose style that will help and we shall examine some of them presently. But the essence of the variety that goes into your style must come from within you. There is no need to strain for newness in what you write. Your relaxed conversation is a good reflection of you as a person. Try to get the best points of this into your writing. Here are three steps toward building a personal writing style:

One: Find yourself.

Two: Find the words.

Three: Find the cadence that makes of those words *you speaking*.

Written words with power have a voice in them. When you read them you hear a human being speaking. If you are acquainted with him you can recognize the "voice."

In these examples you hear a man who has found himself, found the words, and found his voice. From these short passages you may be able to identify the writer:

"July 4. Statistics show that we lose more fools on this day than in all the other days of the year put together. This proves, by the number left in stock, that one Fourth of July per year is now inadequate, the country has grown so."*

* Mark Twain.

Here are three statements in another distinctive voice:

"The British and French Cabinets presented a front of two melons crushed together; whereas what was needed was a gleam of steel."

"Each one hopes that if he feeds the crocodile enough it will eat him last."

"Africa is not a seat, it is a springboard."†

And here are two statements in still another famous voice of this century:

"Marriage is popular because it combines the maximum of temptation with the maximum of opportunity."

"Democracy substitutes election by the incompetent many for appointment by the corrupt few."‡

Here are the words of two other writers whose names are less familiar, but note their distinctive flavor. The first is Jesse Stuart (who finally wrote a novel) talking about himself:

" 'Can I write a novel?' I asked myself. I wondered. I had been told by my friends that I could not. For four years I'd promised my publishers to write one. But when I came to New York on a visit I'd drop in with a new collection of short stories. . . .

" 'I'm a terrible liar,' I told myself. If I never intend to write a novel I should not be telling people that I am going to write one."

"Here's another writer, Ernest Gebler, of Dublin, talking about himself:

"My mother attributed my not going to the university to my father's drinking too much. He was unhappy. A musician. Very frustrated. A Czech. *She* never drank. A pity. An Irish woman."

So "natural," these words of Stuart and Gebler. What could be easier than to write like that? The sentences sound easy

† Winston Churchill.
‡ George Bernard Shaw.

and natural because these men have succeeded in putting their own voices into what they write. But this is no easy thing to do. Each person talks with his own voice, but when he starts to write he often tries to be someone else.

It takes effort, determination, and practice to put your own voice into written words. But it is one of the chief keys to effective writing. And that goes for everything from business letters to novels.

Here is about as simple a business note as we have come across in our work. But it is a good one and effective because it has a human voice in it:

"I was just looking over your last Safety Meeting Minutes and they sure look good. I know you are going to be on top this month.

"I will try to make your next meeting. Could you have it on a Monday morning, say, 10 or 11, March 27?

"Let me know if you need more suggestion blanks."

Once you succeed in putting your voice into your written words you will not have to worry much about variety. Each individual is unique. Once your style of writing fits you it will have its own character. Like your face, it will be different from all others.

Finding yourself

Personal integration is not easy in these days of upset standards and of conflict. Many Americans, the psychologists tell us, fail to grow up emotionally, fail to mature. Or, as we often put it in the vernacular, "Fail to find themselves."

I recall what an old scout told me years ago when I was lost in the woods. I told him I didn't know which way to go.

"Son," he said, "that ain't your trouble. Your trouble is you don't know how you got here. You're never lost if you know which way you come."

The psychiatrists do little more, I suspect, than point out to one where he came from and how he got where he is. Once this is clear, a person is no longer lost and can go forward.

One of the nation's most successful pastors said he asked himself two questions each morning. "Who am I?" and "What am I doing?" Each morning he was "finding himself" in preparation for the day's tasks.

It is helpful to face any task with these two questions. Try giving a few moments' thought to the answers before you set words on paper. It will help you find the words to speak for *you* and to the point.

These questions are simple but can be devastating. There are whole institutions today that could be destroyed by sounding through the halls the question, "What are you doing?" Once a pattern has been established, organizations, as well as individuals, tend to follow it. And they often do so long after the pattern has become meaningless.

Before you can write, or do any other job most effectively, you must find yourself. That means examining the past and planning for the future, and this is not only a long-span process, but a moment-to-moment one as well. Follow it and you will not imitate old patterns that no longer make sense. Instead you will make good use of variety to meet each new situation.

Finding the words

Finding the words is, frankly, more than a lifetime job. I have found the most highly skilled writers in any group to be the ones most eager to learn more about clear expression. The more they write, the more acutely aware they become of the vast possibilities of the language. And the more deeply they feel the inability of any mortal to gain complete control of words. They are seeking any information that may help.

To gain power over words, you must become intimately acquainted with them and their variety. John Dos Passos is one of many who fear that Americans' grasp of language is on the downgrade. He speaks of the "new problem of illiteracy." The *old* problem of illiteracy has almost disappeared; fewer than 3 per cent of the adults in the United States are unable to read and write. The new illiteracy, the vice of fog, has come to take the place of the old problem.

Dos Passos points out that two generations ago regular reading of the Bible in American families "kept a basic floor of literacy under literature as a whole, and under the English language." It kept before a major portion of the population a high standard of style. Today there is no such general experience with excellent prose.

Meanwhile pictures in magazines and on the screens compete with written words, even threaten to displace them. Pictures take up much leisure that used to be spent in reading. And without wide reading no one can gain the command of words and their relationships that a skilled writer requires. Vocabulary, for example, has a direct relationship to the amount of reading a person does. The average student leaves high school with about 12,000 words at his command. Whether that number increases or decreases depends almost entirely upon the amount of reading he does after graduation.

To "find the words," read widely. Read material by skilled writers and, as you do so, note how they exercise variety.

Note the diversity of their sentence length. In most instances you will find some very short sentences from one to five words. Then there will be some longer ones. You may find some, but not many, of more than 40 words.

Note also sentence structure. Some sentences will be simple subject-verb or subject-verb-object statements. Others will include subordinate clauses beginning with "that," "who," or some similar word. And there will be compound sentences linked with "and," "but," or some other conjunction.

Further note the changes in tone, contrast, and shifts in point of view that pluck up your attention with surprises.

Here is a sample of writing picked entirely at random. It is the opening paragraph from a *Saturday Evening Post* travel article by Martha Gellhorn as it appeared in *Reader's Digest*. You will find equal variety in the writing of almost any popular magazine you open:

> Capri is a large limestone and sandstone rock in the Bay of Naples. Its five-and-a-half square mile area is shaped roughly like a figure eight. And it is thoroughly impractical. Although surrounded by the bluest water in the world, there is no water to drink—it must be imported at a dollar a ton. The harbor is scarcely a harbor. The sides of the island are perpendicular cliffs. The surface of the island is more cliffs. Nothing is on the level. There are two roads resembling roller-coaster tracks. When the Bay of Naples acts up, as it often does, you cannot get to Capri or get off it. Nevertheless, more than 100,000 visitors brave the sea-sick-making bay each year in order to see what heaven is like.

The sentences in this short passage have great variety. They range in length from 5 words to 20 with an average of 12. The pattern goes like this: 13—15—5—15—9—6—8—8—5—7—20—20.

Now let us tear the piece apart to find some other samples of its variety. Shifts in sentence structure, tone, and point of view all help to make it interesting:

> Capri is a large limestone and sandstone rock in the Bay of Naples.
>
> (*Simple sentence: Subject-verb-compliment.*)
>
> Its five-and-a-half square miles is shaped roughly like a figure eight.
>
> (*Simple sentence: Passive verb and picturable comparison*).

And it is thoroughly impractical.
(*Simple sentence. "And" at beginning gives emphasis.*)

Although surrounded by the bluest water in the world, there is no water to drink—
(*Complex sentence starting with clause changes rhythm.*)

—it must be imported at a dollar a ton.
(*Actually separate sentence but linked to other with dash.*)

The harbor is scarcely a harbor.
(*Simple sentence.*)

The surface of the island is more cliffs.
(*Simple sentence with surprise.*)

Nothing is on the level.
(*Simple sentence. Humor.*)

There are two roads resembling roller-coaster tracks.
(*Simple-sentence rhythm broken by introduction with "there are." Picturable.*)

When the Bay of Naples acts up, as it often does, you cannot get to Capri.
(*Complex sentence. Shift from third person to "you."*)

Nevertheless, more than 100,000 visitors brave the sea-sick-making bay each year in order to see what heaven is like.
(*Complex sentence, contrast, and surprise.*)

This sample is a piece of light and entertaining cleverness from what the writers call a "slick" magazine. But the same principles should be used in the most factual letters and reports—not to make them light and clever, but simply to make them clearer and more interesting. These principles are techniques of organization. Any writer of a letter or report has a duty of organization. He must not be content to deliver facts to his reader as he would a bushel of leaf lettuce.

Let us take as an example a portion of a "dry" scientific report written by an engineer engaged in research. His superior rejected the report because "the sentences were too short." As we shall see, it is not the shortness of the sentences but the monotony of the structure that makes the piece unappealing. What the report lacks is the sort of variety we have just been examining. Here is a sample of it:

"Three alloys were prepared containing 3, 4, and 5 per cent of tungsten, respectively. Tensile strength tests were run on these samples using standard methods previously described. The tests showed that the tungsten added increased the strength. The increase in strength was proportional to the amount added.

"Three other alloys were prepared containing 3, 4, and 5 per cent of manganese, respectively. Tests of tensile strength were run on these. The alloy containing 3 per cent of manganese showed 10 per cent increase in strength. The alloy containing 4 per cent of the manganese showed 20 per cent increase in strength. The alloy containing 5 per cent manganese was less strong than that containing no manganese and its hardness had decreased, too."

Now let us revise this, using variety of sentence pattern and structure:

"A series of three alloys were prepared containing 3, 4, and 5 per cent of tungsten. When these were tested for tensile strength by the method already described, those with more tungsten proved stronger. The increase proved proportional to the amount of tungsten added.

"Next, three more alloys were prepared with manganese in the same amounts—3, 4 and 5 per cent. Three per cent of manganese increased the alloy strength by 10 per cent; 4 per cent increased it 20 per cent. But when 5 per cent was added the alloy became more brittle and less hard than one containing none of the element."

The second version, through variety of sentence structure,

yields its meaning more quickly. The irritating monotony of the original is gone. And although the second version cuts the length in words by 10 per cent, the average sentence length is the same—16 words.

People in business generally lack flexibility of expression. Those with engineering training are often overly formal in their writing. So are lawyers and accountants. They feel a lack of experience in English and tend to adhere to a stiffness of style. They feel it's safer. Others who have had little formal training in English cautiously follow the forms that have been used in their jobs before. The result is accumulated dullness and verbosity.

There are, of course, a dozen ways of expressing any idea. The parts of an English sentence can be tumbled about like glass chips in a kaleidoscope. One pattern of words will be better than another for certain purposes. Each different version gives a slightly different emphasis. Each has a different rhythm or cadence. Which is best will be determined by the exact meaning you wish to impart and by the way the particular sentence matches those that surround it.

Here, for example, are a few different ways of setting down the idea: "Clear, interesting writing contains all sorts of variety."

> PERSONAL: Variety will give your writing clarity and interest.
>
> CONDITIONAL: If you would employ variety, you would write more interestingly.
>
> SPECIFIC: Variety in words, sentences, tones, and structure is a key to interesting writing.
>
> NEGATIVE: Writing which has no variety lacks sparkle and interest.
>
> COMPARISON: Writing that has variety interests the reader; prose that lacks it is dull.
>
> PREPOSITIONAL BEGINNING: Without variety, prose is dull.

PARTICIPIAL: Lacking variety, prose is uninteresting.

IMPERATIVE: Put variety in what you write in order to interest your reader.

BEGINNING WITH CLAUSE: What your reader likes is variety; give him that and you will hold his interest.

These eight are no more than structural changes and it is easy to see that each one could be varied in several different ways. If one cares to use his imagination and become figurative, the possibilities for variety are unlimited.

We might paraphrase William Cowper, who was writing some 200 years ago, and say, "Variety is the spice of prose." Or we could paraphrase Disraeli and say, "Variety in prose is the mother of enjoyment in reading."

When you have the idea you wish to express clearly in mind, consider the various ways it may be phrased. Then select from that variety the ones that fit you and the occasion.

If you "get caught" writing simply, you have failed. The able writing craftsman works within a strict discipline of simplicity. But he introduces enough variety of sentence length, structure, and vocabulary so that the simplicity is not noticed. The reader, as a result, never thinks of the writing as being choppy or childish.

Variety is a chief ingredient in the art of writing. Only practice can lead to the facility that produces variety. Being aware of the point, however, helps one gain facility more rapidly.

Principle Ten

Write to Express Not Impress

I recall the month my mother prepared her first paper for her literary club. For me it was an uneasy period during a happy childhood. Her subject was the short story. Mother spent hours in the Carnegie Library and other long hours of anguish at her writing desk, sucking her pen.

The paper did not turn out to be a very good one. Mother made the first mistake of nearly anyone not accustomed to a serious job of writing. She confused formality with elegance and supposed long words and long sentences to be the signs of deep thought.

Mother was a sociable, democratic person—but one would never have judged this from her paper.

In the unaccustomed medium of the written word, Mother fell into that trap which awaits, wide open, the inexperienced writer. She was trying to impress rather than express. She was trying to be someone else.

No writing is easy. Mother would perhaps have spent no less time if she had written a good paper. But she should not have wasted time seeking long, unfamiliar words, and in forming meandering sentences.

She should have expressed her own thoughts instead of trying to impress with thoughts borrowed from others. Mother actually knew a great deal about her subject. She had read probably three short stories a week for years, and she was an excellent storyteller herself. In addition she had listened to many papers at the literary club with an incisive critical judgment.

But when it came to writing a paper herself she forgot to write as a listener. Her own fresh views on storytelling would have put life into the heavy rehash she prepared from books of the library. Had she made use of what she knew from experience she would have done a good job of communicating about the short story.

It is not only ladies nervous over their first papers at literary clubs who make this error. Many business conferences, to say nothing of diplomatic conferences, fail for the same reason. Few of us fully escape the temptation of putting more emphasis on impression than expression.

This is not surprising. The roots of the fault go very deep. They could be traced back further than 1066, but that is a good place to begin. In that year the Norman French conquered Britain. The English spoke a Teutonic language brought from the mainland by the Angles, Saxons, and Danes. They had picked up a few Latinian words, because they found them useful, but these were not many.

Language was one instrument the Normans used to keep themselves on top. They decreed that French was to be the language of the courts and schools. High posts in the church and at court went to those who could speak French, and in order to acquire an education a man had to learn French, the language of the schools.

Before the Conquest considerable prose and poetry had been written in English. But for years thereafter English almost disappeared as a literary language. All the upper classes spoke French, while English was left to peasants.

We are not yet beyond the shadow of the Conquest. Those

eager to elevate themselves still try to lord it over others with words of Latin root.

In his *English Words and Their Background* George H. McKnight made an amusing point. He showed that many dignified English words of Latin origin can be traced to slang of the lower stratum. The original Latin of these words can best be expressed in English by terms now classed as slang. McKnight wrote:

> *Recalcitrant* in its origin was equivalent to modern "kicker," *apprehend* to "catch on," *assault* and *insult* to "jump on," *impose* to "put over on," *excoriate* to "take the hide off." In the same way *polite*, in its origin, was equivalent to "smooth," *inveigh* to "sail into," *diatribe* to "rub in," *fool* to "wind bag" or "blow hard," *effrontery* to "face" or "cheek," *interrupt* to "break in on," *perplexed* to "balled up," *precocious* (literally "early ripe") to "half-baked," *delirious* (literally "out of the furrow") to "off one's trolley," *supercilious* to "high brow," *depraved* to "crooked."

The ultimate effect of the Conquest on the English language was, of course, a very good one. The Norman tongue and the native Anglo-Saxon dissolved in one another and made of our language by far the richest in either the Latin or Teutonic family.

Furthermore, during those early years when French was the official language, English was released from the deadening influence of the authorities. No one tried to freeze it or formalize it. So, by 1362, when the English language was reestablished for pleading in the courts it was bursting with new life. That vitality budded in Chaucer and came to full flower in the poetry of Shakespeare and other Elizabethans, and in the prose of the King James Version of the Bible.

The English Bible is the only good writing job I know of that was put together by a committee. Even this achievement might not have been possible if the composition had started from scratch. The churchmen were guided by the simple Greek of the earlier testaments. But they were writing for the people, and agreed on language that stays close to the Anglo-Saxon.

Over much of the world Latin and French continued for centuries to be instruments of awe. Latin was used by the priests, and until very recently French remained the language of diplomacy.

The chance of striking awe by means of big words is about run out in the United States. Readers have almost rid themselves of the yoke of 1066. Few are fooled by fanciness in language. It has been years since I have heard anyone say, in effect, "I can't understand what he is saying; he must be highly intelligent."

The plain fact is, that despite all wailing to the contrary, universal education has worked in the United States. Americans have learned their facts in school and have measured them against experience. They have "been around." Nearly anyone old enough to get about these days has been to California or New York or the state fair, to say nothing of Reykjavik, Okinawa, Tunis, Berlin, and the North Pole.

In his own home, by the time he is ten, an American has inspected, by means of books, magazines, radio, and television, a large slice of the world. We have more means of communication than all the rest of the world put together.

In Germany the Nazis fooled too many with impressive words. In Russia they may not be able to see through them. But I don't see many Americans being fooled by those who try, by means of words, to seem bigger than they are. Most exceptions can be put down to lapses of attention.

As readers, we have recovered from 1066 and have put meaning into the events of 1776. But many—in writing—still act as if readers could be swept away by curled wigs and brocade. The standards of a language for democracy are not yet clear to them.

There is little argument as to the basis of standards for a

language of democracy. First, it should be clear. Second, it should have grace, should fit the tongue. And to remain clear, the language must, of course, remain relatively consistent with history and logic. Meanings must not change too fast.

But pedants of grammar violate many of these principles with their "rules." For years a few who have a narrow view and knowledge of grammar have tried to break individuals and municipalities from using "Go slow." But history as well as literature backs up "slow," as well as "slowly," as a good adverb. It is plain to anyone with no stake in pretending to authority that usage has made one as good as the other.

As for logic, consider the "rule" against a split infinitive. Good writers have split them for centuries without fogging meaning. On the other hand, in some sentences the meaning cannot be made clear *unless* the infinitive is split. Try saying, "You have failed to completely understand me," without separating the two parts of the infinitive "to understand." "You have failed completely to understand me" gives an entirely different idea, and so does, "You have failed to understand me completely."

Next, consider the point of grace. "It is I" and "am I not" are both awkward to the tongue. As a result "it is me" is in general use and has been defended by literary men for at least two centuries. Still it is against the "rules." "Am I not" becomes "ain't I" among the masses and "aren't I" among the fashionable, but grammarians have given way to neither.

Winston Churchill, so the story goes, had his fun with such dealers in precious rules of language. A speech he was to make was submitted to the Foreign Office for comment. It came back with only one change. Churchill had ended a sentence with a preposition and the Foreign Office "corrected" it. Churchill wrote in the margin:

"This is the sort of arrant pedantry up with which I will not put."

Hundreds of examples have been collected that show Shakespeare, Milton, Lamb, Thackeray, Kipling, and nearly every other literary figure have used "incorrect English." The fact is they knew what they were doing. They were using the term best fitted to the sentence and the occasion—the one that seemed graceful and most likely to impart the meaning they intended.

Shakespeare was fortunate. In his day English grammar was taken for granted. Not until after 1700 did scholars begin to center their attention on rules. Before that date there were hardly any books of language criticism. But about 250 were published between 1700 and 1800 in an effort to establish correct English.

In doing readability analyses I have read many thousands of words of industrial, newspaper, and magazine copy a week. Many sentences are unclear. But little of the vagueness results from failure to follow what are customarily called the rules of grammar.

This sentence is from a business letter:

"Everyone in the Atlanta and Birmingham offices are invited to join Harry and I for the Saturday afternoon of the convention."

That's a compound fracture of the correct English: "Everyone in the Atlanta and Birmingham offices *is* invited to join Harry and *me* for the Saturday afternoon of the convention."

The original sentence may mark the writer as lacking in care or education, but it would not confuse plans for a lively Saturday afternoon.

From my point of view, that of clear communication, sentences like the following, though grammatically correct, are more odious. The clear meaning they transfer is very near to zero:

"Unless rising costs and pressures of renewed demand superimpose a further major inflationary advance on the price rise of the last nine years, the readjustment may be effected less painfully than it was in 1920–21, according to a study on the structure of post-war prices just completed by the National Bureau of Economic Research."

And here is an entirely "grammatical" sentence clipped for me from *The New York Times* by B. H. McCormack of the *Wall Street Journal*:

"Asked what they meant by their assertion that the upshot of the week-end bargaining in London between John W. Snyder, Secretary of the United States Treasury, and the British Chancellor of the Exchequer, Sir Stafford Cripps, would decide whether progress toward recovery in Europe would continue or cease, economic experts in Switzerland pointed to numerous specific cases where the volume of intra-European trade was already shrinking because of uncertainty of the future of the pound sterling and for want of some effectual international monetary system, and added that Britain's new discrimination against all hard currencies must act as sand in the wheels of intra-European trade."

What we have been calling "fog" does more damage to clarity and grace in everyday writing than does bad grammar. The fog results from an overdose of complexity and abstraction. And these, in turn result from:

One: Failure of the writer to make his message clear in his own mind before he tries to convey it, and

Two: Failure to take the pains necessary to put his message in language that is clear, concise, and concrete.

Many persons, who talk well enough, freeze up when they start to write for fear they will violate a "don't."

The only "don't" I have for you is: Don't be awed by the rules of grammar. Keep your attention on clear expression and, for the most part, grammar will take care of itself.

This is not to say that grammar is unimportant. Ah, yes, grammar is important. In this land aristocracy by birth is outlawed. Aristocracy by wealth is unsteady. Distinctions based on grammar are one of the few means left by which to maintain social stratification.

If someone tells you, "I done told ya ya shouldn't have ought to of done it," his meaning is perfectly clear, but you know that his upbringing was less than delicate.

Of course, teachers must comb such burrs from the language of their charges. The young, if they have not learned so at home, should be told that "they have went" and "he didn't have no book" are not acceptable English. Not acceptable, that is, to many persons their students may later wish to befriend, court, or work for. Even those exposed to such barbarous English at home usually shed it after a few years of serious schooling or reading.

Beyond errors of this grotesque level there are few that need trouble you. If you say "he don't" when you should say "he doesn't" some of your listeners will be annoyed and may judge you careless. But "errors" like the following are in constant use both in speech and by respected writers. Anyone interested in language as a tool of communication rather than as a scientific study hardly need bother with them: (In parentheses are the "correct" words for those in italics.)

> John talks *like* his brother did. (as)
> At 8 a.m. none of the supervisors *are* on duty. (is)
> We will try *and* have it for you Wednesday. (to)
> Please order us seven of *these* kind of fittings. (this)
> If he *was* going to New York, he could call on the customer. (were)
> *Most* anyone would agree. (almost)
> *Can* I borrow this June report a moment? (may)

Those who teach the language are far more liberal about rules these days than you may think from your schoolday memories. In a recent survey answered by 150 college professors,

77 per cent recognized "it is me" as correct English. A large majority found no objection to "can" in the place of "may" nor to the sentence, "Everyone put on their hats."

The same survey showed high-school teachers, particularly those in small towns; newspaper writers; and editors of women's magazines more conservative about correct grammar than college teachers of English.

Some will consider this amusing. But actually it is easy to understand, and is as it should be. The small-town English teacher is on the front line in the war against illiteracy. Few can be relaxed and philosophical in the heat of battle.

The newspaper writers and editors of magazines, particularly those intended for women, have to be careful. They are preyed upon by that fraction of the population that preens its feeling of superiority by calling attention to broken "rules" in print.

Thus when I used to write a current-events paper used by many high-school English teachers I could not consider splitting an infinitive. There is nothing wrong, as I have shown, with splitting an infinitive. But a split infinitive in my paper would have brought letters from a few well-meaning, conservative teachers. Their *belief* that the divided infinitive is bad grammar would have interfered with communication.

It comes down to this. If you are writing letters and announcements in the course of business, keep your attention on expression and don't freeze up in fear of grammar's "don'ts."

But if you are writing for the public, you need to know what are considered mistakes in grammar. Otherwise, such "mistakes" may interfere with your clear expression in some quarters.

In other words, you need to know grammar not in order to impress but to make sure that you express.

Walt Whitman, who sensed American spirit and purposes

about as well as anyone, once wrote, looking toward the future:

"The Real Grammar will be that which declares itself a nucleus of the spirit of the laws, with liberty to all to carry out the spirit of the laws, even by violating them, if necessary."

It is in that spirit that these Ten Principles have been set down.

PART THREE

Causes and Cures

The Fog in Your Newspaper

Basil Walters had unusual success in the newspaper business. On several occasions he took charge of large newspapers that were slipping and turned them into money-makers. He did this in several leading American cities.

One of Walters's "secrets" was that he could persuade writers to avoid jargon and write in the language of the people. He used to train reporters with a trick of comparing their spontaneous vocal reports and the more stodgy products of their typewriters.

A new man would be sent to cover a big fire. When he returned rosy with excitement and ready to beat out a masterwork, Walters would hail him to the front office: "What have you got?"

In a few minutes of rapid-fire talk the boy would pour out the cold facts and hot, colorful details. Unseen, in the next office, Walters's secretary would be taking them down.

"Good. Go write it," Walters would tell the boy. In 20 minutes the reporter is back with the written story. Walters already has the earlier *vocal* report before him—neatly typed and purged of cuss words by the stenographer.

The story the new man has written goes something like this:

"While firemen struggled hopelessly to negotiate streets made almost impassable by snow and ice, a fire of undetermined origin cost the life of Alvin Smith, 58, of 2548 Maplewood Avenue, early Monday morning, as flames completely consumed his six-room residence causing unestimated damage and rendering his family of five homeless. . . ."

Not a bad job—in the tradition of summary leads, and well decorated with worn jargon—"flames consumed," "undetermined origin," "rendered homeless." But the tidied transcript of the reporter's spoken version goes like this:

"Whale of a big fire way out on Maplewood Avenue. Burned down a six-room house and killed a man name of Alvin Smith. Four kids in the family and they were all in bed. The old man's been sick, and the wife and oldest boy carried him downstairs, right through the flames. But the fumes got him. He died in the front yard in the snow. One kid ran barefoot half a mile in her nightie to get to a phone. But the firemen never did get there. Roads were blocked with snow. Nobody knows how the fire started."

Something between these two is the kind of news story that makes a readable newspaper, the kind that Walters has had exceptional success in getting men and women to write.

Good editors, since newspapers began, have used whatever means they could to influence writers of news to be simple and direct. With the help of the readability research they have made more rapid progress in recent years than they ever have before. The average reading level of some 50 newspapers, which we have checked regularly, used to be between eleventh and twelfth grade. Today the average is between ninth and tenth grade. In other words, the staffs of these papers used to write with the complexity of *Atlantic Monthly* prose. Today their writing is better geared to the reading ability and tastes of average readers. The level of complexity now compares with that of the *Reader's Digest* and *The Saturday Evening Post*.

Still, much of the news in your daily paper is foggy. Remember that newspapers are produced at tremendous speed. An author and the staff of a publishing house may take several years to produce a 75,000-word book. But the staff of a metropolitan newspaper may have two or three times this output every 24 hours. At such high speed, faults in newspaper writing are a matter of no surprise.

However, the greatest faults, once they are understood, can be kept in check even though writers are hurried. An example is the marathon sentence. Only a few years ago nearly every news story began with a sentence of from 35 to 70 words. Some of them ran more than 100 words. Here is a 92-word sentence from *The New York Times* announcing Franklin D. Roosevelt's election to a fourth term:

> Incomplete returns of Tuesday's national election, but much nearer to the final totals than those that were available on election night, disclosed that the President was chosen for a fourth term by an electoral majority and popular vote sharply reduced from 1940, when he broke the two-term tradition, that was more than a century old, but that Democratic gains in the House of Representatives were greater than at any time since Mr. Roosevelt's first re-election in 1936, an increase of twenty over the present membership, with the Senate party line-up apparently unchanged.

In order to understand how such monstrosities developed, you must know something of newspaper organization. In the editorial department of the newspaper you read, there are three types of craftsmen—reporters, deskmen, and editorial writers. (We shall deal later with the frailties of editorial writers.) The fault of the marathon sentence has arisen from a conflict between reporters and deskmen. Reporters gather news and write it. Deskmen read copy, edit it, and write the heads that appear over the printed stories. That these two groups be locked in an eternal cold war seems a requirement of newspaper production.

In the eyes of a deskman a reporter is a lazy, careless, surly illiterate. The reporter, on the other hand, sees the deskman as a sour and insensitive wretch who has given up writing for one of two reasons: (1) He has sold out the creative life for an added ten dollars a week. (2) He has failed as an artist and now thirsts to destroy the beautiful writing of others.

In this conflict the deskman has the upper hand, for he must pass upon what the reporter writes. And the worst thing a deskman can say to a reporter is, "You have missed the lead."

The lead is the first part of a news story, the nub of it, the nail on which all the rest of the details hang. To tell a reporter he has missed the lead is a sharp criticism of his ability to observe and interpret news.

For years editors and journalism teachers have been teaching that the lead of a story should answer the five W's—who, what, where, when, and why. A news story is supposed to start with the most important fact. Other facts are to follow in order of their importance. But no one ever said that all the five W's should be answered in the first sentence. No one ever said the lead of a story is limited to the first sentence. It can be half a dozen sentences. Its only purpose is to get the basic questions answered before getting into less essential details.

The one-sentence summary lead is a victory over deskmen scored by subterfuge of the reporters. If you put every detail you can muster into the first sentence, no one can accuse you of missing the lead. By so doing the reporter avoids the hard work of selecting the most important detail, putting it first, and arranging the other details in the order of their interest. By putting all his facts in one market-bag sentence the reporter escapes the sting of rebuke from the deskman who may have a different opinion as to which fact should come first. In the single summary sentence they *all* come first.

For years this trick fooled deskmen. Meanwhile it sabotaged many a news story for the reader. Deskmen and editors work day in and day out with words. They can read almost any jumble rapidly because of their constant practice. During the period from the beginning of the New Deal to the end of World War II, newspapers climbed steadily in reading difficulty, and few editors noticed it.

I recall a talk with the late John Sorrells, executive editor of the Scripps-Howard Newspapers, when we were beginning the analysis of newspaper writing in 1944. I told him of the basic principles of readability. "We know all that," he said. While waiting to see him I had done some counting of the day's edition of the New York *World-Telegram*. "Do you know the average length of leading sentences on the front page of the *Telegram* today?—45." E. W. Scripps, founder of the newspaper group, favored a leading sentence of about 15 words.

One story on the front page of the *World-Telegram* that day was the work of one of the nation's most outstanding reporters, a Pulitzer prizewinner. It began like this:

"Because of its strict interpretation of Congress' recent prohibition against the dissemination of political propaganda among the armed forces, the War Department is banning one group of national magazines from all army establishments, it was learned today, while permitting another group to circulate freely. . . ."

There are the five W's, all in one sentence, in this order: why, who, what, where, when. Mr. Sorrells agreed that a few periods and revision along this line would have helped the reader:

"One group of magazines is banned from all Army posts to-day. Another group is allowed to circulate freely.

"This results from strict interpretation of Congress' recent action barring 'political propaganda' from Army posts. The War Department issued the order drawing the line between magazines. . . ."

There are the same facts in four sentences. All the five W's are answered, now in this order: what, where, when, why, who. And all the facts of this lead are as near the beginning of the story as they were in the first version, for each version has a total of 44 words.

Today, tests show sentence-lengths average like these for outstanding papers:

Christian Science Monitor, 17 words; *Wall Street Journal*, 21; *The New York Times*, 25; St. Louis *Post-Dispatch* and Chicago *Tribune*, 22 or 23.

The United States has three great daily newspapers of national circulation: *The New York Times*, the *Christian Science Monitor*, and the *Wall Street Journal*. The *Wall Street Journal* prints editions in Chicago, Los Angeles, and Dallas. The *Monitor* is printed daily in Los Angeles as well as in Boston. *The New York Times* is flown daily to every major city in the United States. (For a time in the early 1960s, the *Times* tried a West Coast edition. It was a financial failure but did succeed through its competition in making a good paper out of the Los Angeles *Times*.)

Since we began our work in 1944, each of these three national papers has done much to improve its readability. The *Wall Street Journal* was first to act. That story, and what we did to help, is told in the second chapter of this book. (See page 28.)

The most recent campaign for improved writing among these three has been on the part of the *Christian Science*

Monitor. When DeWitt John took charge of the editorial department in 1965, he set out to give readers "more exclusive news . . . in interesting, highly readable form." *Newsweek* reported:

"To improve readability, the *Monitor* has supplied all members of its staff with copies of *The Technique of Clear Writing*, by readability counselor Robert Gunning. With the book came an announcement from Robert C. Nelson, a *Monitor* editor, that henceforth writers would be graded by a "fog index" created by Gunning."

The *Monitor's* campaign rapidly increased readability. Dr. Fang's tests of the six papers above showed the *Monitor* the most readable of the lot.

The steady improvement of *The New York Times* is chiefly the work of Theodore M. Bernstein. As a *Times* editor, he for years prepared "Winners & Sinners," "an occasional bulletin of second guessing" issued to the 600 (!) writers and editors of the paper. He gave pats for good writing and raps for poor, ponderous, or stodgy writing that had long marked *The Times*.

The sad death of the New York *Herald Tribune* resulted in part from the *Times's* more lively writing. For years many read the *Times* if they had to have a full report, but they bought the *Herald Tribune* for its better writing. Once the *Times* became more readable, a chief competitive advantage of the *Herald Tribune* was wiped out.

The long slow campaign for better writing on *The Times* was triggered on an evening in 1946. Turner Catledge, already a noted newsman, had just joined the *Times* and begun his rise to top editor. The American Press Institute of Columbia University was holding the first of its many seminars.

Arthur Hays Sulzberger, publisher of the *Times*, entertained the 30 visiting managing editors at dinner. On the same day readability had been the topic of discussion at the seminar.

The managing editors were invited to criticize the *Times* and did. John Day of Louisville, a redhead and one of the nation's ablest newsmen, told Mr. Sulzberger the *Times* was "necessary reading" but he objected to its needless complexity. He challenged Catledge, a *Times* executive to read aloud from the front page of the *Times* of that morning. Catledge arose and started with:

"The diversion by the United Nations Relief and Rehabilitation Administration of 6,000 tons of steel rails to Yugoslavia from allocations earmarked for rebuilding China's crippled transportation system was denounced today as 'a strictly irregular deal smacking strongly of fraud' by Representative Roger C. Slaughter, Republican, of Missouri, chairman of a House committee which had spent the day investigating the transaction. . . ."

"I guess this wasn't written to be read," said the *Times* man sheepishly, and sat down.

The meeting had effect. The *Times* at once began putting in more periods. Some reporters, in fact, rode very far indeed in pursuit of brevity. A few weeks later the first paragraph of one *Times* story read, in full:

"Anna Mayer stopped hiccoughing today."

And both the *Wall Street Journal* and *Christian Science Monitor* have turned to long background stories of the type one expects of a magazine. The *Village Voice*, published in New York for the avant-garde and enjoying a growing national circulation, also finds long, talkative articles please its readers.

Radio and TV have changed news readers' habits. News scoops by newspapers are next to impossible these days. Results of elections are often known a few minutes after the polls close. Readers look to newspapers for longer background articles. The *Christian Science Monitor* used to have a policy against "jumping" of news articles from the front page to an inside page. This policy gave way to the new tendency toward longer stories. Readers do not complain, says editor Nelson. Instead they ask for more long articles.

Aside from the three national papers mentioned, there are few great newspapers in the United States today. Dr. Fang chose as local papers for his survey the St. Louis *Post-Dispatch*, the Los Angeles *Times*, the Chicago *Tribune*. One could add as other distinguished papers, the Louisville *Courier Journal*, the Hartford *Courant*, the San Francisco *Chronicle*, the Atlanta *Journal*, and the Cowles papers of Des Moines and Minneapolis.

But most local newspapers have been deteriorating. Their failure, however, is less one of fog than of froth. Years ago, we observed that papers which handled the more important political and economic news were the least readable. At the same time we showed that even heavy concepts could be treated readably. Such papers as the *Wall Street Journal* and the *Christian Science Monitor* have proved this in practice. To write the important news readably does take skill and effort, however. Too few news staffs make the effort. They sidestep fog not by better writing, but by dealing in trivia. We found in a recent extensive survey of newspapers in one of America's most rapidly growing areas that there is little digging for basic news. The news in the same papers twenty years ago was far more penetrating.

John Hay Whitney, who lost a great deal of money trying to maintain the New York *Herald Tribune*, in a college address accused newspapers of having become "captive to the press release and the gentlemanly code of going to great lengths to avoid embarrassing anyone.

"Our task is to cut through the junk in the public mind and, by seeking the order that underlies the clutter of small events, to winnow out of the apparent what is real; to cede to television and radio the mere repetition of activities and to look behind the bare events for meanings."

This goal can be achieved, and the writing can be done in readable English. The three great national newspapers are all doing a better job of this than they did when we first started to survey them in the 1940s. They are also getting sharp competition from some television network programs, particularly that of Walter Cronkite and his team of newsmen. They often dig deep and still report in clear, conversational prose. Dr. Fang's survey showed Cronkite, Huntley-Brinkley, and Peter Jennings reports to be written in simpler language than writing in newspapers.

When a nation loses grip on its language it loses grip on itself. There must therefore always be some guardians about who insist on keeping words in the same harness with meaning. This, as I understand it, used to be the job of poets. But, so far as I can see, most poets these days are up Fog Alley themselves. I'm willing to hand over the job to such custodians as the man who wrote the news story about Dr. Nourse below. May reporters never neglect to pull aside the filigreed curtains of official language to see if there is any real meaning behind them.

There have been periods when the windy words of officialdom blew on and on without challenge. Today, however, an official who prefers the pompous phrase may find himself kidded in the news columns with such a refreshing report as this (from the Washington Associated Press bureau):

> Dr. Edwin G. Nourse has given the nation's military leaders some grave economic advice.
>
> Now they're trying to figure out what it was.
>
> The high brass who heard the President's chief economic adviser at the Pentagon yesterday understood the United States had just signed a mutual defense treaty with 11 other countries.
>
> Apparently it wasn't that simple.
>
> Nourse said that actually "we have turned to horizontal

integration of the defense function to effect operating economies. . . ."

Horizontal integration is apparently going to cost a lot of dough, because Nourse cautioned that "we cannot afford to make the costs of its implementation a simple addition to other military plans as they stood before their new alignment."

The Pentagon was studying Nourse's suggestion that the old adage about an Army traveling on its belly can be changed to read "travels on the economic machine that maintains the physical well-being of the soldiers and keeps them supplied with efficient weapons." No decision has been announced on this matter.

The newspaper profession should be composed of jargon fighters. Unfortunately, one corner of the profession has *cultivated* jargon instead of weeding it from the language. I speak of the editorial writers. This third group is separate from reporters and deskmen who simply observe, write, and edit. Editorial writers are drawn aside and commissioned to ponder. It takes a strong character to avoid stuffness under such circumstance.

For some years now the newspaper editorial has been declining in influence. I have read many articles giving the reasons, but I don't recall seeing a finger placed on the chief fault. Bluntly, it is this: Newspaper editorials are too hard to read.

An editorial writer on his way to work will say to his bus companion:

"I'm glad to see Joe McSweeney get the job of police chief. He's a good man. He'll enforce the law if the Mayor will let him."

Half an hour later the same man writes in traditional editorialese:

"If observation of his previous record be a reliable guide,

Joseph McSweeney is eminently qualified to direct the department of police and will discharge his obligations and duties in a way calculated to achieve maximum effectiveness, provided the Mayor emancipates him from restraints beyond those entirely proper and justified."

For editorial writers in the rut of tradition nothing ever "ends"; it can only be "terminated." Few things "change"; they "undergo modification." Nothing is "thrown out"; it goes by a "process of elimination." "Use" is rarely found for anything. Instead the writer strings syllables like beads and comes up with "utilization." He relishes such words as "castigation," "imprecation," and "impugnment."

The editor of an East Coast daily asked our organization to survey editorials in six papers generally considered leaders in forming opinion. Three out of four of the editorials proved more complex in prose structure than average articles in the *Atlantic Monthly* and *Harper's* magazine. Editorial jargon— made up chiefly of clichés familiar to every editorial reader— accounted for much of the heaviness. In half an hour's search we collected dozens of them. Some examples follow.

If an editorial writer is expressing opposition he dips into the "anti" bin for his clichés and comes up with:

The reprehensible practice	The vicious consequence
The intolerable condition	The flagrant circumstance
The untimely suggestion	The lamentable fact

If, on the other hand, he is expressing support, he draws his clichés from the "pro" bin:

The legitimate grievance	The inadequate facility
The constructive proposal	The salutary experience
The admirable restraint	The inescapable conclusion

More often the editorial writer is on the fence. There is a third bin of worn phrases for this purpose:

The substantial proportion	The prevailing practice
The ultimate objective	The accelerated rate
The attendant circum-	The naturally conducive
stance	situation

The old hand at this trade can produce astonishing veils of fog. How do you like these?:

". . . forgetting the specific implementation of numerous generalized international commitments. . . ."

". . . a transformation attended by a condition that has not previously prevailed on any commensurate scale. . . ."

The Louisville *Courier-Journal* has one of the best staffs of editorial writers in the country. The half-dozen people who contribute to the editorial page all have high literary qualifications, and they write very well indeed. However, the first survey we did for the paper showed that the editorials averaged 13 in reading level—above the *Atlantic Monthly* level of complexity.

One of the editorial writers suggested, "I suppose we write complexly because of the tradition of Henry Watterson."

Watterson, possibly the greatest of the personal journalists, wrote for the *Courier-Journal* from 1868 until 1919, when he and the new owner of the paper broke over the League of Nations issue. Watterson's reputation for thundering prose was international.

I told the editorial writer that I was confident that Watterson's editorials would prove less complex than our tests had shown the current issues of the *Courier-Journal* to be. My guess was that no one who had won so wide an audience as Watterson could have done so by writing on a 13 level. When we tested a collection of Watterson editorials this guess proved true. His average over his 50-year career was 9—somewhat lower than the present reading level of *The Reader's Digest*.

Watterson most certainly wrote long rumbling sentences

at times. Take this first sentence from his Pulitzer Prize editorial of 1917:

> It is with solemnity, and a touch of sadness, that we write the familiar words of the old refrain beneath the invocation to the starry banner, the breezy call of hero-breeding bombast quite gone out of them; the glad shout of battle; the clarion note of defiance; because to us, not as to Nick of the Woods and his homely co-mates of the forest, the rather as to the men of '61, comes this present call to arms.

But Watterson also used simple direct sentences. Even in this solemn editorial he used an equal number of simple sentences and complex sentences. And throughout his writing, clumps of hard-hitting simple sentences are even more typical than the rolling thunderers. Take this example from one of his last editorials, an attack upon the League of Nations:

> Inevitably Woodrow Wilson would be caught by such a whimsy as the League of Nations. We must do the President no wrong. He is our file leader. He possesses a fruitful, speculative mind. He is unafraid. What a journalist he would have made! I wonder that, instead of the schoolroom, when groping for a livelihood, he did not take to the newspaper. In France the statesmen usually begin with journalism.
>
> But the League of Nations! It is a fad. Politics, like society and letters, has its fads. In society they call it fashion and in literature originality. Politics gives the name of "issues" to its fads. . . .

There we have only one complex sentence to a dozen simple ones.

Most present-day editorial writers remember the long sentences of literature and forget the short ones. They make their mixtures too rich. The *Courier-Journal* editorial writers have been reminded now. Today they write a page much better suited to the tastes of their readers. But here is the beginning of an editorial selected at random from the days before the change. It contained a dozen sentences—not one of them simple in structure. Here are the first three:

> Even if the threatened railroad strike has been averted by the Government's seizure of the roads in default of a settlement, the institution of fact-finding boards as a device for resolving labor disputes may have been dealt a mortal blow and the Administration—and the public—forced to look to something else.
>
> The stubbornness with which the engineers and trainmen have refused to accept the recommendations of the President's fact-finding, although these carried an increase of $1.28 a day in basic wage, is evidence of labor's intention to discourage this process of wage agreements. The point becomes plainer when it is observed that the brotherhoods have offered to recede from their original demand of $2.50-a-day increase, but not quite down to the level recommended by the fact-finders and accepted by the roads. . . .

When Watterson wrote he was speaking for himself. During all but the last couple of years of his career he owned the paper for which he wrote. This gave him an advantage which very few other writers of editorials have. No matter how clear the thought and style of a writer he will gather some fog in trying to fit his words to the attitudes of the publisher. Arthur Krock puts it this way in his introduction to the collection of Watterson editorials:

"A hired journalism, however zealous, however loyal, however entrusted, however brilliant, cannot be great because it speaks through the mist of subordination."

The hired journalist will often find his thoughts in harness.

He will feel called upon to build his sentences with caution and qualification. But all this is not sufficient excuse for writing the complex prose that is heavy going for most readers.

Our tests show that newspaper editorials are improving in readibility. But some editorial writers are still in a rut of complexity and formality.

Earlier in this chapter we discussed the news-story form called the "inverted-pyramid" style which places the five W's (who, what, where, when, and why) first, then follows with the details. As the diagram in the chapter about Principle Six showed, this method begins with the basic facts and builds downward with facts of less and less importance. Recently in the effort to free news writing of long-sentence fog, some have suggested that the inverted-pyramid style is at fault. They suggest that news stories should be told in narrative form instead.

The narrative form is often quite effective in news writing—particularly for "feature" stories. But to write all news, or even a major part of it, in narrative form would make a newspaper ridiculous. The narrative or chronological form is best for swaying the emotions, for creating atmosphere, for entertainment. You recognize this principle when you tell an anecdote, joke, or funny story. The news writer follows the same principle when writing a sob feature story:

"John Jones walked slowly last night through the new-fallen snow. He thought of his five children and the presents he had just bought for their Christmas. . . ." At length you discover that Jones never got home. He was hit by a truck and ended up in the hospital.

But the narrative form will never replace the five W's inverted-pyramid form for delivering information quickly. If you doubt the psychology of this, imagine having been present when President Kennedy was assassinated in Dallas. Soon after, you pick up a friend at the airport. You say to him:

"I have just come from downtown Dallas. There was a tremendous crowd there because of the President's visit. The day was unseasonably warm. I found a good place to watch the procession from that little slope in front of the Texas School Book Depository. Presently there was excitement in the crowd. The President's car, a long black Lincoln with the bubbletop off, was coming down the grade to the underpass at the intersection of Elm, Main, and Commerce streets. The President was dressed in a dark blue suit and his wife was seated beside him. Suddenly a shot rang out . . ."

No one would report startling news in such a manner. Experience tells us what the listener wants. We have learned to come to the point.

If you had actually seen the terrible event you would run up to your friend and cry out:

"Good Lord, President Kennedy has just been shot. In downtown Dallas. I saw it happen. Just an hour ago. He's at Parkland Memorial Hospital. They don't know who did it yet. They don't know whether he will live."

And there in a few words you have the five W's. You will add details as your listener asks questions or as you foresee the questions he is about to ask. He will want to know: How badly was the President hurt? Just how did it happen? What sort of a fellow shot him?

Time has made a great success with the narrative approach to the news. But such a feature approach is almost necessary for a magazine. By the time the magazine has reached you, you already have read or heard the "spot" news. News magazines have to rely on interesting you in the background of the news, and for this purpose the narrative form is excellent.

But the inverted pyramid should never, and, of course, will never, be discarded as a means of handing on information. It is the normal, most efficient way of passing along facts, whether they are in a scientific report or in gossip about the girl next door. The form is efficient because it allows the listener or reader to stop when he has all the information he wants.

In thumbing through the daily paper, the man of the house will be interested in the fact that Mary Smith finally got the Pratt boy; his wife will want to read on to see whether the bride's bouquet was forget-me-nots or lilies of the valley. On the other hand, the man of the house will want to know just how the rookie pitcher retired three strong hitters in the eighth; his wife will be satisfied with the leading paragraph which should, by all means, make it clear to her whether the Yankees won or lost the game.

Aside from marathon sentences, the chief cause of fog in newspapers is the jargon of other professions which sifts into news writing. If his job is to be done right a reporter must be a good translator. If a diplomat speaks of a "bilateral concordat," the newsman should let his readers know that the document in question is a "two-way pact." When the county prosecutor announces that he has "nolled" a burglary case, the reporter is careless if he uses this unusual term in his story. He need say no more than that the prosecutor has dropped the case with permission of the court.

The able reporter also quickly detects windy statements and deflates them for the reader's sake.

> *Senator Sounder says*
>> I anticipate a disposition on the part of my colleagues to expedite additional labor legislation.
>
> *The reporter translates*
>> Senator Sounder looks for Congress to hurry along new labor law.
>
> *The bureaucrat issues a statement*
>> The state will be unable to satisfy financial commitments unless additional revenue is forthcoming in the immediate future in order to meet expenditures.

The reporter chases the fog

If the state doesn't get more tax money quickly, it won't be able to meet its bills.

Many times you have read in your paper that a victim "suffered lacerations and contusions." The reporter who is interested in protecting the language from obesity writes simply that the victim "was cut and bruised." I have a copy of a New York *Post* accident story in which a young woman suffers "bruises and contusions." The writer did not know "contusion" is the doctors' fancy term for "bruise."

Below are some samples of routine articles from newspapers as they appeared originally and as they were rewritten to eliminate fog.

Over the years, padding has accounted for millions of unnecessary words in news stories. With space as tight as it is now, deliberate padding by news writers is unlikely. Unnecessary words put in without thought, however, are just as wasteful.

One of the chief causes of unnecessary words in news stories is poor organization. And this, in turn, can usually be blamed on the speed with which news is written. A minute spent organizing a mass of details will often save several minutes in their writing.

The organization of the following story runs up both the Fog Index and wordage. The rewrite saves nearly one word out of four and cuts the Fog Index from 17 plus to 9.

Fog Index 17 plus 164 WORDS NEW SCHOOL AGE LAW WILL CUT EXPENSES	*Fog Index 11* 115 WORDS NEW SCHOOL AGE LAW WILL CUT EXPENSES
Passage of the bill which makes once again six years of age the starting time for youngsters in school will more than pay for the	By once again setting the age for starting school at six years, the Legislature saved the public schools more money than was

cost of the extraordinary special sessions of the Legislature in amounts saved in public school expenses.

That is the opinion of A. R. Meadows, Alabama State Superintendent of Education, stated in a letter to city and county superintendents of schools urging them to express their appreciation to the governor and members of the Legislature for passing the bill.

The state superintendent pointed out that employed elementary teachers who would have been required to handle the large number of younger children who would have come into public schools this Fall, can now be shifted from first grade to other overcrowded grades and that the demand for emergency teachers in elementary grades could consequently be reduced.

Also, he said, the delay will benefit the younger children by requiring them to wait until they are more nearly ready to enter school before enrolling.

spent on the special sessions, according to A. R. Meadows, State Superintendent of Education.

By letter he has urged city and county superintendents to thank the governor and members of the Legislature for passing the bill.

Meadows pointed out that many teachers who would have been needed to handle the many first-graders this year can now be shifted to other overcrowded grades. As a result there will be less need for emergency teachers.

Children will benefit, too, he said: By waiting until they are six, they will be more nearly ready for school.

Much heavy language bloated with unnecessary words turns up in official handouts. Here's an example of one that slipped into a paper with very little change. In the rewrite 98 words do the work of 164 as the Fog Index falls from 17 plus to 10.

Fog Index   17 plus
164 WORDS
ARMY INSTALLATIONS
WILL HELP VETERANS
Former Employes to
Be Given Old Jobs

The War Department's policy of expediting the re-employment of returning veterans to the jobs they formerly held as civilian employes in Army installations will be pursued vigorously at all Memphis Army installations in response to a Fourth Service Command order, Lieut. Col. Paul O. Mitchell, executive officer of the Memphis Army Service Forces Depot, said yesterday.

In line with a standard War Department policy, all installations in the Fourth Service Command—which has its headquarters at Atlanta—will seek to effect the return of these men to their old jobs. If the installation at which the veteran was employed is no longer active or if the job to which he was assigned no longer exists, every effort will be made to place him at another nearby installation.

Veterans seeking new employment in Army installations are given preference for any job in which they might qualify. Approximately 41,000 have been employed by the War Department in recent months on this preferential system.

Fog Index   10
98 WORDS
ARMY INSTALLATIONS
WILL HELP VETERANS
Former Employes to
Be Given Old Jobs

Discharged veterans who used to work at Memphis Army posts as civilians can look for quick return to their old jobs, says Lieut. Col. Paul O. Mitchell, executive officer of the Memphis Army Service Forces Depot.

A Fourth Service Command order from Atlanta stresses the War Department policy of rehiring returning service men and women.

If the job a veteran held no longer exists, other work will be sought for him at a nearby post.

Any veternan qualified for a civilian job with the Army is given preference. The War Department has hired some 41,000 under this system.

Note how the Fog Index is lowered from the original in the rewritten items below:

Fog Index   17 plus
ACTION TO OUST
STIRONE DISMISSED

A twice-amended bill in equity filed against Nick Stirone, former kingpin of the A. F. of L. Common Laborers' Union here, was dismissed today without prejudice by Judge Harry H. Rowand of Common Pleas Court.

The bill, filed by Attorney Harry Alan Sherman in behalf of Ross Adams, ousted business agent of Stirone's Local 1058 of the Hod Carriers and Common Laborers, contained "impertinent and irrelevant" matter, the Judge said.

Such matters, he said, would "have no bearing on the final action in this case and we are of the opinion they are entered for the purpose of embarrassment and vilification of the defendant, and therefore have no relevancy."

He said the plaintiff could if he sees fit, "bring further action confined to the allegations he expects to prove. . . ."

The Adams' bill sought to regain his position as business agent of Local 1058, asked Stirone's ouster as president and asked an accounting of all union funds.

Fog Index   9
ACTION TO OUST
STIRONE DISMISSED

Ross Adams, ousted union business agent, failed today in a court effort to get his job back, Judge Harry H. Rowand of Common Pleas Court told Adams, however, he is free to try again.

Adams filed action against Nick Stirone, former kingpin of the A. F. of L. Common Laborers' Union here. He asked to be restored as business agent of Stirone's Local 1058 of the Hod Carriers and Common Laborers. Adams also asked that Stirone be ousted as president of the local and that there be an accounting of union funds.

The bill of equity filed for Adams by Attorney Harry Alan Sherman had already been changed twice before the judge turned it down. Judge Rowand said it held "impertinent and irrelevant" matter that did not bear on final action of the case. He said he believed it was put in only to embarrass Stirone.

Fog Index 17
GAS STATION CASE
CARRIED TO COURT

Counsel for Gus Percoco, 848 Gaylord Ave., applicant for a gasoline service station at the corner of West and State streets, today obtained a writ for Supreme Court review of the denial by the Zoning Board of Adjustment to rescind its action in recommending that the City Commission grant the permit.

The court action caused postponement, without date, of a public hearing on the issue by the City Commission today in City Hall.

Arthur Greisheimer, counsel for Percoco, contends the zoning board and not the commission has the right to grant his client's application and unsuccessfully sought to have the zoning board rescind its action of March 31 at a special meeting Friday night.

Fog Index 17
DALY ASKS SEWER TAX DELAY

Despite the fact that the proposed sewer rental ordinance provides for a new tax levy of $150,000, which will be apportioned among all types of property owners with an average of $10 per year for single-family dwellings, only two of the approximately 10,000 property owners affected at-

Fog Index 8
GAS STATION CASE
CARRIED TO COURT

Gus Percoco, 848 Gaylord Avenue, who wants to build a filling station in the residential West End, carried his fight to the Supreme Court today.

By so doing he avoided the public hearing set for today at City Hall. City Commissioners called it off.

Three months ago the Zoning Board of Adjustment said Percoco could build at the corner of State and West streets. At the same time the board asked the City Commission to approve the action.

Friday night Percoco's attorney, Arthur Greisheimer, told the board to leave the City Commission out of its decisions. The board refused. Now Greisheimer wants the Supreme Court to rule that zoning board decisions are final.

Fog Index 9
DALY ASKS SEWER TAX DELAY

Only two out of 10,000 persons about to be saddled with a new city tax showed up at City Hall today to speak against it. And neither of the two raised much objection in what was scheduled as a public hearing.

The proposed levy would require property owners to pay rent

Fog Index 17

DALY ASKS SEWER TAX DELAY

tended a public hearing today on the measure at City Hall.

Tax assessor Anthony F. Daly of 171 Ward Street, speaking as a private taxpayer, and Andrew Weingart, Church Street property owner, were the only property owners to appear and neither entered strenuous objections to the measure.

Daly said he was in favor of a sewer rental ordinance but he was against the ordinance up for final hearing today because, he alleged, it was discriminatory. Daly suggested that a citizens committee investigate all phases of the city's finances. Weingart said the measure was just another tax and "taxes in New Brunswick were too high already."

Fog Index 9

DALY ASKS SEWER TAX DELAY

on sewers. A total of $150,000 is to be collected. The owner of an average single-family home would pay about $10 per year.

One of the two who appeared at the hearing was Anthony F. Daly of 171 Ward Street. Daly is the city tax assessor, but he spoke as a private citizen. He said he has nothing against a sewer tax as such, but he doesn't like the one that was up for final hearing today. He called it "discriminatory."

The tax assessor wants the measure held up until a citizens committee can look into all phases of city finance.

Protest of the other citizen, Andrew Weingart, Church Street property owner, was general. He said, "This is just another tax and taxes in New Brunswick are too high already."

Fog Index 15

TAXI FIRMS FAVOR LICENSE FEE BOOST

Councilman James E. Hale, chairman of Council's finance committee, today dropped his proposed taxicab plan of one-cent-per-meter-flip in favor of a counter proposal by the cab companies that the cost of their city licenses be increased.

The cab companies now pay the city $25 per year for each

Fog Index 9

TAXI FIRMS FAVOR LICENSE FEE BOOST

Taxi companies say they would rather pay a higher license fee than charge an extra penny for each flip of their meters.

As a result Councilman James E. Hale, chairman of Council's finance committee, dropped his one-cent-per-flip plan today. Aim of the plan was to raise money for the City Recreation Department.

Fog Index 15
TAXI FIRMS FAVOR
LICENSE FEE BOOST

cab. Mr. Hale said the cab companies have suggested this be increased to approximately $125 per year which would provide the City Recreation Department with $19,000 to operate the remainder of this year, Mr. Hale said.

The Recreation Department's need for operating cash prompted the proposal for increased taxing of taxicabs. N. J. Barack, recreation director, said he needed $21,000 for the remainder of the year.

Council will meet at 7 p.m. tomorrow to consider an ordinance now being drawn. Mr. Hale said he considered the $100 per year boost in a cab license as considerable, but that it appeared satisfactory to the companies. He said . . .

Fog Index 9
TAXI FIRMS FAVOR
LICENSE FEE BOOST

Cab companies now pay $25 per year for each cab in operation. Mr. Hale says the companies suggest this be raised to about $125 a year.

This would provide the recreation department with $19,000 for the rest of the year. N. J. Barack, recreation director, says $21,000 is needed.

Council will meet at 7 p.m. tomorrow to consider an ordinance now being drawn. Mr. Hale says although . . .

Fog Index 17 plus
TB CONTROL PROGRAM
TOPIC AT MEETING

"The military tuberculosis control program, through rejection from service, early diagnosis and medical care, insured early treatment for a large group of the population with corresponding saving of life and great reduction in future exposure," declared Dr. Esmond R. Long, director, Henry Phipps Institute, University of Pennsylvania and director

Fog Index 10
TB CONTROL PROGRAM
TOPIC AT MEETING

The military tuberculosis control program saved many lives and helped check spread of the disease, Dr. Esmond R. Long told the fifty-fourth annual meeting of the Pennsylvania Tuberculosis Society of Harrisburg.

He suggests a similar plan be applied to the entire nation.

Dr. Long is head of the Henry Phipps Institute, University of

Fog Index   17 plus
TB CONTROL PROGRAM
TOPIC AT MEETING

of the Delaware County Tuberculosis and Health Association, in addressing the fifty-fourth annual meeting of the Pennsylvania Tuberculosis Society in Harrisburg.

Dr. Long spoke from experience as chief consultant on tuberculosis in the office of the surgeon general of the Army, where he was responsible for general control of tuberculosis in the Army.

Discussing the subject, "Tuberculosis Control in Military Service—Its Relation to the Anti-Tuberculosis Campaign," Dr. Long pointed out that the plan followed provided "far larger routine diagnosis than ever before attempted. There is no reason why, with certain modifications, the method should not be applied to the entire nation.

"A most significant feature of this tuberculosis control program has been the universal X-ray examination practiced on separation from service. About 12,000,000 men and women have been examined. . . ."

Fog Index   10
TB CONTROL PROGRAM
TOPIC AT MEETING

Pennsylvania, and of the Delaware County Tuberculosis and Health Association. During the war he was in charge of Army control of tuberculosis. He served as chief consultant on the disease in the office of the Army surgeon general.

The Army's diagnosis program was the greatest ever tried, Dr. Long said. An outsanding feature of the plan is X-ray examination of every person leaving service.

"About 12,000,000 men and women have been examined. . . ."

Fog Index   17 plus
LOW RENT BARS NEW BUILDING
REALTOR SAYS

Saying that continued rent prices at the present low levels are blocking the creation of new

Fog Index   7
LOW RENT BARS NEW BUILDING
REALTOR SAYS

Rents frozen at low levels are holding back the building of new homes for rent, Samuel Warwick,

Fog Index   17 plus
LOW RENT BARS NEW BUILDING
REALTOR SAYS

rental housing units, Samuel Warwick, president of the Chester
Real Estate Board, today threw
his support behind the plea of
the National Association of Real
Estate Boards which is before the
Senate Banking and Currency
Committee, in which some relief
for the owners of rental properties was asked.

The association requested that
the government be directed to
grant dollar for dollar an increase
in rents where the property owner
can show increases in operating
and maintenance costs since their
rentals were frozen, according to
Warwick.

"Nearly 80 per cent of the nation's residential property owners
are small owners and they have
had to meet increased costs in
fuel and maintenance costs. . . ."

Fog Index   7
LOW RENT BARS NEW BUILDING
REALTOR SAYS

president of the Chester Real
Estate Board, declared today.

Warwick says he is backing the
plea of the National Real Estate
Board now before the Senate
Banking and Currency Committee. The National Board seeks relief for landlords through breaking rent ceilings. Dollar-for-dollar
raises in rent are called for when
the owner can show upkeep has
gone up since rents were frozen.

He said, "nearly 80 per cent of
the nation's rental property
owners (landlords) are small
owners. They have had to meet
growing costs in fuel and maintenance. . . ."

Fog Index   17 plus
WOOD ADVISES VETERANS ON
MEDICAL TREATMENT

Disabled veterans training under
Public Law 16, the Vocational
Rehabilitation Act, were reminded Friday by officials of the
Hartford Veterans Administration
Regional Office that they may be
treated for disability, service-
connected or otherwise, by private
physicians if, in the opinion of
the chief medical officer, such

Fog Index   12
WOOD ADVISES VETERANS ON
MEDICAL TREATMENT

If you are taking job training
under the veterans'-aid bill and
need medical treatment, you may
be able to get it free from your
own doctor.

The chief medical officer of the
Veterans Administration Regional
Office will have to give his per-
mission for the treatment first.
But he will do so if he believes

Fog Index 17 plus
WOOD ADVISES VETERANS ON MEDICAL TREATMENT

treatment is necessary to prevent interruption of training.

Harry T. Wood, manager, also advised veterans that although VA medical facilities must be fully utilized, in cases where the veteran would suffer undue hardship or training would be interrupted, he may request an authorization for treatment by a private physician.

Authorization for treatment under these conditions must always be obtained in advance, according to Wood, except in cases of emergency. . . ."

Fog Index 12
WOOD ADVISES VETERANS ON MEDICAL TREATMENT

the service of a private physician is needed to keep you from missing training, Harry T. Wood, manager of the Hartford VA office, said Friday.

A veteran must use regular VA medical service when he can. Only when this is too difficult will treatment by a private physician be allowed, said Mr. Wood.

Authority for private treatment must be granted in advance except in an emergency. . . .

Fog in Business Writing

The pile of papers on the plant manager's desk was formidable.

"How many letters, memos, reports come to you a day?" I asked him.

"Between 40 and 50 on the average," he replied.

"How do you get them read and still do the rest of your work?"

"Most of them don't get read thoroughly. They are too long. Needlessly long. Many I don't grasp well. They have too much complex specialized detail. Still others fail to come to the point. I don't have time to *dig* for meaning and main ideas. That's why we have you here to work with our staff."

This busy executive's predicament is typical. Robert Gunning Associates works with scores of corporations conducting writing seminars and training courses. Everywhere these same complaints are raised by those who have to read and make decisions. Letters, memos, and reports are too wordy, too complex, and poorly organized.

The larger the corporation, the greater the problem. At IBM we found Albert L. Williams using a helpful training device. He would rewrite wordy memos sent him and return his revisions to the original authors to show how the messages could have been worded to be more helpful to him. As president of IBM he did much to promote better writing.

Here is an example:

ORIGINAL MEMO
Subject: Douglas Bill to Require Reporting of Pension Fund Investments

Our Washington counsel advised me today that the situation of the House Committee on Education and Labor has changed from that of last week, due to the passage by the Senate last week of the Kennedy-Ives Bill.

The House Committee initially was opposed to the Douglas Bill (which would require reporting of pension fund investments). This led the press and others to believe that no action would be taken on the Douglas Bill this Session. However, the passage of the Kennedy-Ives Bill, which is more unpopular with the House Committee, coupled with the pressures that are building up for some kind of labor legislation this Session, may lead to the passage of the Douglas Bill as a compromise. . . . (Note—This continued for another 50 words.)

WILLIAM'S REWRITE
Subject: Publicity Regarding Pension Funds.

The Senate has passed a bill which requires public disclosure of certain information regarding corporate pension funds. The House is considering similar legislation. If this bill passes, we will be required, probably starting April 1, to report details of Retirement Fund for the cost, value and investments for the previous year.

This is advance notice of the *possibility* of final passage. Will advise if *finally* passed, together with applicable details.

The first, written from the writer's viewpoint, gives all the details, but does little to digest them. The rewrite comes to the point and tells the busy executive the *meaning* of the message. This is what executives want, but get too seldom. To write a good memo for the boss requires thought—and also a little courage. The writer has to decide what are the important points and take a stand.

Would you accept the following as a definition of executive ability?

One: Skill in untangling detail and absorbing its meaning, *plus*

Two: Skill in passing the meaning on to others in a form that will result in action.

You might use the same words to describe ability in communication.

Few top executives have had training as professional writers. Now and then a corporation chooses as its head a public-relations or advertising man whose trade, in part at least, has been writing. But even this is unusual. The accustomed path to the top is by way of production, finance, or sales.

Still, the typical American executive is good at communication. He has to be to get to the top and stay there. He may be poor at *formal* speechmaking and often lacks a smooth writing style. Both oratory and the development of clear writing require practice and usually special instruction as well to root out bad habits formed in old-fashioned schools.

But even though his speaking and writing may lack professional polish, the man at the top is still able to use language to get ideas from others, relate them, and transmit them into action. And, in doing this job, an executive is constantly reminded of the failings of others in the use of English.

Each executive finds the reading he must do in his job far heavier with fog than the magazines and books he reads outside the office. One reason for this is that business writing is a pool into which flow many muddy streams of jargon. Any large business organization has within it professionals of many talents. And when experts work together they try to impress one another with their specialties. Their effort to impress the boss is never absent.

It crops up in the oddest ways. We find that even when the head of a corporation seeks cooperation to simplify writing, his helpers may pledge aid in elaborate language. The president of one firm asked for sample letters to be used in a Readability Clinic. The head of the sales department returned his with this note:

"In reference to communications as required for the Readability Clinic the attached memos are herewith respectfully submitted as requested."

That's courteous palaver for the head man. But it should have been clear, this time at least, that the better way to say it would have been a simple:

"Here are sample memos for the Readability Clinic."

The temptations of fancy language are, of course, very great. And who can deny that he has seen it used to occasional advantage. The obscure technical phrase dropped at just the right moment may serve to show how easily you find your way through mountains of fact that remain uncharted for your colleagues.

Then there are times when one has pushed his argument too far beyond an established position. A rapid burst of high-sounding words, preferably with a sprinkle of Latin, may throw up a smoke screen sufficient to cover a rapid retreat.

An alert executive sees through such verbal tricks. But even the most able person needs help in battling the waste of words in business. For most departments give no heed to word conservation.

When the executive calls upon his lawyers to explain the rules, they feel compelled to make the explanations sound oracular. An accountant who is asked for figures usually feels obliged to send along some jargon, as a stamp of his professionalism. The time-motion and the computer people, because their professions are rather new, outdo the others in giving unfamiliar names to familiar situations.

All this more or less friendly competition for status is very costly to industry. It wastes time, money, and paper and is hard on the nervous systems of managers.

Each time the legal department, the accounting department, or the sales department looks over a news release or an annual report, it is likely to come back with complexity added.

And the experts are prepared to defend their additions. The lawyer will argue "protection." The accountant will cite "precedent." The sales department points to "pride and propriety." The engineer has added his words for "precision."

All these "pr" words—"protection," "precedent," "pride," "propriety," and "precision"—are virtues to be retained in business writing. But they should not be allowed to interfere with business nor with another "pr"—"public relations."

The experts in law, science, accounting, and sales need to be confronted and balanced with another expert—one who stands for simple direct English and who is able to defend it. Most businesses lack such a person or fail to make use of him.

It is in the public-relations department that an executive is most likely to find help in clearing the fog from business communications. This is the only department likely to be staffed by men and women who are professional writers. And, only a mature person with long writing experience can be expected to have the professional knowledge that will carry weight against professionals of other types who tend to write complexly.

Usually a specialized writing job for a corporation is best accomplished by a team. If a lawyer *and* a professional writing man sit down together to draft a pension booklet, they may be able to produce one that can be read by employees. If a lawyer drafts it alone, it is likely to be a booklet that only lawyers can read.

Much of the complication of business language today results from a failure to adjust to a human scale. It is cold, formal, and impersonal and would fit better into the nineteenth century. Such language goes with autocracy, and is not the language of men working as a team.

A generation or so ago it was possible to run a business like a grand duchy and still be successful. Workers could be regarded as mechanisms and orders could be written in military style. An inflexible system could be set up and run relatively smoothly for years without change.

This never was the most effective way to run a business, as many realized even then. But still it was possible 50 years ago for several reasons:

First, the world was changing more slowly. Once the members of an organization learned the details of a job they could carry on from year to year without change. An accountant didn't have to *keep on* learning. A stockman didn't have to keep abreast of dozens of new materials and new parts each month. A selling organization could follow old patterns without being overrun by competition.

Second, schooling was limited. The great majority of workers in a plant and many in the office had not completed high school. They were prepared to do less thinking for themselves, were more willing to take orders from above.

Third, the broad goals (those other than mere wages and profits which alone are never enough to inspire fullest teamwork) were more plainly defined half a century ago. Development of industry had only begun. It was clearly to the advantage of all to build America. The workman, as well as the executive, felt important taking part in this big job.

So, it was possible, then, to operate a business with little regard for anything but immediate financial gain.

The great depression shook business into recognizing human values along with profit values. It became necessary to consider community responsibility. It became necessary to treat employees, customers—and, yes, even shareholders—more like human beings.

Our shift toward greater speed, wider schooling, and more democratic human values is reflected in language. A static society depends heavily on nouns and noun forms to carry its meaning. A more dynamic organization places more burden of its expression on strong, active verbs. In our more highly interdependent society, information must be spread more widely. More people who are nonexperts wish to know what the experts are doing, and their writing, if it is to serve the wider audience, must be comparatively free of unfamiliar technical words. And, last, a society of greater equality in human relations calls for a more personal language. Blunt or formal orders from high places will tend to get less cooperation than more friendly, conversational, persuasive English.

The public-relations profession has risen to help business and industry to adjust to these changes. In some quarters the shift has been made with great success. The Bell Telephone System, for example, is conspicuous for its good relations with the public. In most foreign countries it is taken for granted that the telephone system should be operated by the government but in the United States such a suggestion is hardly ever heard. The automobile industry, too, has generally good public relations.

In giving telephone service and in providing automobiles, companies are in constant contact with the people. This is a great advantage. It produces within a company respect for the people's needs and aspirations, on the one hand, and an understanding of the necessity to get along with them, on the other. Executives in such industries often become national leaders. Their business experience teaches them to deal with people and lead them.

Such an industry as steel, on the other hand, is at a disadvantage in making adjustments to the new industrial and social climate. Although steel plays a part in the daily life of everyone, the makers of steel themselves have little direct contact with the public.

Back in 1950 some persons of considerable influence in the government were suggesting that the steel industry be taken over. Steel executives were troubled with one Congressional investigation after another.

As a small indication of how the industry was muddling along with the written word at that time, consider this single 168-word sentence taken from a letter to stockholders. The U.S. Steel Corporation issued it on Feb. 27, 1950, to explain new benefits to be given employees:

> In order to provide adequately for discretion in the Board of Directors of the Corporation with respect to providing non-contributory and contributory pensions for employees under varying circumstances as occasion may require, it is considered necessary, as set forth in the attached plan for employee pension benefits, to continue the authority of the Board of Directors of the Corporation to authorize adoption of the pension provisions heretofore described and to authorize amendments or revisions of such provisions and benefits so as to provide different pension benefits or employee contributions from those set forth, to provide for the same or different pension benefits for other groups of employees, and to designate employees as being within or no longer within the coverage of any such pension benefits, all as the Board of Directors of the Corporation shall, in its discretion, from time to time believe to be required by the differing situations of various employees or groups of employees and in the best interests of the Corporation and its stockholders.

There are very few large firms in the country today that lack public-relations departments. But some are set up as little more than gestures. They act as defensive buffers between the press and management, but are allowed little part in forming company policy or in informing the public and shaping opinion.

In only a comparative handful of corporations has a professional in public relations—one who is skilled both in writing and in public contact—been placed in a top policy-forming position. But in each case that I have observed the move has been highly successful.

There must be a genuine interest in human relations all through a company before its communication can markedly improve. But even those companies that have made this adjustment still lag badly in language.

Public-relations departments themselves often set a poor example.

In our work for newspapers we find that the business and industrial news releases that come during a day to a city editor's desk average 13 or 14 in Fog Index. This means their complexity of style is greater than that of average material in the *Atlantic Monthly* and *Harper's*. During the same day the local news in papers we have worked with will average about the style complexity of the *Reader's Digest*.

Only a small percentage of the press releases that come to the city desk get into a paper. Many go into the wastebasket at once because they are not clear to the city editor himself on first reading.

Many press releases are poor because the persons who prepare them are not adequately trained. On the other hand, we have found that many able writers, who wrote simply and directly when they worked on magazines or newspapers, shift to a more complex style when they begin writing for industry.

There are a number of reasons for this. The first is that a writer who starts serving industry is likely to begin writing to please the executives first and readers second. He is apt to shift to a more formal and complex style simply because he feels this is the language of business. This is an error he would not make if the need to capture and hold an audience were still his first aim.

Because the editing of some newspapers is lax, many foggy press releases do get into papers. This is considered a sufficient end by some press agents, who can show the clippings as proof that they are doing their job. But what good has a printed piece done if it is too complex to be read or understood? The job of a press release has not been discharged until it has been read and remembered, and has helped to shape opinion.

A most frequent piece of evidence that a publicity writer is addressing his executive rather than the public is a news item that begins like this:

"Mr. Alfred M. Lighthouse, Jr., division manager of the Acme Plow and Rake Corporation, subsidiary of the Willmark Farm Equipment Manufacturing Co., announced today that William Meens, 418 Sixth St., will be retired Thursday after forty years service in the local corporation's sales department."

The news about Meens is of far more interest to the public than the name and detailed title of the man who made the announcement. The order should be reversed:

"William Meens, 418 Sixth St., salesman of the Acme Plow and Rake Corporation for 40 years, will retire Thursday.

"The announcement was made by Alfred M. Lighthouse, Jr., manager of the local plant, a subsidiary of Willmark Farm Equipment Manufacturing Co. . . . etc."

The most transparent toadying of a press agent to the boss and the grossest error in preparing publicity copy is the inclusion of "boosting" words. It is surprising to find, in watching the business news releases that come to a city editor's desk, how many are in this tone:

"An exciting as well as educational afternoon is planned for the huge crowds who are expected to inspect the beautiful new offices of the Watson Corporation, Sixth and Walnut Streets, Saturday afternoon.

"Extensive plans have been executed . . . etc."

Such boosting words as "exciting," "huge," "beautiful," and "extensive" would be cut out of this copy by any competent newspaperman. More often an editor would toss such copy into the wastebasket rather than take pains to put it into standard news form.

Many other unnecessary words fog the general flow of language that business addresses to the public. Most of it is padded, and although padding may make a piece of writing look impressive, it repels readers.

When a piece of writing must be approved by a number of people in a business organization, they, rather than the writer himself, may be responsible for the unnecessary words. The legal department, the accounting department, and all the others tend to put in a few more terms or qualifications just to show, if nothing else, that they are on the job.

Fog gets into business writing chiefly because it is comparatively difficult to set standards for writing. Standards for law, accounting, engineering, and so on are more firmly established.

It would be ridiculous to picture an accountant who would falsify his books simply to give his superior a rosy feeling. His first duty is to show truly whether or not the company is making a profit. The standard here is so clear that no one can *unconsciously* vary from it. But it is easy to vary from the aims and principles of good writing without being noticed. Many writers actually fool themselves into believing that they are writing for the public when they are actually writing to impress the boss. But an executive who understands the principles of clear writing will not be fooled.

Both the executive who needs helps in taking the fog out of his firm's writing and the industrial writer who needs facts to back up his professional opinion find readability research useful. It gives them a set of objective standards to use in judging written material.

Many times an industrial writer is overwhelmed in an argument with someone from, say, the legal department. While the writer's arguments are written off as personal opinions, the lawyer makes his stand on years of court decisions. But a writer armed with a knowledge of readability research has powerful ammunition to meet the arguments of other departments. He can say to a lawyer, for instance:

"You say that the way you have written this is correct, and I do not doubt it. But I know that if it is published that way it won't be read or understood.

"Here is another version I'd like to offer. It seems to me to say the same thing and it is far easier reading. In this form it won't be a waste in print. If I'm wrong in believing that the meaning is the same, show me where it is wrong. We'll revise it further. But when we do, let's keep *both* our purposes in mind. We want to protect the company, of course. But we *also* want to get our message read."

In nearly every chapter of this book are examples of foggy business writing that ignore one principle or another. Here are a few more that further illustrate the need in business organizations for experts who will constantly put forward the plain fact that words are for communication.

One of our clients used to have an order blank with a note at the bottom: "This material to be furnished subject to conditions printed on the back of this order."

I won't trouble you with *all* the small-print "GENERAL INSTRUCTIONS" that appeared on the back. But here is No. 11, word for word:

"If it becomes necessary for the Seller, either as principal or by agent or employee, to enter upon the premises or property of the Buyer, in order to construct, erect, inspect or deliver hereunder, the Seller hereby covenants and agrees to take, use, provide and make all proper, necessary and sufficient precautions, safeguards and protections against the occurrence or happenings of any accidents, injuries, damages or hurt by whomsoever caused and whether by the negligence or not of the buyer, to any person or property during the progress of the work herein covered, and to be responsible for any to indemnify and save harmless the Buyer from the payment of all sums of money by reason of all, or any, such accidents, injuries, damages or hurt that may happen or occur upon or about such work and all fines, penalties and loss incurred for or by reason of the violation of any city or borough ordinance or regulation, or the law of the State, or United States, while the said work is in progress."

No one could remember that this paragraph had ever been called into use. I strongly doubt if anyone who was supposed to, had ever read it through. It was there as "protection," but it is highly doubtful if it would have meant much one way or another in a court case. This was not a legal paper to be signed. The law covering the responsibility in such cases is rather fully developed. A simple warning like the following would have had as much weight with a jury. What is more important this notice would have had some chance of being read and understood by those to whom it was directed:

"In fulfilling this order the Seller agrees to be responsible for any damages or fines that result from negligence he or his agents commit on the property of the Buyer."

Financial releases that many companies send to newspapers are clogged with special terms that would not be clear to the average reader. In a day when companies are eager to have a wide base of ownership for their common stocks it is sensible to inform the public about a company's financial progress without mystification.

The story to the left below was released to newspapers. Only the name of the company and the figures have been changed. The words in italics would be perfectly familiar to anyone who deals in finance. But they raise the Fog Index of the piece to 16. The revision tells the same story, but omits the difficult words. This is a short example but it makes an important point. The revision tests 9 and would be easy reading for the great majority:

ORIGINAL

The Amalgamated Box Company yesterday reported *third quarter* earnings of $720,439.42 or $2.22 per share of common stock *outstanding* after preferred dividends and *deductions of all reserves* including Federal taxes.

This compares with earnings of $290,463.72, or $1.07 per share of common stock *after preferred dividends* in the third quarter of the previous year, according to L. E. Rains, treasurer.

During the first quarter this year *all remaining oustanding cumulative convertible preferred shares* of the company were either *converted* into common stock or *redeemed*. The company is now fully relieved of *its preferred stock obligations* with only common stock outstanding, it was announced.

REVISION

The Amalgamated Box Company earned $720,439.42 from July 1 to September 30 this year, the company reported today. This is equal to $2.22 per share of common stock.

Less than half that much was earned by the firm during the same period last year. Earnings then were $290,463.72, or $1.07 per share of common.

The figures for both periods are after taxes and preferred dividends, according to L. E. Rains, treasurer.

During the first quarter of this year the company has bought up or exchanged common stock for all preferred shares. Today there is only common stock outstanding, the report said. . . .

The great savings to a business come, of course, from general readability training that keeps simple messages like that on the right from becoming swollen and foggy as it was in the original:

ORIGINAL	REVISION
41 WORDS 30% POLYSYLLABLES	31 WORDS 0% POLYSYLLABLES
We believe that the procedures governing the preparation of this revised tabulation are sufficiently explicit to enable your organization to prepare this report without any difficulty; however, if further clarification is required on a particular point, your advice will be appreciated.	We believe the revised table will give you no trouble. The way to prepare it is set forth plainly. However, if you do want us to clear up any points, please ask.

At the head of each tariff sheet issued by railroads there is a sentence of complicated legal language. It is supposed to be read by station agents and businessmen who are trying to find out how much it costs to ship goods from one place to another. In Baltimore and Ohio Railroad tariffs the sentence read like this:

"Subject to provisions of Notes 1, 2, 3 and 4 below, from any point of origin from which a commodity rate on a given article to a given destination and via a given route is not named in this tariff, which point is intermediate to a point from which a commodity rate on said article is published in this tariff via a route through the intermediate point over which such commodity rate applies to the same destination, apply from such intermediate point to such destination and via such route the commodity rate in this tariff on said article from the next point beyond from which a commodity rate is published herein on that article to the same destination via the same route."

In a Readability Clinic held for Baltimore and Ohio Company executives, we offered the following revision:

"In this rule 'rate' means a commodity rate on a given article to a given destination.

"Subject to the Notes below, the rate from a point of origin not named in this tariff may be found as follows: Use the rate from the next point beyond if it applies via a route through the unnamed point."

Aside from being within range of human understanding, that version requires only half as many words as the other. Attorneys for the railroad admitted that the second version said what they were trying to say in the first, but claimed they wrote the first version because of the Interstate Commerce Commission. Roy White, then president of the road, replied to them, "The ICC may require us to do strange things, but it does not require us to be incomprehensible."

Quite right. Neither the ICC nor anyone else requires business writing to be weighed down with complexity. But most of it is, and will continue to be until executives awake to the fact that foggy language is wasteful and set about to dispel it.

On the pages that follow are a variety of samples of writing that we have run across in our work with corporations. The original passages are set beside our suggested revisions.

ORIGINAL	REVISION
Recommended Procedure for the Administration of Your Nasal Medication	How to Use Your Nose Drops
TO ALL DEPARTMENT HEADS:	TO ALL DEPARTMENT HEADS:
In order to determine the division's role in the forthcoming ABC sales program it is requested that each addressee of this notice submit to this office a memo stating the division's responsibilities in all those areas which are the responsibility of the agency headed by the respective department chief addressed. It is further requested that these responsibilities be defined and explained to such an extent that it will be improbable for misunderstanding or confusion to result.	Each of you is asked to send this office a clear, concise memo outlining what the division must do, in the department under your direction, in order to carry out the ABC sales program.

Fog Index   17 plus
109 WORDS 5 SENTENCES
25 POLYSYLLABLES-22%
AVG. SENTENCE LENGTH-22 WORDS

Mr. Robert Gunning
Robert Gunning Associates, Inc.
Blacklick, Ohio
Dear Mr. Gunning:

The June 18th issue of Public Relations News mentions a reading ability study your organization has just completed.

I am interested in this material because I have felt for quite a while that publicity material and, in general, public-relations copy is written too formalistically, which is not conducive to the greatest possible acceptance by the public.

From the statement in the Public Relations News it would seem that your material will supply the necessary impetus for revising many ideas concerning the production of copy.

I should appreciate information concerning the procedures to follow in obtaining a copy of your study.

Thank you for your assistance in this matter.

Sincerely yours,

Fog Index   8
46 WORDS   4 SENTENCES
4 POLYSYLLABLES-9%
AVG. SENTENCE LENGTH-11 WORDS

Mr. Robert Gunning
Robert Gunning Associates, Inc.
Blacklick, Ohio
Dear Mr. Gunning:

In Public Relations News I saw mention of your study of reading ability.

I agree that public-relations writing often misses its audience. Seems to me your work will bring about some copy changes.

Please tell me how I can get a copy of your study.

Thank you,

Fog Index   16
107 WORDS

For some time there has been under consideration the policy of adopting a practice to alleviate the adverse effect on employees of

Fog Index   11
72 WORDS

For some time we have been aware that employees back from long trips abroad need time to readjust themselves to home.

Fog Index 16
107 WORDS

extended trips abroad. One way of at least partially solving this problem would be to afford the returning traveler a brief period to adjust himself before fully resuming his home office duties.

Therefore, the following policy is established effective immediately:

As soon as conveniently possible, after a trip of one month's duration or more, an employee shall be allowed a few days' paid leave of absence. The employee concerned will arrange his leave of absence with his immediate superior in conformity with the policy above.

Fog Index 11
72 WORDS

Therefore, this policy is to take effect at once:

When an employee returns from a trip of a month or more, he is to be given a few days' paid leave of absence. The leave should be arranged with his immediate superior, and should be granted as soon as conveniently possible.

Fog Index 17 plus
121 WORDS

Subject: Arrangements for 20 April Celebration

The number of persons to attend any one of the various functions planned for 20 April cannot, of course, be reliably estimated until shortly before that date. It is therefore desired that detailed planning be based, and that tentative but noncommitting preparatory measures be initiated, on the assumption that there will be capacity attendance at all functions and that there may be an overflow for the afternoon and evening lecture. In other words, planning and prearranging are to be done so that all last-minute

Fog Index 10
66 WORDS

Subject: Arrangements for 20 April Celebration

We have no way of telling until shortly before April 20 how many will attend the functions that day. We had best plan, therefore, for capacity crowds at each event with possible overflow attendance at the afternoon and evening lectures.

By planning this way we can make last minute changes more easily if crowds prove small. Keep this principle in mind in planning the following events:

Fog Index   17 plus
121 WORDS
Subject: Arrangements for 20
    April Celebration

adjustments will be downward adjustments, and therefore feasible with minimum difficulty on short notice. This principle will apply particularly to such events as the following, regarding which further word may issue from time to time if found desirable:

Fog Index   10
66 WORDS
Subject: Arrangements for 20
    April Celebration

The examples that follow are from manuals on writing or other sources where one might expect excellence. The rewrites reveal how fog can be cut even in these.

Fog Index   15
118 WORDS

The abstract is essentially a summary or review of the report, designed to serve three types of reader. For the co-worker in the author's own field, the abstract is the means for deciding whether to read the report in detail. For the supervisor in other fields, it is the means for deciding whether to pass the report on to his subordinates. For top administration, it is the contact with work in progress. A properly prepared abstract should serve all three functions: the brief, general description of the work needed by the co-worker; the concise accurate summary needed by the supervisor; the relationship between the report and other work and a statement of important conclusions needed by top administration.

Fog Index   10
93 WORDS

The abstract summarizes a report for three types of reader. Think of the needs of each as you write an abstract:

Your co-worker in the same field. He needs a brief description of the work to help him decide whether to read the report in detail.

The supervisor in another field. He wants a clear, concise summary to help him decide whether to pass the report on to those under him.

The top administrator. Give him a quick review of work in progress that relates the report to other work and presents conclusions.

Fog Index   17 plus
130 WORDS

A technical journal should not have as one of its criterion for publication the presence or lack of understanding of the article by its average readership or, indeed, even by the majority of its readers. Those articles which by their very novelty and imaginativeness will be understood by but a few of the membership upon first publication will in the end contribute more to the growth of professional standards in the society than any other one factor which can be named. The *Journal* and the society should do all within its power to encourage its membership to original thinking and should provide the mechanism, through publication, whereby products of such creative work can be brought to the attention of the whole membership for their present and future use and appreciation.

Fog Index   12
91 WORDS

The standard for publication of an article by a technical journal should not be that most of the journal's readers will be able to understand it. When first published, a highly novel and imaginative article may be grasped by only a few. Still the same piece may, at length, contribute greatly to the society's professional standards. The *Journal* and the society should do all they can to stimulate the membership to original thought. And publication should bring the fruit of such work before the whole membership for present and future use.

Fog Index   17 plus
86 WORDS

According to literary standards, a good report is one which is clear, concise, well organized, uses concrete terms, conforms to rules of grammar and punctuation, employs standard abbreviations, avoids slang and trade terms and is readily understood. The good research report must not only meet these qualitative specifications but is expected to contain

Fog Index   11
65 WORDS

The prose of a good report should be clear and easy to understand. It should be well-organized and grammatical and should employ concrete terms and standard abbreviations. Slang and trade terms (jargon) should be avoided. Beyond this, a good research report should contain enough data to enable a qualified reader to evaluate the work,

Fog Index 17 plus
86 WORDS

sufficient data to enable a qualified reader to evaluate the work by verifying calculations and judgments entailed in arriving at the findings and conclusions or permit him to extend the investigation or study.

Fog Index 11
65 WORDS

check its calculations and conclusions, and extend the study, should he wish.

Fog Index 17 plus
137 WORDS

The cost and workload in technical library operations are progressively increasing along with the staggering growth in volume of engineering and scientific material written today and predicted for the future. Libraries must keep up with the increasing volume of material, or library operations will cease to have the desired value to research, development, and other scientific organizations. Action must be taken to control the increasing costs which will continue to grow year after year, and this can best be done by studying the problems, developing ideas, and establishing new procedures.

Many activities and individuals are devoting considerable efforts in applying machines—computers —to the information retrieval problem. However, not enough effort is being devoted to the study of the problems and the reduction of costs in the work that is necessary prior to retrieval by the machines.

Fog Index 11
87 WORDS

Both costs and workload in technical libraries are growing at the same staggering rate as the volume of scientific writing. If libraries are to serve science and research they must keep pace with this ever-increasing volume of written material, and their best hope of doing so is to cut costs. Problems must be studied; new methods established.

Much effort has gone into applying machines—computers—to the information-retrieval problem. Not enough has been done, however, to cut costs of work required prior to retrieval by machines.

Probably the foggiest writing found in business and industry is that of the National Electrical Code. The Code is a guide for installing electrical equipment so it will meet safety standards. The jargons of engineers, lawyers, and government officials mingle in the Code, the work of a committee. Engineers and electricians spend hours puzzling over the wording. Months are wasted as builders, officials, and insurance men battle over Code meanings.

Plant Engineering, an industrial magazine, conducted a campaign to have the Code written in clearer language, and asked us to show how the job could be done. Some original excerpts and rewrites follow:

As It Now Appears in Code 107 words	Suggested Revision 47 words
500–4. *Class I Locations.* Class I locations are those in which flammable gases or vapors are or may be present in the air in quantities sufficient to produce explosive or ignitible mixtures. Class I locations shall include the following:	Hazardous Locations are classified as follows:
(a) *Class I, Division 1.* Locations (1) in which hazardous concentrations of flammable gases or vapors exist continuously, intermittently, or periodically under normal operating conditions, (2) in which hazardous concentrations of such gases or vapors may exist frequently because of repair or maintenance operations or because of leakage, or (3) in which breakdown or faulty operation of equipment or processes which might release hazardous concentrations of flammable gases or vapors, might also cause simulta-	500–4. *Class I, Division 1.* Where concentrations of flammable gases or vapors exist (1) continuously or periodically during normal operations; (2) frequently during repair or maintenance or because of leakage; or (3) due to equipment breakdown or faulty operation which could also cause failure of electrical equipment.

AS IT NOW APPEARS IN CODE
107 WORDS

neous failure of electrical equipment.

SUGGESTED REVISION
47 WORDS

135 WORDS

(b) *Class I, Division 2.* Locations (1) in which volatile flammable liquids or flammable gases
are handled, processed or used,
but in which the hazardous
liquids, vapors or gases will
normally be confined within
closed containers or closed systems from which they can escape
only in case of accidental rupture
or breakdown of such containers
or systems, or in case of abnormal operation of equipment,
(2) in which hazardous concentrations of gases or vapors are
normally prevented by positive
mechanical ventilation, but which
might become hazardous through
failure or abnormal operation of
the ventilating equipment, or (3)
which are adjacent to Class I,
Division 1 locations, and to which
hazardous concentrations of gases
or vapors might occasionally be
communicated unless such communication is prevented by ade-
quate positive-pressure ventilation
from a source of clean air, and
effective safeguards against ventilation failure are provided.

65 WORDS

Class I, Division 2. (1) **Where**
flammable *volatile liquids, vapors*
or *gases* are confined in closed
containers or systems from which
they cannot escape except in case
of rupture, breakdown, or abnormal operation of equipment;
(2) where concentrations of explosive gas or vapor, normally
prevented by ventilation, would
occur if the equipment failed;
(3) areas next to Class I, Division
1 locations not protected by positive-pressure, clean-air ventilation,
safeguard against failure.

106 WORDS

500–5. *Class II Locations.* Class
II locations are those which are
hazardous because of the presence

55 WORDS

500–5. *Class II, Division 1.* (1)
Where, at any time during normal
operations, there could be enough

As It Now Appears in Code
106 words

Suggested Revision
55 words

of combustible dust. Class II locations shall include the following:

(a) *Class II, Division 1.* Locations (1) in which combustible dust is or may be in suspension in the air continuously, intermittently, or periodically under normal operating conditions, in quantities sufficient to produce explosive or ignitible mixtures, (2) where mechanical failure or abnormal operation of machinery or equipment might cause such mixtures to be produced, and might also provide a source of ignition through simultaneous failure of electrical equipment, operation of protection devices, or from other causes, or (3) in which dusts of an electrically conducting nature may be present.

combustible *dust* in the air to explode or ignite; (2) where failure or abnormal operation of machinery or equipment might cause such explosive mixture and, at the same time, the means of igniting it; (3) where dusts that can conduct electricity may be present.

Legal Prose

"But, judge," argued the young lawyer before Judge E. W. Fitch of Akron, *"res ipsa loquitur."*

"How's that?" asked the judge.

"Res ipsa loquitur—the facts speak for themselves," the attorney repeated.

"Young man," the judge told him gruffly, "if the facts speak for themselves, let them speak English."

Judge Fitch, like many distinguished men of his profession, hated pomposity and tried to take the fog out of legal language.

Harrison W. Tweed, as chairman of the American Law Institute, led an effort to guide the language of the law into clearer, simpler, English. He asked: "How can two laymen follow the terms of a contract between them if they cannot understand the language? Entirely too much time is wasted on old-fashioned terms that mean little or nothing to our clients, or to the courts."

There are many, many reasons why legal language is complex. One of them is probably justified. This is the fact that law deals with certainty. Legal phrasing must, if it is properly drawn, have only one meaning.

You can say to your friend, "I'll sell you my lot on Sixth Street for a thousand dollars."

"I'll take it," says he and the deal is made. But it is not yet closed legally. The community has an interest in this transaction. It must be clear that the lot is yours to sell and that all dower rights are released. Just what "lot" means in this instance must be established down to the inch. All this information goes into the deed and the other legal papers of the transfer.

When a rich man provides for the division of his estate or when a legislature lays down the rules under which businessmen may compete, the language needs to be certain. And usually a great many words are required to close all the loopholes in such complicated affairs.

These tasks are for masters of English, but too few are found in law offices or on the bench. In the 6 or 7 years that law students must spend in college, the usual requirement for English is a few months of a freshman course. No wonder the average lawyer is so unsure of his own expression that he is fearful of leaving out qualifications that are meaningless. He is so poorly versed on the relationship of words that he often dumps all he has to say into one sentence. This shifts the chief burden of composition, that of properly relating ideas, onto the reader. Here is a sample of such a jerry-built traditional legal sentence of 277 words:

"While it is true that equity will not extend relief by cancellation of a contract merely because the obligations assumed by the plaintiff, one of the contracting parties, are improvident and heavy, or that the consideration accruing to her is inadequate, or that she has been induced to sign through the persuasion of the other contracting party, however, where it appears that the plaintiff is a person of limited ability, illiterate, and wholly unacquainted with business matters, and that the defendant, the other contracting party, is a friend and confidant of plaintiff, whose husband, an attorney at law, the plaintiff has had occasion in the past to employ professionally, and who drew the contract in question, and who was present when plaintiff was urged to sign it by the defendant and the plaintiff's daughter, a close friend of the defendant, and that the obligations assumed by defendant are ambiguous, indefinite, and uncertain, and that plaintiff is evidently unacquainted with the implications of the obligations assumed by her, which may be extended to limit any sale, lease, or other disposition of two valuable pieces of real estate, upon one of which is a residence occupied by the defendant and her husband, and which, under the terms of the contract, the defendant is permitted to occupy for life or until an indefinite obligation is performed by the plaintiff, a case requiring the intervention of a court of equity is presented, and such contract will be annulled and the title to the real estate of plaintiff involved quieted against any claim arising under such contract, the plaintiff not being represented by or receiving professional counsel as to her rights and obligations."

This is an Appellate Court decision and a fairly recent one. Such monstrous sentences are becoming rarer, however. Other lawyers, who have to read what their colleagues write, have been insisting that marathon sentences be broken up. They know that such a method is the lazy way to write a decision. Short sentences are just as legal. The only difference is that they put the drudgery of clear and logical organization of facts upon the writer, where it should be, rather than upon the reader.

About half the cases that come into court are those in which different lawyers derive different meaning from the same samples of legal prose. Some of the disagreement, of course, is manufactured for tactical reasons. A great portion, however, comes from fog in the words themselves. And not all this fog results from ignorance and lack of skill in language. Unfortunately, the legal profession is open to temptations that beset few of the rest of us.

In most professions the interest and the advantage lie with clear communication. Although they often fail to achieve it, the novelist, the journalist, the engineer, the accountant all have a high stake in clarity of their prose. The more readily they make themselves understood the more likely they are to increase both earnings and stature in their professions.

This is not always true for lawyers. As we pointed out in an earlier chapter, if a man draws a document that only he can interpret, he has built himself a degree of security. He must be retained to interpret it. On the other hand, if a legal instrument is drawn in such simple terms that a client can readily understand it, the client will begin to wonder: "Coudn't I have done this myself?"

Often, of course, the lawyer can throw the blame for vague words back on his clients. A man seeking a patent will want his attorney to draw his claim as broad as possible. And some unreliable insurance companies have been known to have lawyers bury escape clauses in complexly written fine print which the policyholder may not take time to read or understand.

A newspaper publisher once showed me an amusing letter from his lawyer. It came in answer to three legal questions the publisher had asked. The letter was several pages of closely typed legal verbiage. At the end the lawyer had added a postscript;

"The answer to your questions are—
    "1—No.
    "2—No.
    "3—Yes."

The fact is this lawyer was doing his job better than most. For often the communication job in law is twofold. There is one type of language qualified according to hundreds of years of court tests. And there is another type that is quickly expressive. The body of the letter of the attorney satisfied the first; his postscript the second.

The more earnest the lawyer and the higher his skill in English composition, the more nearly a court version will tend to resemble a layman's version. We have found that once a lawyer becomes convinced of the need for broad communication he will go very far in simplifying his language. But not enough of them have given the matter thought.

H. Bartow Farr, Jr., a top legal executive of IBM, is one who has been concerned about making legal language readable. Speaking before a meeting of the company's lawyers he urged them to use ordinary language whenever possible.

"A good contract," he said, "should be concise, contain no irrelevant clauses and no legalistic phrasing. It should avoid redundant, overly protective clauses; relics from other contracts and other times. It should not only serve to protect the company's legal rights, but should also enhance its public image as a company. It should reveal the company as one easy to do business with and reasonable in its requirements. Few contracts meet these criteria. In fact, most violate all of them."

Farr then cited a number of typical sections from contracts, commented on them and rewrote them.

Here, for example, is the original of a familiar statement about patent rights:

ORIGINAL 144 WORDS	FARR'S REWRITE 58 WORDS
Contractor will assign to X, its successors and assigns, any said invention upon X's request and the same shall become and remain X's property whether or not patent applications are filed thereon. Contractor shall, upon, X's re-	Any invention, discovery or improvement resulting from services performed under this Agreement belongs to X, whether or not patentable. Contractor will assist X in any way requested in filing patent applications wherever X

Original 144 words	Farr's Rewrite 58 words
quest and at X's expense, cause patent applications to be filed thereon in countries selected by X, through solicitors designated by X and forthwith assign all such applications to X, its successors and assigns. Contractor shall give X and its solicitors all reasonable assistance in connection with the preparation and prosecution of any such patent applications and shall execute all such assignments and other instruments and documents as X may consider necessary or appropriate to carry out the intent of this paragraph. X agrees to grant and hereby does grant to Contractor an irrevocable, nonexclusive, nontransferable, fully paid-up license in (country) under any said inventions assigned to X.	wishes it. Contractor will assign such applications to X. Contractor will be given an irrevocable, nonexclusive, nontransferable, fully paid-up license under any invention so assigned.

Consider this sentence dealing with the use of a name:

"If Smith disapproves the use of his name in connection with X's proposed use of his work, or by any other party authorized by X to use his work he shall so notify X. In such circumstances X agrees that Smith's name will not be used in conjunction with such work."

Farr's comment: "It would be sufficient to say in all but the rarest of cases: 'Smith may disapprove the use of his name in any use of his work.' "

Windy passages like the following are often included in contracts in what seems a near hysterical effort at protection:

Seller agrees to indemnify buyer and save it harmless against any losses, claims, damages or liabilities regarding employees or agents of seller and of its subcontractors, joint or several, to which buyer may become subject, insofar as such losses, claims, damages or liabilities (or acts in respect thereof) pertain to injury to or death of persons or damage to property that may have been or may be alleged to have been caused directly or indirectly by seller, its subcontractors and employees or agents or by buyer, its employees or agents, in connection with or in any manner growing out of the work contracted for, including, but not limited to, the whole of the foregoing losses, claims, damages, or liabilities arising in whole or in part from negligence or breach of duty, statutory or otherwise, on the part of the buyer. Seller will reimburse buyer for any legal or other expenses reasonably incurred by buyer in connection with investigating or defending any loss, claim, damage, or liability or action referred to in the preceding sentence. If buyer's machinery or equipment is used by seller in the performance of the work called for under this contract, such machinery or equipment shall be considered under the sole custody and control of seller during the period of such use by seller and if any employee or employees of buyer should be used to operate said machinery or equipment during the period of such use, such person or persons shall be deemed during such period of operation to be an employee or employees of seller.

Farr comments:

"This provision is not only virtually incomprehensible, but also patently unfair—no seller would even consider agreeing to it unless:

(1) it was unrelated to his activity or
(2) he didn't read it or couldn't understand it or
(3) he needed the business so badly he would agree to anything."

The next time you ride an airplane, note the back of the ticket. Here legal language reaches its height of absurdity and its vanishing point of readability. You will need a magnifying glass to decipher the tiny print beneath the heading "Conditions of Contract." In a space that a man's hand will cover are crowded more than 1,500 words, the equivalent of about four pages of this book. The first sentence is 109 words long.

In discussing this curious botch of pretended communication with Farr, I said, "if I am accused of doing something that the back of this ticket says I shouldn't do, I'll fight the matter in court on the basis that this cannot be read."

"I'll take the case," replied Farr, "and we will win it."

One of our clients formerly issued a pension-plan booklet containing a draft of the legal document which was the base of the pension plan. Sentences were very long. This one, for example, runs 211 words:

"If, on any date prior to January 1, 1954, this Plan is discontinued, (1) no monthly pension payment commencing at or after age sixty-five which is payable after such date to any such member shall exceed one-twelfth of the greater of (a) $1,500, or (b) a pension, which on the basis of the mortality tables and interest rate used in the reserve calculations in 1944, shall have a value as of the date of such discontinuance equal to twenty per cent (20%) of such member's regular salary, not in excess of $50,000 per annum, received during the years commencing with January 1, 1944, and continuing up to such date of discontinuance, plus such pension as can be provided on the basis of such mortality tables and interest rate from the contributions made by such member, and (2) no monthly pension payment under subsection (2) of Section Four or under subsection (6) of Section Eight which is payable after such date to or with respect to any such member living on such date shall exceed the amount which would have been payable under such subsection and commencing at the same time if the pension otherwise payable commenc-

ing at age sixty-five were the greater of the amounts (a) or
(b) in this sentence."

The booklet went to the company's thousands of employees.
No one expected them, however, to read the body of the plan
with understanding, so a series of questions and answers about
it were incorporated in the booklet. These were to serve as an
explanation. The language was simplified. There were no
more 211-word sentences, but there were sentences of the
length of this one, containing 96 words:

"Until the first payment on account of a member's pension
becomes due, he may elect to receive, in lieu of the normal or
early pension which he would otherwise have been entitled
to receive, a modified pension for himself for life, with the
provision that after his death it shall continue for the life of
his designated beneficiary, or he may elect a modified pension
for himself for life, with the provision that after his death a
pension at one-half the rate of his modified pension shall be
continued during the life of his designated beneficiary."

After a Readability Clinic, the Legal Department revised
the pension-plan booklet. The questions and answers were
made easy reading throughout and still remained as "legal"
as before. The complicated sentence above, for instance, was
revised into several with a Fog Index of 9. They answered the
question:

"May a member have his pension changed so that after his
death a pension will continue to his wife or some other beneficiary?"

And the revised answer was:

"Yes. A member can assure his wife or another beneficiary
a pension after his death. He does this by accepting a *modified*
pension instead of the *early* or *normal* pension due him. There
are two plans. Under one the same rate is paid first to the
member until his death and then to the beneficiary during

his or her life. A second plan sets the rate of the beneficiary's pension at one-half that paid the member during his life. The choice is open until the first payment of the member's pension falls due."

In writing the basic document of a pension plan, attorneys can be excused for complex language. They are addressing other lawyers. But if they retain complexity in an explanation for employees they defeat their purpose. There is a limit in adding protective armor plate. Beyond a certain point it sinks the ship.

Legal terms have their place. But they should be dropped, whenever possible, from annual reports of business firms, employee reports and letters to stockholders.

Furthermore, most of the legal terms that appear in newspapers could be and should be avoided. If a newspaper reporter clearly understands legal terms he can translate them and save burdening the reader.

For instance, he seldom needs to say, "The prisoner was *arraigned* before Judge Smith." Few newspaper readers are clear about the meaning of "arraignment." Usually it is enough to say, "The prisoner was brought before Judge Smith."

The following often appears in papers: "The prisoner waived extradition and will be returned to the custody of New York police." Usually one need say no more than— "The prisoner agreed to return to New York for trial."

Anyone will understand: "Judge Smith said he would decide the case later." But many are left in the dark by, "Judge Smith took the case under advisement."

It is short to write: "The prosecutor nolled three burglary cases." But few aside from lawyers will understand. The clearer version is: "The prosecutor dropped three burglary cases with the court's consent."

There are scores of legal terms. Here are a few translated.

If a writer understands them he can usually make their meaning clear to the reader with other words:

AFFIDAVIT—written statement signed and sworn to before an officer.

ALLEGE—say, state, assert.

CAPIAS—writ of arrest.

DEMURRER—statement that the facts that the other fellow relies on show on their face that he has no case.

DEPOSITION—written statement taken under oath in the presence of lawyers for both sides.

DISMISS WITH PREJUDICE—throw a person's case out of court and bar him from suing again on the same facts.

DISMISS WITHOUT PREJUDICE—throw a person's case out of court but allow him to start over again if he wants to.

ENJOIN, OR ISSUE AN INJUNCTION—forbid someone to do some specific thing or class of things.

FEE SIMPLE—without limitation. (A property held in fee simple is owned absolutely.)

GRANT CERTIORARI—agree to hear a case on appeal.

GRANT CHANGE OF VENUE—permit trial by another court (usually in another county).

HABEAS CORPUS—writ by which a person is brought before a judge to determine if he is being legally held by authorities.

INTERLOCUTORY DIVORCE—a temporary one, not yet final.

MANDAMUS—writ to compel a public officer to do some specific act.

MISTRIAL—trial in which errors have prevented a fair result.

NOLO CONTENDERE—plea of "no contest." Pleader accepts penalty without admitting guilt.

RECOGNIZANCE BOND—money or property pledged to be forfeited if a person fails to appear in court when ordered to do so.

SUBPOENA—order to appear in court.

VACATE (an order or injunction)—cancel.

In translating legal terms a headline writer in Oklahoma City some years ago went rather far. A town character who was beyond libel was brought into court on a gambling charge. He pleaded *nolo contendere*.

The deskman headed the story:

JOE WILK PLEADS GUILTY IN LATIN

Fortunately lawyers themselves are becoming increasingly conscious of the need of simplified language, and writing courses in law schools are on the increase.

There is no profession in which clear writing is more important than in law. But the work of lawyers and those who imitate them accounts for a very large portion of the fog in business communication and the writing of every-day life. For example, a busy real-estate man of my acquaintance found this missive in his morning mail:

> Sirs:
>
> I have been referred to your office with respect to the leasing of a single-occupancy apartment within the City of Pottsville, Pa., for a minimum period of one year commencing June 1, and wish to receive certain preliminary information prior to calling upon your office in Pottsville personally, to-wit: descriptive information regarding the better apartments available for occupancy at the time noted, *supra,* the annual or monthly rates thereof, and the locations of such apartments within the City of Pottsville. At such time as this initial information is received, it will be evaluated forthwith and you will be informed of the listings in which I am most interested in order that they may be shown during my next visit to Pottsville.
>
> Inasmuch as I am desirous of executing a lease within the near future, the prompt attention of your office to this matter will be appreciated.
>
> Very truly yours,

All he wished to say was:

> I wish to lease an apartment for one in Pottsville for at least a year beginning June 1.
>
> Please send me information about apartments available, where they are, and what is their monthly rental.
>
> I will let you know in which ones I am interested and you can show them to me on my next trip to Pottsville.

Technical Writing

Willard Gibbs was one of the greatest of American scientists. Henry Adams, among others, called him *the* greatest. Gibbs is known to engineers, but few others can identify him.

This quiet Yale mathematician laid the foundation for physical chemistry. The plastics industry, the rubber and steel industries, and many others owe their development to discoveries made by Gibbs. In stature he rates close to Darwin and Einstein, whose names are known to nearly everyone. But the name of Gibbs means next to nothing to the public that is so deeply indebted to him.

Gibbs, unlike most of the men who become famous, had a sadly limited understanding of the purposes of the written word. Lack of recognition both during his lifetime and since has been his penalty.

Although he wrote with precision, his prose was leadened with complexity. He made no effort to prepare his readers for new ideas he presented. He felt no duty to see that what he wrote was understood and used. As a result, some important discoveries made by Gibbs lay buried in obscure language until they were rediscovered later by other men. It became a scientific joke that it was easier to "rediscover Gibbs than it was to read him."

Here is Gibb's own abstract of his great paper, *On the Equilibrium of Heterogeneous Substances:*

> It is an inference naturally suggested by the general increase of entropy which accompanies the changes occurring in any isolated material system that when the entropy of the system has reached a maximum the system will be in a state of equilibrium. Although this principle has by no means escaped the attention of physicists, its importance does not appear to have been duly appreciated. Little has been done to develop the principle as a foundation for the general theory of thermodynamic equilibrium.
>
> The principle may be formulated as follows, constituting a criterion of equilibrium:
>
> 1. For the equilibrium of any isolated system it is necessary and sufficient that in all possible variations of the state of the system which do not alter its energy, the variation of its entropy shall either vanish or be negative.
>
> The following form, which is easily shown to be equivalent to the preceding, is often more convenient in application:
>
> 2. For the equilibrium of any isolated system it is necessary and sufficient that in all possible variations of the state of the system which do not alter its entropy, the variation of its energy shall either vanish or be positive.

Gibb's language is neat and precise but hardly any who read it in early years suspected the great discoveries it held.

Today all of us who hope to live outside a lead-lined cellar have a personal interest in how well scientists communicate. Our future depends to considerable degree on how well research men and technicians can inform one another. To fail in the use of language as Gibbs failed is clearly an unsocial act.

The men of science who are remembered were skilled in communication. Louis Pasteur's paper on the prevention of rabies and Madame Curie's account of the discovery of radium are readable, exciting pieces of prose. The writing of both Darwin and Einstein is excellent.

The principal discoveries of Einstein are deep mathematics clear to only a few. But even though he wrote in that heaviest of languages, scholarly German, Einstein could write prose that is clear and direct. His concepts are complex, but he does not add to their complexity with foggy language. The following sample, although a translation, reveals his conversational style.

> If we ponder over the question as to how the universe, considered as a whole, is to be regarded, the first answer that suggests itself to us is surely this: As regards space (and time) the universe is infinite. There are stars everywhere, so that the density of matter, although very variable in detail, is nevertheless on the average everywhere the same. In other words: However far we might travel through space, we should find everywhere an attenuated swarm of fixed stars of approximately the same kind of density.
>
> This view is not in harmony with the theory of Newton. The latter theory rather requires that the universe should have a kind of center in which the density of the stars is a maximum, and that as we proceed outward from this center the group density of the stars should diminish until finally, at great distances, it is succeeded by an infinite region of emptiness. This stellar universe ought to be a finite island in the infinite ocean of space. . . .

And here is a sample, from *The Descent of Man,* of Darwin's vivid, concrete prose (It has a Fog Index of 10).

> The main conclusion arrived at in this work, namely, that man is descended from some lowly organized form, will, I regret to think, be highly distasteful to many. But there can hardly be a doubt that we are descended from barbarians. The astonishment which I felt on first seeing a

party of Fuegians on a wild and broken shore will never be forgotten by me, for the reflection at once rushed into my mind: Such were our ancestors. These men were absolutely naked and bedaubed with paint, their long hair was tangled, their mouths frothed with excitement, and their expression was wild, startled, and distrustful. They possessed hardly any arts, and like wild animals lived on what they could catch; they had no government, and were merciless to everyone not of their own tribe. He who has seen a savage in his native land will not feel much shame if forced to acknowledge that the blood of some more humble creature flows in his veins.

The big men of science, the ones whose ideas have most influenced our lives, the ones whose names are widely remembered, were very able with words.

Today some of the best and some of the poorest English being written is the work of technical men and women—engineers, doctors, social scientists. Technical writers start with an advantage. Their basic material is concrete facts and events. And the main object is to describe such and show the relationships between them. Fiction is, of course, out of the question, and biography and philosophy (which can lead rapidly to fog) are discouraged.

The best technical writing is being done by persons at the top of their professions who have done important work, understand its meaning, and write about it with confidence. They are bold enough to write simple, direct English.

Too many others, who haven't done much or who understand less clearly what they have done, write with an uneasiness that leads to fog. They are likely to smother their meaning in qualification. The man who is sure of himself includes, of course, qualification that is required. But he also recognizes the surplus that can be safely shed. This is an important part of wisdom and essential to clear communication.

Most technical men and women are able in oral communication. They talk clearly and concretely and can explain to a
layman or to a bright youngster what they are doing. But let
them begin to write and they shun simple English and slip
into an odd jargon they consider traditional and safe.

A chemist once came to me with his writing problems. He
was trying to perfect a new cigarette lighter which a businessman hoped to manufacture and sell. There were technical
problems involved that the chemist found difficult to make
clear to the businessman.

"You see," the chemist said to me. "We must make the flame
visible. But this flame burns so perfectly you can hardly
see it. We have tried to color the flame but that doesn't work
too well. What I want to do is to change the torch so it does
not burn as well as it does now. Then like a match flame, it
will show up. You know yourself how you can smoke up a
piece of glass with a match flame. That's because there are
particles of carbon in the flame that don't get burned. When
they are hot they are bright yellow and make the flame easy
to see."

You see, the chemist was having no trouble making himself
clear.

Then I looked at the letter he had written the businessman.
It covered the same point. But clear English had been re-
placed by jargon:

"Neither volatile nor solid additives have proved themselves
as flame colorants. It is recommended that the flame be made
softer, for in unsaturated hydrocarbons this is a means of increasing the visibility of the incandescent gas."

The letter was *addressed to* the businessman but it was
not *written for* him. It was written for other chemists.

Speaking face-to-face the chemist had put his explanation
into picturable terms. He sensed the need of linking his idea
with my experience through the illustration of the match flame
and smoked glass. But in writing he was afraid to do this.

Not that the chemist was a timid man. Good engineers never are. But how can his retreat into obscure technical language be explained except by lack of courage and confidence? He was afraid his writing might seem unprofessional.

It is never unprofessional, in the sciences at least, to make oneself clear.

Long, technical words used by experts have been the butt of much poor humor. If the jokes are directed at pedantry they do a service. The technical vocabularies of the English language themselves, however, deserve respect, for they are among its greatest riches. Our English technical words are a measure of our culture, a measure of our knowledge of ourselves and our environment. Education, in fact, consists chiefly of making technical terms meaningful.

Technical vocabularies, like all other useful inventions, are open to abuse. A man new to a profession is prone to use its special vocabulary at every opportunity, to show that he belongs. Unconfident persons often overwork ornate words to try to persuade others (and perhaps convince themselves) that they know a great deal.

And there are still others so deeply involved in their work that its special language has become second nature to them. They overlook how awkward, bundlesome, and puzzling this jargon can become when allowed to clot on paper.

The vast majority of technical words that have established themselves in English have done so because they are useful. If an architect were denied such words as "jamb," "facia," "stud," "plate," and "module," he would have to invent others to take their places.

New words like "penicillin" and plutonium" come into common use because they are needed as scientific knowledge expands. "Hay fever" becomes a ragweed or other type of "allergy" as we learn more about it.

If we overlook unsettled areas such as psychiatry, the greater portion of technical terms are concrete. They stand for substances, tools, or objects that can be pointed out or for processes that can be demonstrated. Thus there is little question about the meaning of such terms once they become familiar. They are not fuzzy in outline like many of the cumbersome terms so frequent in general business writing.

However, the technical fields are not free of that taste for high-sounding language that causes fog in every trade and profession. It spawns complicated words that could be dropped and never be missed. The metallurgist could deny himself "comminution" and get along very well with "crushing" or "grinding." The botanist would never miss "desquamation" if he confined himself to the familiar term "scaling off." And it is difficult to support the doctor's substitution of "rhinitis" for "common cold," or "myopia" for "nearsightedness," on the basis of either need or precision.

Poor workmanship in making new technical words also causes needless complexity in scientific language. Technicians who are rarely schooled in either Latin or Greek make a habit of digging into these languages to form new names. The classical languages have given science many stems and parts of words that are now familiar and give hints of the meaning in new words. Using old parts helps make a new word like "videogenic" meaningful. But the use of Greek to manufacture such tongue twisters as "stoichiometrically" or "xerography" does small service to clear communication.

Such words are invented by men who sit at desks. Those who work in the shop make words that are better fitted to the tongue. The best short, crisp, and descriptive technical words are of this origin.

In pottery, ceramists have acquired such terms as "spall" (for the chips of broken ceramic materials), "sinter" (to describe the way clays knit when fired), "frit" (the sandy material from which glass is made), and "blunge" (to mix with water by stirring). Workmen have contributed "floc" for the precipitate in ore processing and "gangue" for the waste material of ore. In contrast, the educated metallurgist seeking a term for the process of purifying ore comes up with "beneficiation."

There are thousands upon thousands of technical terms unfamiliar to each of us. Opening an unabridged dictionary to nearly any page will reveal this. When a technical man writes for those outside his field he should take care to avoid or explain technical terms that are not generally familiar.

Furthermore, in writing for people within his own field, a technical writer should sift technical words through these self-critical questions: Am I using these words to express or to impress? Am I using them because they are necessary to make my ideas clear or am I using them merely to signal that I am an expert?

Many long terms are necessary in technical writing, and they seem to have magnetic properties, attracting nontechnical terms that could be simplified or omitted.

Here are a few examples along with revisions in which the unnecessary complexity has been removed (note that such precise technical terms as "viscous," "modulus of elasticity," and "linear" are retained in these revisions while the Fog is dispelled):

> ORIGINAL: Experiments conducted to determine the lowest temperature at which the reduction reaction could be initiated indicated reduction began at 27 degrees Centigrade.
>
> REVISION: Experiments showed the lowest temperature at which reduction began was 27 degrees Centigrade.
>
> ORIGINAL: Comparison of data obtained with these paints using Barco with those using Lenol reveals that use of Barco solvent slows the drying appreciably (approximately doubling the time in most cases) but has very little effect on the viscosity characteristics obtained.

REVISION: The data show(s) paints using Barco are no more viscous than those using Lenol, but dry only about half as fast.

ORIGINAL: An approximately linearly decreasing relationship of modulus of elasticity with increasing temperature resulted.

REVISION: Modulus of elasticity decreased as temperature rose. The relationship was roughly linear.

Very few engineers write as well as they talk. This is easy to judge from the lively oral discussions that are often printed following the dry scientific papers of technical meetings. Engineers have told me that, as a means of saving time, they habitually skim the articles, then read closely the oral discussions.

Good scientific writing should be objective, impersonal, and precise. Unfortunately, however, virtues are often twisted into writing faults. A spendthrift can defend himself on the basis of generosity. And in the same way I have known engineers to defend poorly organized, dull, and vague reports on the basis of the three virtues just mentioned. Let us consider them separately.

One—objectivity vs. disregard of the reader

Technical writing is due for a Copernican revolution. Before Copernicus the earth was considered the center of everything. Ptolemy had described how the skies, as hollow spheres, turned about it.

Copernicus upset all this. He showed that the earth revolves around the sun—and he was persecuted as a heretic. Many in high places regarded Copernicus as a traitor to the human race as well as to his habitat. But he was merely revealing facts others could observe were true.

His discoveries made the earth no less important. Nothing was changed but the relationships which he revealed in their true order.

Many technical papers are composed with a concept of relationships as out-of-date as Ptolemy's. Facts are of first importance in a report. But in attending to them a writer should not forget the reader.

Any piece of writing should revolve around the intended reader. This does not mean that the facts become less important. But it does mean that they should be related to the reader's experience. A report should prepare a reader for what it is about to tell him. The piece should be written so that it leads the reader's attention and enables him to gain facts and their relationships in the shortest possible time. The simple setting down of facts is only half a job of report writing. The facts should be weighted and their significance shown through arrangement and emphasis.

Anyone who writes a paper has spent time gathering facts and contemplating their meaning. The interpretation of meaning is usually the more important part of a paper. The author owes it to the reader to make clear the meaning he has been able to draw from the facts—without, of course, neglecting to underline points that are still unclear or unsolved. To sum up this advice: "Write for the reader, not for the filing cabinet."

Two—impersonal vs. inhuman

Technical reports are supposed to be strictly impersonal. The idea is that any trained person carrying out the same experiment will get the same results. But the need to be impersonal is not an excuse for being inhuman. Most of the great technical papers have a degree of warmth. Even Einstein, writing of relativity, draws homely analogies with the aid of "our old friend, the railway carriage."

But some writers of reports shun the first person so completely that they would not use "we" to refer to the human race. They prefer, for example, such dull and awkward constructions as, "At present information available on these alloys is extremely limited" to, "We know little about these alloys."

The effort to be impersonal causes a deadening overuse of the passive voice in scientific prose. An engineer preparing a report will write over and over again: "Tests were made." He may feel barred from writing "We made tests." However, he could usually avoid the passive, and cover the ground faster, by writing "Tests showed. . . ."

The technical writer should make special effort to avoid a monotonous series of passives, for active verbs are more readable. Sentences can often be recast to the active voice and still be kept impersonal. Example:

> PASSIVE: The melting point of the alloy was lowered 50 degrees by adding 10 per cent of aluminum.
> ACTIVE: Adding 10 per cent of aluminum lowered the melting point 50 degrees.

A close look at some of the most formal scientific journals, such as *The Physical Review* or the *Journal of the American Chemical Society*, shows that much good scientific writing is written in the first person and always has been. You may not find an "I," but "we" is plentiful. The ASTM (American Society for Testing Materials), certainly not a radical organization, advises going still further. Here are some excerpts from an editorial in an ASTM publication:

> The ASTM has decided to stop publishing whodunits. From now on readers of ASTM papers will be told whose research is being reported, whose opinions and beliefs are being aired, whose conclusions are being stated. We have decided that our authors are no longer going to be forced to adopt the hallowed third person in their discourses for the sake of some bogus "objectivity."

Use of the third person has nothing whatever to do with objectivity. "I believe" is no less objective than "the author believes," and it is a good deal shorter. "I believe" is not one whit less objective than "it is believed," and it is a good deal more precise.

As most everyone has agreed for some time now, use of the third person in a technical paper not only adds nothing to scientific objectivity, it renders the paper gutless and lifeless. A strong active verb gives muscle to an English sentence, and the sound of the human voice gives it spice. The third person smothers the voice behind the verbs, and, even worse, the no-person sentence compels the use of flaccid, passive verbs. . . .

Scientists of the 19th century (Darwin, T. H. Huxley, Freud, et al.) wrote sensibly and clearly in the first person and turned out some very respectable prose. No one seems quite sure how and when the third-person cult arose. . . .

Let us begin anew. . . .

1. Write in the first person. If you are the sole author use "I," if not, use "we."

2. Use active verbs. Do not say, "The specimens were examined." Say "I examined the specimens."

And here is a statement from "Instructions for Contributors" compiled by the editors of *Science*:

"Use first person, not third; do not use first person plural when singular is appropriate."

In performing his primary work, the engineer or scientist asks such questions as these: What is the problem? How can we solve it better today than we have previously? But when he writes, the technical man too often begins by asking, "How have we always done this?"

Throughout this book we have, in a sense, invited those who must set words on paper to "engineer" their writing. Applying this approach to the matter of active verbs and first person, we can sum up with these guides for thought (not rules, which are substitutes for thought).

1. In general, soft-pedal the first person for the sake of modesty.

2. On the other hand, don't get into awkwardness from avoiding it. Don't write, "Correspondence has been initiated with the supplier in order to ascertain," when all you mean is, "We have written the supplier to find out."

3. Be aware that much of the best formal scientific writing in journals and even in the military services freely uses the first person.

4. Even if you have an aversion to the first person, try to keep your verbs active. Avoid such reverse English as, "Through pumping of gas into the cylinder, increases in pressure are accomplished and cost savings are realized." Rather write, "Pumping gas into the cylinder increases pressure and saves on costs."

Three—precision vs. hedging

Nothing, of course, is more important in a technical report than accuracy. The technical writer tries to present his facts to the reader as exactly as possible and to write in such a way that nothing may be challenged. These two aims can pull in opposite directions. The struggle for exactness is an important part of clear communication. But avoiding challenge can become more self-protection than an honest effort at communication. Thus it may lead to fog.

Let me give only one example. In working with a team of engineers who were preparing a report on a new fuel, I came upon this sentence:

"So great is the spread between the production cost of this new fuel and gasoline that the cost of gasoline would have to increase substantially before the new fuel would be competitive."

"Substantial" is a vague word, handy for hedging. Literally

it means anything more than zero. As a gasoline consumer I would consider 5 or 10 per cent a "substantial" increase in price.

The engineers explained that the word had been inserted because the precise amount of increase necessary was a matter of controversy. But the argument was whether the cost of gasoline would have to increase *100 or 200 per cent* before the new fuel would be competitive. The sentence was rewritten as follows to inform the reader more precisely and still safely skirt the controversy:

"So great is the spread between the production cost of this new fuel and that of gasoline that the cost of gasoline would have to double at least before the new fuel would be competitive."

Caution that is prompted more by self-protection than by an effort to make the message clear and precise for the reader produces sentences like this:

"The data indicate that cold drawing is beneficial as far as energy consumption in machining is concerned."

This in clear, precise English means:

"The data showed machining of cold-drawn steels required less energy."

Here is another instance of complexity caused by hedging:

ORIGINAL: Measurements of the lengths of the rod-shaped particles tend to indicate a different basic length for the straight rods as compared to the crooked rods and lead to the possible supposition that either two different viruses are involved, or two different phases of the same virus.

REVISION: The straight rods are generally shorter than the crooked ones. This suggests that either two different viruses are present, or two phases of the same virus.

These remarkable hedges have been handed me by technical men. This one to explain difficulty with an electronic circuit:

"The trouble was apparently caused by spurious signals which came from extraneous sources caused by random phenomena."

This one from a chemist trying to explain a negative result:

"The reason for this denouement does not reveal itself with facility."

And how about this for a New Year's resolution?

"No more drinking! No less, of course, but no *more* either."

Language is flexible. There are many ways of stating each set of facts. There is always some way to cast a sentence so that it will say precisely what you mean and still not mislead on controversial points.

On the firing line in the battle against fog in technical writing are the hundreds of editors of technical, professional, and trade journals. Some of them work for little or no pay to keep information about new ideas in physics, education, sociology, medicine, and a hundred other specialties flowing. We are all much in their debt.

These men and women know that although technical and professional people generally are poor writers, they read no better and are no less easily confused by fog than the rest of us. The task facing many of these editors is next to impossible. They would need infinite time, fanatical zeal, and complete knowledge to make readable material of the periodic crop of pages they receive. They would have to be at the same time dictators and diplomats.

Many of them worry painfully over how far they should go in editing. In some instances, the editor is expected to do little more than see that the precise wording of papers is printed and circulated. On the other hand, most technical men, I have found, cheerfully welcome the aid of a good editor.

Our firm had for some years a working arrangement with a group of Middle Western farm papers. A large portion of the copy for these useful publications is written by university professors—experts in soils, horticulture, animal husbandry, and other subjects.

At one university we held a meeting for the editors and the professors who contributed to the papers. The writers made it clear to the editors that help was welcome. The consensus of the writers was this:

"Although the writing we do for you is but a small part of our work, we consider it highly important. We wish we had more time to give to the writing of these pieces, but we have to turn them out fast. You editors understand the subjects about which we are writing well enough to be of great help in making what we write clearer. You are more skilled at writing than most of us who are experts in other fields. Any time you spend on improving the expression of the articles we will greatly appreciate. We don't want you to alter facts, of course, but we trust you to keep the meaning we have intended."

Now and then the editor of a professional publication speaks out about foggy copy. Here are two worth listening to.

The first, as Thomas Creighton, editor of *Progressive Architecture*, said:

> We've rejected a number of manuscripts by city and regional planners during the last year, because they were examples of what Churchill called "hocus-pocus such as the substitution of six-syllable words for the shorter ones used by common folk to say the same thing." If planning is a democratic process, which it must be, then why can't planners express themselves simply and clearly? . . . I've just sent back a manuscript which argued that architects are small peanuts in the planning process, because planning is so important and different that they can't be expected to understand it. The author said:
>
> "The uniqueness of comprehensive planning is established: a) in the philosophical and theoretical base on which it rests, b) the composite and distinctive knowledge

comprising its intellectual corpus, c) the particular methodology of planning, d) the features of operation which it exhibits, and e) the existence of a substantial and rapidly expanding literature dealing specifically with the subject."

That's what's the matter with planning. What does the man mean? As far as I can figure out, when the fancy words are removed it stands as a rather unimpressive statement:

Planning is different from architecture because a) it is a theory, b) requires study, c) it is logical, d) (I give up on this one) and e) people write about it.

Dr. Henry A. Davidson, as editor of the *Journal of the Medical Society of New Jersey*, writing in *Medical Economics*, had this to say:

A doctor in staff room conversation talks simply. Yet when scratching that itch to write, he often develops a fondness for fancy language. He wants to be impressive. Instead, he is hard to understand. . . .

Higher standards of medical education have not promoted a simpler style of medical writing. Here is how one medical-school teacher recently described Addison's Disease:

"The exact date of onset is indeterminate. The patient can rarely point with any exactness to the initiation of his sense of lassitude. The *facies,* on examination, seem pallid, the ocular sclera exhibit translucency, and the patient complains of dyspnea on exertion."

Compare that with Addison's original description in 1855:

"This disease makes its approach in so slow a manner that the patient can hardly fix a date to the earliest feeling of languor. The countenance gets pale, the whites of the eyes pearly, the frame flabby; and on attempting exertion, there is marked breathlessness."

Latin is an affectation in modern medical writing. There

is no reason for using *in situ, facies, modus operandi, locus minoris resistentiae,* or *morbilli.* Nor is it often necessary to write the words "etiology" or "causation" instead of "cause," or to write "dosage" for "dose." Only special circumstances justify words like "cholelithiasis" when "gall stones" will do, or "neoplasm" when "tumor" is meant. Even legitimate words ought to be avoided if their meaning is obscure to most readers. For instance, "staphylectomy" is the proper word for "removal of the uvula," and "agrypnia" is a valid synonym for "insomnia." But most physicians are unfamiliar with these words. They slow the reading and drive him to the next article rather than to the dictionary.

Physicians, as Dr. Davidson indicates, have no logophobia (fear of words). They can always give a longer and less familiar name to a familiar ailment. To them nosebleed is "epistaxis" and bellyache is "enteralgia." If you are extremely drunk you have "temulensy." If you think you are a wolf you have "lycanthropy." If you have a desire to leap and sing you are suffering from "tarantismus." If you are unable to concentrate you have "aprosexia"; if you loathe society, "apanthropia."

The doctor inexperienced at writing rarely escapes the temptation to exhibit his technical vocabulary. The heavy writing typical of medical journals results. But it is poor logic to deduce that this is the language that doctors prefer to read.

Many writers who face the job of writing for a technical group believe their first task is to lengthen sentences and increase the mixture of polysyllables. They read technical publications in the new field, noting all odd departures from standard English. Thus, in addition to picking up the technical vocabulary they are after, they absorb the bad habits of written expression that have impeded communication in the field for years.

This process of inbreeding made a tiresome hodgepodge of business writing for many years. Then along came the *Wall Street Journal* and made a brilliant success by throwing out jargon. *The Scientific American* has shown that the same is possible in science.

Here is a paragraph written by an editor working for one of our clients, a food company. The piece discusses the process by which cows make vitamins within their own bodies. It was to appear in a circular distributed to doctors and farm and nutrition experts. More than one word in three of the following has three syllables or more:

"*Location of Synthesis*—Regardless of quantity synthesized the animal will obtain little or no benefit unless the synthesized vitamin is actually absorbed into the system and utilized. A prime factor in determining the availability of intestinally synthesized vitamins is the location of such synthesis in the intestinal tract. As previously pointed out, if the vitamins are synthesized high up in the intestinal tract where absorption is maximal, the animal will derive full benefit from the vitamins; if the vitamins are synthesized in the lower portion of the intestinal tract where absorption proceeds at a minimum, bacterial synthesis will have very little significance with respect to fulfilling essential requirements."

The following says the same in 20-per cent fewer words. Although necessary technical terms are retained, the polysyllable count has dropped to less than one word in ten:

"Vitamins synthesized within the body of an animal must be taken up and used by the animal's system to be of benefit. Therefore, the point within the intestinal tract where the synthesis takes place is important. If the vitamins appear high in the tract most of them will be absorbed and the animal will get full benefit. If, on the other hand, they appear low in the tract, they will aid the animal little, for only a small part will be absorbed and used."

Tom Burns Haber writing in the *Scientific Monthly* once recommended Basic English to scientists. To the 850 terms of Basic, 100 others have been added particularly for scientific writing:

Professor Haber says:

> It is not urged here that all writers of college texts in science adopt at once the Basic English vocabulary. The Spartan simplicity of Basic, though it is the handmaiden of truth, does not always serve other ideals as faithfully. Variety and subtlety, for example, are not main properties of Basic. These virtues and other qualities of a pleasing style ought not to be lacking from the books our science students read. Nevertheless Basic English could have a tonic effect upon these books. It could dispel much foggy thinking, which is the real cause of bad writing. If an author thought in Basic first, he would not write "heliotropic inclination toward the illuminating source." He would see that the meaning of his first word is repeated needlessly in the five that follow and might decide that his whole phrase could be put thus: "turning in the direction of the light"—which is good science and good Basic. No one can compose in Basic without having in his mind a pretty clear idea of what he wants to say.
>
> Is there, for example, any reason why a book in psychology should be written in this style?
>
> "The apperception of self-motivation is a psychological fact. A concomitant phenomenon is the consciousness that the origin of this motivation is internal and not external."
>
> Is not this what the writer means?
>
> "The mind is conscious that it is self-moving; and at the same time, that the motion comes from within itself."
>
> The last sentence above is written in Basic English.

In these days, more than ever before, the reading time of a technical man is precious. Few of them like the task of writing. They would prefer to be in the laboratory. At the same time writing is the chief means they have of handing on what they have learned.

If a technical man will analyze his writing from the point of view of the reader, and if he will break away from the bad habits that have hampered much scientific writing, he will be on his way to clear writing. The men who have won names for themselves in science have almost all succeeded in doing this.

APPENDIXES

Appendix A

On page 34 of the chapter "Readability Yardsticks" seven factors of reading difficulty are mentioned. Of those that can be measured objectively, these are the ones that we have found most helpful in the analysis of reading difficulty.

Let us see how these factors of analysis apply to a piece of American prose familiar to all, Lincoln's Gettysburg Address, which has a reading level of 10.

Fourscore and seven years ago our fathers brought forth on this continent a new nation, conceived in liberty, and dedicated to the proposition that all men are created equal.

Now we are engaged in a great civil war, testing whether that nation, or any nation so conceived and so dedicated, can long endure. We are met on a great battlefield of that war. We have come to dedicate a portion of that field as a final resting place for those who here gave their lives that that nation might live. It is altogether fitting and proper that we should do this.

But, in a larger sense, we cannot dedicate—we cannot consecrate—we cannot hallow—this ground. The brave men, living and dead, who struggled here, have consecrated it far above our poor power to add or detract. The world will little note nor long remember what we say here, but it can never forget what they did here. It is for us, the living, rather, to be dedicated here to the unfinished work which they who fought here have thus far so nobly advanced. It is rather for us to be here dedicated to the great task remaining before us—that from these honored dead we take increased devotion to that cause for which they gave the last full measure of devotion; that we here highly resolve that these dead shall not have died in vain; that this nation, under God, shall have a new birth of freedom; and that government of the people, by the people, for the people, shall not perish from the earth.

Average sentence length

The address has a good variety of long and short sentences. The count runs like this: 29—24—10—27—11—16—21—12—9—26—82. That last sentence of 82 words contains a series of "that" clauses all having about the same weight and the same relationship to the rest of the sentence. This is the "list" type of sentence discussed in Principle One. Relationships in such sentences are not as difficult as their length indicates. Therefore, in both testing and analysis we except such sentences from our counts. Note that Lincoln's 82-word sentence is carefully constructed. And even with it, the average sentence length of the address is 24 words, considerably less than we have found in much news and business copy. Excepting the "list" sentence, the average sentence length is 18.5 words, slightly more than the average of news magazines. Reading tends to be hard if sentences average much more than 20 words in length.

Simple sentences

Of the 10 sentences in the Gettysburg Address only one is simple in form, the third one: "We are met on a great battlefield of that war." All others are complex or compound.

Thus the address contains only 10 per cent of simple sentences. This is a low percentage for readable prose, but it is rather typical of formal subject matter such as this. On the other hand, simple sentences are often used by good writers to relieve material which would otherwise be heavy with formality. The editorials of Henry

Watterson, discussed in the chapter on newspaper writing, are an example of this. About half the sentences in his editorials were simple in form.

In readable magazine stories and articles the percentage of simple sentences runs as high as 60 per cent. In average newspaper material the range is 30 to 40 per cent. When the percentage drops below 20, the long sentences tend to become heavy going for a reader. The relationships within the sentences is a chief source of reading difficulty in the address. Fortunately Lincoln balanced this with a number of other factors that tend to make reading easy.

Verb force

Lincoln knew how to put force in his verbs. Active verb forms are numerous in the address. Lincoln used passives only for variety or where sense required. There is no evidence of the smothering action of weak verbs linked with nouns derived from verbs. He says, "We have come to dedicate" not, "We are here to make dedication."

Active verbs in the address number 26. Here they are in the order they appear: brought, engaged, endure, met, come, gave, live, do, dedicate, consecrate, hallow, struggled, consecrated, note, remember, say, forget, did, fought, advanced, take, gave, resolve, died, have, perish.

The number of words in the address that are active verbs is high—just under 10 per cent. Any piece of prose so rich in verb force is likely to be readable.

In addition there are three active infinitives: "to dedicate," "to add," (to) "detract." These also add force to the piece.

Portion of familiar words

By the time a person leaves high school he has a working vocabulary of about 10,000 words. The number of words outside the 10,000 most frequently used in print is a good guide, then, to reading difficulty. E. L. Thorndike's work has established which words are most frequently used, and the *Thorndike Century Senior Dictionary* indicates the frequency of use of each word.

Only two words in the address are outside the 10,000 used most often. They are "detract" and "nobly." "Nobly" we do not count because it is a variation of "noble" which is among the 2,000 words most often used.

The portion of familiar words in the address, therefore, is very close to 100 per cent—99.63 per cent, to be exact. Even *Time* has only 1 to 2 per cent of words outside this list of 10,000. The less familiar words should be used only sparingly if writing is to be kept readable.

Portion of abstract words

Principles Seven and Eight show the important links between abstract words and reading difficulty. But where the line is to be drawn between concrete and abstract words is always open to argument.

All would probably agree that the words "liberty," "proposition," "sense," "power," "devotion," "cause," and "freedom" from the address are abstract words. These are the ones we count as abstract. They cannot be pointed out or pictured like "fathers," "men," "field," "ground," and "war." Nor can they be measured like "year," nor demonstrated like "work."

Measuring abstraction objectively requires long arbitrary lists of words. And the counting calls for much effort and concentration. But the details need be of little concern for other than experts. The various other counts of long or hard words relate closely to counts of abstraction. When you count one you usually come close to measuring the other as well.

Percentage of personal references

This is the only objective count that relates closely to subject matter. The others deal with the *structure* of words and sentences. And complex structure is the factor of hard reading that we are treating in this book. At the same time everyone knows that some subjects make easier, more interesting reading than others. An *objective* way of measuring the appeal of subject matter to people generally is next to impossible. However, nearly all readers are interested in people and a count of the references to people in a piece of writing is a clue to its readability. It is also important for writers to remember that anything they put on paper deals in one way or another with people. Dryness in writing results from losing sight of this fact. Try to say what you have to say in human terms whenever possible.

Note that Lincoln does this. He uses the words "fathers," "men," and "people" repeatedly. The address is rich in personal pronouns, "our," "we," "us," "they." Nine per cent of the words in the address are personal references. This is a very high count and is one factor that helps the address as a piece of communication.

In counting personal references in your own copy, include proper names of people, personal pronouns, and words like "father," "mother," "people," "man," "woman," and others that refer directly to humans. Do not include occupational and other labels like "doctor," "player," etc.

Percentage of long words

There are many ways of measuring the hard-word factor of prose. We have found that the best from the twin viewpoint of reliability and ease of use is the simple counting of words of more than two syllables. Three types of words are excepted from the count: (1) capitalized words, unless, of course, the reason for capitalization is that they begin a sentence; (2) words composed of simple familiar words, such as "bookkeeper" and "inasmuch"; (3) verb forms which are made three syllables because *-ed* or *-es* has been added. Examples: "departed," "transgresses."

In the address the word "battlefield" and the word "created" are not counted. The first is a combination of simple words; the second is a verb form that would be two syllables without the "ed."

The long-word count of the address includes these words: continent, liberty, dedicated (used 6 times), proposition, altogether, consecrate (used twice), remaining, devotion (used twice), remember, unfinished, government.

The total is 18, or 7 per cent. This is relatively low and helps the address communicate readily and clearly.

A further note

Much of the great flexibility and power of English comes from its double root in the Latin and the Teutonic languages. These two great language families came together as a result of the Norman Conquest. For a few hundred years thereafter the early Anglo-Sazon English was the spoken language of field and kitchen. Norman French or Latin were used in the courts and universities. Consequently long and abstract words in modern English are derived for the most part from Latin. The short, concrete words we use are mostly from the Anglo-Saxon side of our language.

The Gettysburg address has a number of strong words of Latin derivation such as *continent, liberty, dedicated, consecrate, proposition, devotion.* However, the mixture of such words is quite lean.

Clark E. Carr, in his book *Lincoln at Gettysburg* (A. C. Mc-Clurg & Co., 1907), commented on Lincoln's preference for Anglo-Saxon words. Carr heard Lincoln's address and was on the commission that set up Gettysburg National Cemetery. He wrote, "A careful analysis shows that Lincoln's Gettysburg address contains 32 words of Latin origin which with repetitions of the same word, or other forms of the same word, make 45 Latin derivatives, all told. There are 267 words in the address, leaving the balance, 222, Anglo-Saxon.

"That is, one-fifth or 20 per cent, are Latin words, while four-fifths or 80 per cent are Anglo-Saxon."

Appendix B

The following list of 3,000 words was prepared by Dr. Edgar Dale of Ohio State University. The words included "are known in reading by at least 80 per cent of the children in Grade IV."

Dr. Dale points out that no one is intended to confine his writing to this list, for it excludes many important words. The word "nation" is an example; it tested slightly below the 80 per cent mark but is no doubt generally familiar to adults.

Writing that averages 20 words per sentence or less can include as many as 20 per cent of words outside this list and still remain within the easy-reading range (Fog Index 10 or less).

The words in this list that exceed two syllables (except for proper nouns and words formed from simpler words) have been italicized to emphasize how few there are. They total only 4 per cent.

DALE LIST OF 3,000 FAMILIAR WORDS

a	*accident*	add	afternoon
able	account	address	*afterward*(s)
aboard	ache(ing)	admire	again
about	acorn	*adventure*	against
above	acre	afar	age
absent	across	afraid	aged
accept	act(s)	after	ago

agree	anybody	author	basement
ah	anyhow	auto	basket
ahead	anyone	*automobile*	bat
aid	anything	autumn	batch
aim	anyway	*avenue*	bath
air	anywhere	awake(n)	bathe
airfield	apart	away	bathing
airport	*apartment*	awful(ly)	bathroom
airplane	ape	awhile	bathtub
airship	apiece	ax	battle
airy	appear	baa	battleship
alarm	apple	babe	bay
alike	April	baby(ies)	be(ing)
alive	apron	back	beach
all	are	background	bead
alley	aren't	backward(s)	beam
alligator	arise	bacon	bean
allow	*arithmetic*	bad(ly)	bear
almost	arm	badge	beard
alone	armful	bag	beast
along	army	bake(r)	beat(ing)
aloud	arose	baking	*beautiful*
already	around	*bakery*	*beautify*
also	arrange	ball	beauty
always	arrive(d)	balloon	became
am	arrow	*banana*	because
America	art	band	become
American	artist	bandage	*becoming*
among	as	bang	bed
amount	ash(es)	banjo	bedbug
an	aside	bank(er)	bedroom
and	ask	bar	bedspread
angel	asleep	barber	bedtime
anger	at	bare(ly)	bee
angry	ate	barefoot	beech
animal	attack	bark	beef
another	attend	barn	beefsteak
answer	*attention*	barrel	beehive
ant	August	base	been
any	aunt	baseball	beer

beet
before
beg
began
beggar
begged
begin
beginning
begun
behave
behind
believe
bell
belong
below
belt
beneath
bench
bend
bent
berry(ies)
beside(s)
best
bet
better
between
bib
bible
bicycle
bid
big(ger)
bill
billboard
bin
bind
bird
birth
birthday
biscuit
bit

bite
biting
bitter
black
blackberry
blackbird
blackboard
blackness
blacksmith
blame
blank
blanket
blast
blaze
bleed
bless
blessing
blew
blind(s)
blindfold
block
blood
bloom
blossom
blot
blow
blue
blueberry
bluebird
bluejay
blush
board
boast
boat
bob
bobwhite
body(ies)
boil(er)
bold
bone

bonnet
boo
book
bookcase
bookkeeper
boom
boot
born
borrow
boss
both
bother
bottle
bottom
bought
bounce
bow
bowl
bow-wow
box(es)
boxcar
boxer
boy
boyhood
bracelet
brain
brake
bran
branch
brass
brave
bread
break
breakfast
breast
breath
breathe
breeze
brick
bride

bridge
bright
brightness
bring
broad
broadcast
broke(n)
brook
broom
brother
brought
brown
brush
bubble
bucket
buckle
bud
buffalo
bug
buggy
build
building
built
bulb
bull
bullet
bum
bumblebee
bump
bun
bunch
bundle
bunny
burn
burst
bury
bus
bush
bushel
business

busy	canyon	*cereal*	chorus
but	cap	certain(ly)	chose(n)
butcher	cape	chain	christen
butt	*capital*	chair	Christmas
butter	captain	chalk	church
buttercup	car	*champion*	churn
butterfly	card	chance	*cigarette*
buttermilk	cardboard	change	circle
butterscotch	care	chap	circus
button	careful	charge	*citizen*
buttonhole	careless	charm	city
buy	*carelessness*	chart	clang
buzz	carload	chase	clap
by	*carpenter*	chatter	class
bye	carpet	cheap	classmate
cab	carriage	cheat	classroom
cabbage	carrot	check	claw
cabin	carry	checkers	clay
cabinet	cart	cheek	clean(er)
cackle	carve	cheer	clear
cage	case	cheese	clerk
cake	cash	cherry	clever
calendar	cashier	chest	click
calf	castle	chew	cliff
call(er)(ing)	cat	chick	climb
came	catbird	chicken	clip
camel	catch	chief	cloak
camp	catcher	child	clock
campfire	*caterpillar*	childhood	close
can	catfish	children	closet
canal	catsup	chill(y)	cloth
canary	cattle	chimney	clothes
candle	caught	chin	clothing
candlestick	cause	china	cloud(y)
candy	cave	chip	clover
cane	ceiling	chipmunk	clown
cannon	cell	*chocolate*	club
cannot	cellar	choice	cluck
canoe	cent	choose	clump
can't	center	chop	coach

coal	corner	cross(ing)	dare
coast	correct	cross-eyed	dark(ness)
coat	cost	crow	darling
cob	cot	crowd(ed)	darn
cobbler	cottage	crown	dart
cocoa	cotton	cruel	dash
coconut	couch	crumb	date
cocoon	cough	crumble	daughter
cod	could	crush	dawn
codfish	couldn't	crust	day
coffee	count	cry(ies)	daybreak
coffeepot	counter	cub	daytime
coin	country	cuff	dead
cold	county	cup	deaf
collar	course	cupboard	deal
college	court	cupful	dear
color(ed)	cousin	cure	death
colt	cover	curl(y)	December
column	cow	curtain	decide
comb	coward(ly)	curve	deck
come	cowboy	cushion	deed
comfort	cozy	custard	deep
comic	crab	*customer*	deer
coming	crack	cut	defeat
company	cracker	cute	defend
compare	cradle	cutting	defense
conductor	cramps	dab	delight
cone	*cranberry*	dad	den
connect	crank(y)	daddy	dentist
coo	crash	daily	depend
cook(ed)	crawl	dairy	*deposit*
cook(ing)	crazy	daisy	describe
cooky(ie)(s)	cream(y)	dam	desert
cool(er)	creek	damage	deserve
coop	creep	dame	desire
copper	crept	damp	desk
copy	cried	dance(r)	destroy
cord	croak	dancing	devil
cork	crook(ed)	dandy	dew
corn	crop	danger(ous)	*diamond*

did	dot	dust(y)	English
didn't	double	duty	enjoy
die(d)(s)	dough	dwarf	enough
difference	dove	dwell	enter
different	down	dwelt	*envelope*
dig	downstairs	dying	equal
dim	downtown	each	erase(r)
dime	dozen	eager	errand
dine	drag	eagle	escape
ding-dong	drain	ear	eve
dinner	drank	early	even
dip	draw(er)	earn	evening
direct	draw(ing)	earth	ever
direction	dream	east(ern)	every
dirt(y)	dress	easy	everybody
discover	dresser	eat(en)	everyday
dish	dressmaker	edge	everyone
dislike	drew	egg	everything
dismiss	dried	eh	everywhere
ditch	drift	eight	evil
dive	drill	eighteen	exact
diver	drink	eighth	except
divide	drip	eighty	exchange
do	drive(n)	either	excited
dock	driver	elbow	*exciting*
doctor	drop	elder	excuse
does	drove	eldest	exit
doesn't	drown	*electric*	expect
dog	drowsy	*electricity*	explain
doll	drug	*elephant*	extra
dollar	drum	*eleven*	eye
dolly	drunk	elf	eyebrow
done	dry	elm	fable
donkey	duck	else	face
don't	due	elsewhere	facing
door	dug	empty	fact
doorbell	dull	end(ing)	*factory*
doorknob	dumb	*enemy*	fail
doorstep	dump	engine	faint
dope	during	*engineer*	fair

fairy
faith
fake
fall
false
family
fan
fancy
far
faraway
fare
farmer
farm(ing)
far-off
farther
fashion
fast
fasten
fat
father
fault
favor
favorite
fear
feast
feather
February
fed
feed
feel
feet
fell
fellow
felt
fence
fever
few
fib
fiddle
field

fife
fifteen
fifth
fifty
fig
fight
figure
file
fill
film
finally
find
fine
finger
finish
fire
firearm
firecracker
fireplace
fireworks
firing
first
fish
fisherman
fist
fit(s)
five
fix
flag
flake
flame
flap
flash
flashlight
flat
flea
flesh
flew
flies
flight

flip
flip-flop
float
flock
flood
floor
flop
flour
flow
flower(y)
flutter
fly
foam
fog
foggy
fold
folks
follow(ing)
fond
food
fool
foolish
foot
football
footprint
for
forehead
forest
forget
forgive
forgot(ten)
fork
form
fort
forth
fortune
forty
forward
fought
found

fountain
four
fourteen
fourth
fox
frame
free
freedom
freeze
freight
French
fresh
fret
Friday
fried
friend(ly)
friendship
frighten
frog
from
front
frost
frown
froze
fruit
fry
fudge
fuel
full(y)
fun
funny
fur
furniture
further
fuzzy
gain
gallon
gallop
game
gang

garage
garbage
garden
gas
gasoline
gate
gather
gave
gay
gear
geese
general
gentle
gentleman
gentlemen
geography
get
getting
giant
gift
gingerbread
girl
give(n)
giving
glad(ly)
glance
glass(es)
gleam
glide
glory
glove
glow
glue
go(ing)
goes
goal
goat
gobble
God(g)
godmother

gold(en)
goldfish
golf
gone
good(s)
good-by(bye)
good-looking
goodness
goody
goose
gooseberry
got
govern
government
gown
grab
gracious
grade
grain
grand
grandchild
grandchildren
granddaughter
grandfather
grandma
grandmother
grandpa
grandson
grandstand
grape(s)
grapefruit
grass
grasshopper
grateful
grave
gravel
graveyard
gravy
gray
graze

grease
great
green
greet
grew
grind
groan
grocery
ground
group
grove
grow
guard
guess
guest
guide
gulf
gum
gun
gunpowder
guy
ha
habit
had
hadn't
hail
hair
haircut
hairpin
half
hall
halt
ham
hammer
hand
handful
handkerchief
handle
handwriting
hang

happen
happily
happiness
happy
harbor
hard
hardly
hardship
hardware
hare
hark
has
harm
harness
harp
harvest
hasn't
haste(n)
hasty
hat
hatch
hatchet
hate
haul
have
haven't
having
hawk
hay
hayfield
haystack
he
head
headache
heal
health(y)
heap
hear(ing)
heard
heart

heat(er)	his	hour	in
heaven	hiss	house	inch(es)
heavy	*history*	housetop	income
he'd	hit ·	housewife	indeed
heel	hitch	housework	Indian
height	hive	how	indoors
held	ho	however	ink
hell	hoe	howl	inn
he'll	hog	hug	insect
hello	hold(er)	huge	inside
helmet	hole	hum	instant
help(er)	*holiday*	humble	instead
helpful	hollow	hump	insult
hem	holy	hundred	intend
hen	home	hung	*interested*
henhouse	homely	hunger	*interesting*
her(s)	homesick	hungry	into
herd	honest	hunk	invite
here	honey	hunt(er)	iron
here's	honeybee	hurrah	is
hero	honeymoon	hurried	island
herself	honk	hurry	isn't
he's	honor	hurt	it
hey	hood	husband	its
hickory	hoof	hush	it's
hid	hook	hut	itself
hidden	hoop	hymn	I've
hide	hop	I	*ivory*
high	hope(ful)	ice	ivy
highway	hopeless	icy	jacket
hill	horn	I'd	jacks
hillside	horse	idea	jail
hilltop	horseback	ideal	jam
hilly	horseshoe	if	January
him	hose	ill	jar
himself	*hospital*	I'll	jaw
hind	host	I'm	jay
hint	hot	*important*	jelly
hip	hotel	*impossible*	jellyfish
hire	hound	improve	jerk

jig	knife	lean	lion
job	knit	leap	lip
jockey	knives	learn(ed)	list
join	knob	least	listen
joke	knock	leather	lit
joking	knot	leave(ing)	little
jolly	know	led	live(s)
journey	known	left	lively
joy(ful)	lace	leg	liver
joyous	lad	lemon	living
judge	ladder	lemonade	lizard
jug	ladies	lend	load
juice	lady	length	loaf
juicy	laid	less	loan
July	lake	lesson	loaves
jump	lamb	let	lock
June	lame	let's	*locomotive*
junior	lamp	letter	log
junk	land	letting	lone
just	lane	lettuce	lonely
keen	language	level	lonesome
keep	lantern	*liberty*	long
kept	lap	*library*	look
kettle	lard	lice	lookout
key	large	lick	loop
kick	lash	lid	loose
kid	lass	lie	lord
kill(ed)	last	life	lose(r)
kind(ly)	late	lift	loss
kindness	laugh	light(ness)	lost
king	laundry	lightning	lot
kingdom	law	like	loud
kiss	lawn	likely	love
kitchen	lawyer	liking	lovely
kite	lay	lily	lover
kitten	lazy	limb	low
kitty	lead	lime	luck(y)
knee	leader	limp	lumber
kneel	leaf	line	lump
knew	leak	linen	lunch

lying
ma
machine
machinery
mad
made
magazine
magic
maid
mail
mailbox
mailman
major
make
making
male
mama
mamma
man
manager
mane
manger
many
map
maple
marble
march(M)
mare
mark
market
marriage
married
marry
mask
mast
master
mat
match
matter
mattress

may(M)
maybe
mayor
maypole
me
meadow
meal
mean(s)
meant
measure
meat
medicine
meet(ing)
melt
member
men
mend
meow
merry
mess
message
met
metal
mew
mice
middle
midnight
might(y)
mile
milk
milkman
mill
miller
million
mind
mine
miner
mint
minute
mirror

mischief
miss(M)
misspell
mistake
misty
mitt
mitten
mix
moment
Monday
money
monkey
month
moo
moon
moonlight
moose
mop
more
morning
morrow
moss
most(ly)
mother
motor
mount
mountain
mouse
mouth
move
movie
movies
moving
mow
Mr., Mrs.
much
mud
muddy
mug
mule

multiply
murder
music
must
my
myself
nail
name
nap
napkin
narrow
nasty
naughty
navy
near
nearby
nearly
neat
neck
necktie
need
needle
needn't
Negro
neighbor
neighborhood
neither
nerve
nest
net
never
nevermore
new
news
newspaper
next
nibble
nice
nickel
night

nightgown	oil	owl	patter
nine	old	own(er)	pave
nineteen	old-fashioned	ox	pavement
ninety	on	pa	paw
no	once	pace	pay
nobody	one	pack	payment
nod	onion	package	pea(s)
noise	only	pad	peace(ful)
noisy	onward	page	peach(es)
none	open	paid	peak
noon	or	pail	peanut
nor	orange	pain(ful)	pear
north(ern)	orchard	paint(er)	pearl
nose	order	painting	peck
not	ore	pair	peek
note	organ	pal	peel
nothing	other	palace	peep
notice	*otherwise*	pale	peg
November	ouch	pan	pen
now	ought	pancake	pencil
nowhere	our(s)	pane	penny
number	ourselves	pansy	people
nurse	out	pants	pepper
nut	outdoors	papa	peppermint
oak	outfit	paper	perfume
oar	outlaw	parade	perhaps
oatmeal	outline	pardon	person
oats	outside	parent	pet
obey	outward	park	phone
ocean	oven	part(ly)	*piano*
o'clock	over	partner	pick
October	overalls	party	pickle
odd	overcoat	pass	picnic
of	overeat	*passenger*	picture
off	overhead	past	pie
offer	overhear	paste	piece
office	overnight	pasture	pig
officer	overturn	pat	pigeon
often	owe	patch	piggy
oh	owing	path	pile

pill	police	proud	rag
pillow	policeman	prove	rail
pin	polish	prune	railroad
pine	polite	public	railway
pineapple	pond	puddle	rain(y)
pink	ponies	puff	rainbow
pint	pony	pull	raise
pipe	pool	pump	raisin
pistol	poor	pumpkin	rake
pit	pop	punch	ram
pitch	popcorn	punish	ran
pitcher	popped	pup	ranch
pity	porch	pupil	rang
place	pork	puppy	rap
plain	*possible*	pure	*rapidly*
plan	post	purple	rat
plane	postage	purse	rate
plant	postman	push	rather
plate	pot	puss	rattle
platform	*potato*(es)	pussy	raw
platter	pound	pussycat	ray
play(er)	pour	put	reach
playground	powder	putting	read
playhouse	power(ful)	puzzle	reader
playmate	praise	quack	reading
plaything	pray	quart	ready
pleasant	prayer	quarter	real
please	prepare	queen	*really*
pleasure	present	queer	reap
plenty	pretty	question	rear
plow	price	quick(ly)	reason
plug	prick	quiet	rebuild
plum	prince	quilt	receive
pocket	princess	quit	recess
pocketbook	print	quite	record
poem	prison	rabbit	red
point	prize	race	redbird
poison	promise	rack	redbreast
poke	proper	radio	refuse
pole	protect	radish	reindeer

rejoice
remain
remember
remind
remove
rent
repair
repay
repeat
report
rest
return
review
reward
rib
ribbon
rice
rich
rid
riddle
ride(r)
riding
right
rim
ring
rip
ripe
rise
rising
river
road
roadside
roar
roast
rob
robber
robe
robin
rock(y)
rocket

rode
roll
roller
roof
room
rooster
root
rope
rose
rosebud
rot
rotten
rough
round
route
row
rowboat
royal
rub
rubbed
rubber
rubbish
rug
rule(r)
rumble
run
rung
runner
running
rush
rust(y)
rye
sack
sad
saddle
sadness
safe
safety
said
sail

sailboat
sailor
saint
salad
sale
salt
same
sand(y)
sandwich
sang
sank
sap
sash
sat
satin
satisfactory
Saturday
sausage
savage
save
savings
saw
say
scab
scales
scare
scarf
school
schoolboy
schoolhouse
schoolmaster
schoolroom
scorch
score
scrap
scrape
scratch
scream
screen
screw

scrub
sea
seal
seam
search
season
seat
second
secret
see(ing)
seed
seek
seem
seen
seesaw
select
self
selfish
sell
send
sense
sent
sentence
separate
September
servant
serve
service
set
setting
settle
settlement
seven
seventeen
seventh
seventy
several
sew
shade
shadow

shady	shout	ski	snuff
shake(r)	shovel	skin	snug
shaking	show	skip	so
shall	shower	skirt	soak
shame	shut	sky	soap
shan't	shy	slam	sob
shape	sick(ness)	slap	socks
share	side	slate	sod
sharp	sidewalk	slave	soda
shave	sideways	sled	sofa
she	sigh	sleep(y)	soft
she'd	sight	sleeve	soil
she'll	sign	sleigh	sold
she's	silence	slept	soldier
shear(s)	silent	slice	sole
shed	silk	slid	some
sheep	sill	slide	somebody
sheet	silly	sling	somehow
shelf	silver	slip	someone
shell	simple	slipper	something
shepherd	sin	slipped	sometime(s)
shine	since	*slippery*	somewhere
shining	sing	slit	son
shiny	singer	slow(ly)	song
ship	single	sly	soon
shirt	sink	smack	sore
shock	sip	small	sorrow
shoe	sir	smart	sorry
shoemaker	sis	smell	sort
shone	sissy	smile	soul
shook	sister	smoke	sound
shoot	sit	smooth	soup
shop	sitting	snail	sour
shopping	six	snake	south(ern)
shore	sixteen	snap	space
short	sixth	snapping	spade
shot	sixty	sneeze	spank
should	size	snow(y)	sparrow
shoulder	skate	snowball	speak(er)
shouldn't	skater	snowflake	spear

speech	station	strawberry	swan
speed	stay	stream	swat
spell(ing)	steak	street	swear
spend	steal	stretch	sweat
spent	steam	string	sweater
spider	steamboat	strip	sweep
spike	steamer	stripes	sweet(ness)
spill	steel	strong	sweetheart
spin	steep	stuck	swell
spinach	steeple	study	swept
spirit	steer	stuff	swift
spit	stem	stump	swim
splash	step	stung	swimming
spoil	stepping	subject	swing
spoke	stick(y)	such	switch
spook	stiff	suck	sword
spoon	still(ness)	sudden	swore
sport	sting	suffer	table
spot	stir	sugar	tablecloth
spread	stitch	suit	tablespoon
spring	stock	sum	tablet
springtime	stocking	summer	tack
sprinkle	stole	sun	tag
square	stone	Sunday	tail
squash	stood	sunflower	tailor
squeak	stool	sung	take(n)
squeeze	stoop	sunk	taking
squirrel	stop	sunlight	tale
stable	stopped	sunny	talk(er)
stack	stopping	sunrise	tall
stage	store	sunset	tame
stair	stork	sunshine	tan
stall	stories	supper	tank
stamp	storm(y)	suppose	tap
stand	story	sure(ly)	tape
star	stove	surface	tar
stare	straight	surprise	tardy
start	strange(r)	swallow	task
starve	strap	swam	taste
state	straw	swamp	taught

tax
tea
teach(er)
team
tear
tease
teaspoon
teeth
telephone
tell
temper
ten
tennis
tent
term
terrible
test
than
thank(s)
thankful
Thanks-
   giving
that
that's
the
theater
thee
their
them
then
there
these
they
they'd
they'll
they're
they've
thick
thief
thimble

thin
thing
think
third
thirsty
thirteen
thirty
this
tho
thorn
those
though
thought
thousand
thread
three
threw
throat
throne
through
throw(n)
thumb
thunder
Thursday
thy
tick
ticket
tickle
tie
tiger
tight
till
time
tin
tinkle
tiny
tip
tiptoe
tire
tired

'tis
title
to
toad
toadstool
toast
tobacco
today
toe
together
toilet
told
tomato
tomorrow
ton
tone
tongue
tonight
too
took
tool
toot
tooth
toothbrush
toothpick
top
tore
torn
toss
touch
tow
toward(s)
towel
tower
town
toy
trace
track
trade
train

tramp
trap
tray
treasure
treat
tree
trick
tricycle
tried
trim
trip
trolley
trouble
truck
true
truly
trunk
tunnel
turkey
turn
turtle
twelve
twenty
twice
trust
truth
try
tub
Tuesday
tug
tulip
tumble
tune
twig
twin
two
ugly
umbrella
uncle
under

understand	village	weather	who'll
underwear	vine	weave	whom
undress	*violet*	web	who's
unfair	visit	we'd	whose
unfinished	*visitor*	wedding	why
unfold	voice	Wednesday	wicked
unfriendly	vote	wee	wide
unhappy	wag	weed	wife
unhurt	wagon	week	wiggle
uniform	waist	we'll	wild
United	wait	weep	wildcat
States	wake(n)	weigh	will
unkind	walk	welcome	willing
unknown	wall	well	willow
unless	walnut	went	win
unpleasant	want	were	wind(y)
until	war	we're	windmill
unwilling	warm	west(ern)	window
up	warn	wet	wine
upon	was	we've	wing
upper	wash(er)	whale	wink
upset	washtub	what	winner
upside	wasn't	what's	winter
upstairs	waste	wheat	wipe
uptown	watch	wheel	wire
upward	watchman	when	wise
us	water	whenever	wish
use(d)	watermelon	where	wit
useful	*waterproof*	which	witch
valentine	wave	while	with
valley	wax	whip	without
valuable	way	whipped	woke
value	wayside	whirl	wolf
vase	we	whisky	woman
vegetable	weak(ness)	whisper	women
velvet	weaken	whistle	won
very	wealth	white	wonder
vessel	weapon	who	*wonderful*
victory	wear	who'd	won't
view	weary	whole	wood(en)

woodpecker	worst	written	yonder
woods	worth	wrong	you
wool	would	wrote	you'd
woolen	wouldn't	wrung	you'll
word	wound	yard	young
wore	wove	yarn	youngster
work(er)	wrap	year	your(s)
workman	wrapped	yell	you're
world	wreck	yellow	yourself
worm	wren	yes	yourselves
worn	wring	*yesterday*	youth
worry	write	yet	you've
worse	writing	yolk	

Appendix C

The following list will help you find short words (or phrases) for long words. The list is not meant to do the job of either a dictionary or a thesaurus. The suggested substitute(s) will often not fit the longer words' meaning.

You will find the list helpful when your writing begins to become heavy with polysyllables. You are presumed to be familiar with both the long words and the substitutes and to be able to judge whether they are possible and accurate in the sense you wish to convey.

The substitutes offered are in each case either shorter or more familiar. In some instances, two or more words (or phrases) are offered as substitutes. This is done to provide another expression for an over-worked word.

THE SHORT FOR THE LONG

abandon—give up, desert
abatement—decrease
abbreviate—shorten
abdicate—give up, resign
abdomen—belly
abduct—kidnap
abeyance—waiting
abhorrent—disgusting, hateful

ability—skill
abjure—renounce
ablution—cleansing
abolish—do away with
abominable—disgusting, hateful
abrasion—scratch
abridge—shorten
abrogate—cancel, do away with

abscond—go off and hide
absolutely—wholly
accede—give in
accelerate—hasten
acceptable—welcome
accessible—easy to reach
accidental—chance
accommodating—obliging
accompany—go with
accomplish—carry out
accomplished—expert
accordingly—therefore
accurate—correct
accusation—charge
acknowledge—admit, express
  thanks for
acquiesce—agree, accept
acquire—gain
acquit—set free
acrimonious—sharp, bitter
actuate—put in action, move
adamant—hard
adapt—make fit
additional—added
address—speech
adhere—stick fast
adjacent—next to
adjustment—settlement
administer—manage
admonish—warn
admonition—warning
adroit—skillful
adverse—harmful
adversity—distress
advocate—speak for
affable—pleasant
affectionate—loving
affluent—rich
affray—fight
aggrandize—make greater

aggravate—provoke
aggregate—total
agitate—shake, stir, excite
alacrity—speed
alienate—turn against
allay—quiet
allegation—assertion
allegiance—loyalty
alleviate—make easier
allotment—share
allude—refer
alteration—change
altercation—dispute
alternate—take turns
alternative—choice
amalgamate—combine, blend,
  unite
ambiguous—not clear
ameliorate—improve
amendment—change
amicable—friendly
amorphous—shapeless
amplify—make greater
amputate—cut off
anathema—curse, accursed
animadversion—blame
animation—life
animosity—hatred
annihilate—destroy
annually—yearly
anomalous—abnormal
anonymous—nameless
anterior—front
anticipate—expect
antipathy—dislike
antiquated—out-of-date
antithesis—opposite
apathetic—indifferent
aperture—gap, hole
apex—tip

apparent—clear, plain
appease—calm
appellation—name
append—add
appliance—device
apply—put on, use, ask
appoint—name
apportion—divide
apprehend—seize
apprehensive—uneasy
approbation—praise
appropriate—proper (adj.), set aside (verb)
approval—praise, consent
approximately—about
aqueous—watery
arbiter—judge, umpire
arduous—hard
armistice—truce
artifice—craft
ascend—climb
ascertain—find out
aspersion—slander
asphyxiate—suffocate
aspiration—longing
assay—try, test
assemble—gather
assembly—meeting
assent—agree
assimilate—absorb, digest
assistance—help
assuredly—surely
astute—shrewd
atrophy—waste away
attain—gain
attempt—try
attire—dress
attractive—pleasing
audacious—bold
augmentation—increase

austere—harsh, stern
authentic—real
authorize—give power
autonomous—independent
available—ready
avarice—greed
avaricious—greedy
aversion—dislike

banal—trite
barbarous—coarse, brutal
bargain—deal
bashful—shy
beatitude—blessing
becoming—fitting
beleaguer—besiege
bellicose—warlike
belligerent—warlike
benediction—blessing
beneficence—kindness
beneficial—helpful
benevolent—kindly
benignant—kindly
bereavement—loss
beseech—beg
besmirch—soil
bespeak—order, reserve
biannual—twice a year
bilateral—two-sided
bizarre—odd, queer
bona fide—in good faith

cadence—rhythm
caitiff—coward
cajolery—coaxing
calumniate—slander
capacity—ability, power, position
captivate—charm
carboniferous—coal-bearing
carnivorous—flesh-eating

cartilage—gristle
catalogue—list
catechism—set of questions
categorical—positive
censure—blame
certainly—surely
cessation—stop, pause
character—nature
characterize—describe
charlatan—quack
chicanery—trickery
chimerical—unreal
chivalrous—gallant
circuitous—roundabout
circumspect—careful
circumvent—get around
clarify—make clear
clemency—mercy, mildness
coagulate—thicken
coalesce—grow together
coalition—union
cognitate—ponder
cognizant—aware
collaborate—work together
collection—mass, heap
comical—funny
commence—begin
commencement—start
commendation—praise
commerce—trade
commiseration—pity
commitment—pledge
commodious—roomy
compassion—pity
compensate—pay
competent—able
component—part
compose—make up
composed—calm, quiet
composition—make-up

compunction—regret
concealment—hiding
conceive—think up
conception—thought, idea
concern—firm
conciliate—win over, soothe
conclude—end
conclusion—end
conclusive—final
concrete—real
concussion—shock
condescend—stoop to
conformity—likeness
confront—meet
confuse—mix up
congeal—freeze
congenital—inborn
congruous—fitting
conjecture—guess
conjunction—union
connoisseur—expert
conscious—aware
consequence—result
considerable—much
consolation—comfort
consolidate—unite, combine
constant—fixed
consternation—dismay
constitute—make up, form
constitution—make-up, form
construct—build
constructive—helpful
consume—use up
contaminate—taint
contemplate—think about
contempt—scorn
contemptible—mean
contemptuous—scornful
contiguity—nearness
contiguous—touching, near

contingency—chance
continue—keep on
contort—twist, bend
contradict—deny
contribution—gift
contusion—bruise
convenient—handy
conversation—talk
conversion—change
convolution—coil, fold, twist
cooperate—work together
coquette—flirt
corporation—company, firm
corporeal—bodily
correct—true, right
correspond—agree
corroborate—confirm
corrugate—wrinkle
corruption—decay
counteract—hinder
counterfeit—false
countermand—cancel, recall
counterpart—copy
courageous—brave
courteous—polite
cozen—cheat
criterion—rule, test
criticize—blame
cryptic—secret
curriculum—course of study
custody—care, keeping
customary—usual

debilitate—weaken
decapitate—behead
decentralize—scatter
declination—downward slope
decline—go down; refuse
dedicate—devote
deduct—take away
de facto—real

defective—faulty
deficiency—lack
deficit—shortage
definitive—final
defunct—dead
delectable—pleasing
delete—strike out
demonstrate—show
depart—go
deplete—empty
depreciate—lessen
depress—lower
description—kind
designate—name
determine—settle
detest—hate
detrimental—harmful
development—growth
deviate—turn aside
difficult—hard
digress—turn aside
dilatory—not prompt
diminution—lessening
diplomacy—tact
diplomatic—tactful
disagreeable—cross
disarrange—disturb
disburse—pay out
discerning—keen
disconnected—undone
discontented—uneasy
discontinue—give up
discount—take off
discordant—harsh
discredit—doubt
discussion—talk
disdain—scorn
disembark—land
disengage—free
disentangle—free
disguise—hide

disintegrate—break up
disinter—dig up
dismember—take apart
dispatch—send
dispel—drive away
dispense—give out
disperse—scatter
display—show
dispossess—put out
disregard—ignore
disrespectful—rude
disrupt—split
disseminate—scatter
dissimilar—unlike
dissipate—scatter, waste
dissolute—evil
distend—stretch out
distinguish—tell apart
distort—twist
distribute—spread
disturbance—trouble
divert—turn aside
divest—strip off
divine—foresee
divulge—tell
doctrine—belief
domesticate—tame
domicile—home
dominant—ruling
dominate—control
domineer—rule over
donation—gift
dormant—asleep
dorsal—back
dubious—doubtful
duplicate—copy

ebullient—bubbling up
eccentric—odd, not circular
economical—thrifty
edification—benefit

edifice—building
educate—teach
efface—rub out
effect—bring about
effective—getting results
effeminate—womanish
effervescent—bubbling, gay
effusive—pouring out
egregious—very great
egress—exit
ejaculate—exclaim
elect—choose
electrode—pole
elevate—raise, lift up
elevation—height
elicit—draw out
eliminate—throw out
elongate—stretch
elucidate—make clear
elude—slip away
emaciated—thin
emanate—go out from
emancipate—free
emasculate—weaken
embellish—adorn
emerge—come out
eminence—high place
eminent—high
emolument—salary, fees
emphasize—stress
employ—hire
employment—work
encounter—meet
encumbrance—burden
endeavor—try
endorsement—support
endownment—gift
enervate—weaken
engender—cause, breed
engrave—carve
enigma—riddle

enigmatic—puzzling
enjoin—order
enmity—hate
entirely—wholly, fully
entirety—whole
entreat—beg
enumerate—count
epistle—letter
equable—even
equitable—fair
equivalent—equal
erratic—uncertain
erroneous—wrong
erudite—learned
evident—plain
exaggerate—stretch
exaltation—rapture
excessive—too much
execute—carry out
exhausted—worn out, used up
exhibit—show
exigency—need
existence—being
exorbitant—much too high
expand—spread out
expedience—fitness
expedite—make easy, hurry along
expeditious—quick
expenditure—spending, expense
expensive—costly
explicit—clear
expound—make clear
expunge—wipe out
extemporaneous—offhand
exterior—outside
exterminate—destroy
external—outer

fabricate—build, make
facilitate—make easy
fallacious—misleading

fallacy—error
fantastic—odd, unreal
fascinate—charm
fatuous—silly
feasible—can be done
felicitous—apt
felicity—bliss
felonious—wicked
ferocious—fierce
fictitious—made-up
finical—fussy
firmament—sky
fissure—cleft
fluctuate—rise and fall
fluctuation—wavering
forbearance—patience
forfeit—lose, give up
formulate—draw up
fortunate—lucky
fracture—break
fragile—frail
fragment—piece
frequently—often
frivolous—silly
frugality—thrift
frustration—defeat
fundamental—basic

generate—produce
genuine—real
germinate—sprout
gigantic—huge
glutinous—sticky
gratify—please
gratuity—gift, tip
gravitate—settle
guarantee—backing, promise

habitation—house
hazardous—risky
heterogeneous—varied

homogeneous—similar
humid—damp
humorous—funny

identical—same
ignoble—base, mean
ignominious—shameful
illumination—light
illustration—picture
imbue—fill
imitate—copy, mimic
imitation—copy
immaculate—pure, spotless
immediately—at once
immense—huge, vast
imminent—near
immoral—evil, wicked
immovable—firm, fixed
impair—harm
impartial—fair, just
impeccable—faultless
impecunious—poor
imperative—urgent
imperceptible—very slight
imperfection—fault, defect
impertinent—rude, saucy
impetuous—rash
impinge—strike
impolite—rude
importunate—urgent
imposter—cheat, fraud
impotent—helpless
impregnate—fill with
improvident—not thrifty
imprudent—rash
inaccuracy—mistake
inactive—idle
inadvertent—careless
inadvisable—unwise
inanimate—lifeless
inapplicable—not suitable

inattentive—careless
inaugurate—begin
inauspicious—unlucky
incipient—beginning
incision—cut
incisive—cutting
incite—rouse
inclement—harsh, stormy
incoherent—confused
incombustible—fireproof
incompetent—unfit
inconsiderate—thoughtless
inconstant—fickle
inconvenience—bother
incorrect—wrong
increase—gain, grow
incredulity—doubt
increment—growth, increase
incubate—hatch
incumbrance—burden
indebtedness—debts
indefatigable—tireless
indefinite—vague
indelicate—coarse
indemnify—repay
indentation—notch
independent—free
indeterminate—vague
indicate—show
indication—sign
indigent—poor, needy
indiscriminate—confused
individual—person
indolent—lazy
indorsement—support
indubitable—certain
ineffectual—useless
inelegant—crude, vulgar
inexhaustible—tireless
inexpedient—unwise
infection—catching

infirmity—weakness
inflexible—stiff, rigid
information—news
infrequent—rare
infuriate—enrage
ingenious—clever
ingenuous—frank, open
inhibit—check, hinder
inhibition—restraint
inhuman—cruel
inimitable—matchless
iniquitous—wicked
initial—first
initiate—begin
injudicious—unwise
injunction—order
innocuous—harmless
innovation—change
inoperative—not working
inquire—ask
inquisitive—curious, prying
insecure—unsafe
insensible—unaware
insidious—wily, sly, tricky
insinuation—hint
insipid—weak
insolvent—bankrupt
institute—set up, begin
instruct—teach
instrument—tool
insubstantial—flimsy
insufficient—not enough
insurgent—rebel
insurrection—revolt
intention—aim
interdict—forbid
interminable—endless
intermission—pause
internecine—deadly
interrogate—question

interrupt—hinder, stop
intersection—corner
intimate—hint
intimidate—frighten
intractable—stubborn
intrepid—fearless
intrigue—plot
inundate—flood
invaluable—priceless
invert—upend
inviolable—sacred
inviting—tempting
irrelevant—off the subject
irreproachable—faultless
irritability—impatience
isolate—set apart

jocular—funny
jocund—gay
judicious—wise

laceration—cut, tear
laggard—slow
languish—droop
languorous—listless
lenient—mild, gentle
lethargic—dull
liberate—free
liquidate—pay
liveliness—vigor
locality—place
lucent—bright
lucid—clear
lugubrious—sad
luminous—bright

magnificent—grand
malediction—curse
malevolence—spite
malformation—bad shape

manifest—clear, plain
manufacture—make
masticate—chew
meditate—reflect
melancholy—sad
mendacious—lying, false
mendicant—beggar
mentality—mind
mercurial—quick, fickle
meritorious—worthy
meticulous—very careful
militate—fight
minimal—smallest
minuteness—smallness
misadventure—mishap
misapprehension—wrong idea
miscellany—mixture
miserable—wetched
mitigate—make mild, soften
modification—change
mollify—soothe
morbid—sickly
mordant—biting
municipality—city
mutable—fickle

narration—telling
narrative—story
nauseous—sickening
nebulous—hazy, vague
negation—denial
neglectful—careless
negotiate—talk business
neutralize—offset
nonsensical—foolish, absurd
notation—note
notification—notice
notify—let know
numerate—count
nutriment—food

obdurate—stubborn
objective—aim, goal
obligate—pledge
obligation—duty
oblige—compel, force
oblique—slanting
obliterate—blot out
oblivious—forgetful
obloquy—abuse, shame
obscene—vile
obscure—dim
obsequious—fawning
observation—remark
observe—note
obsess—haunt
obsolete—out-of-date
obstinate—stubborn
obstreperous—unruly
obstruction—block, hurdle
obtuse—dull, blunt
obviate—wipe out
obvious—plain
occasion—event, cause
ocassionally—now and then
occupy—take up, fill, live in
occurrence—event
odious—hateful
odium—hatred, blame
officious—meddling
operate—work, run
opportunity—chance
oppose—be against, fight
oppressive—harsh, unjust, severe
opprobrium—scorn, abuse
option—choice
opulent—rich
ordinance—rule, law
orifice—opening, hole
original—first
originate—invent

ostentation—show, display
ostracize—banish
outrageous—shocking

pacify—make calm
palatable—pleasing
panacea—cure-all
pandemonium—uproar
paragon—model
parallelism—likeness
paralyze—cripple
paramount—top, chief, supreme
pariah—outcast
parlance—talk
parlous—shrewd
parsimonious—stingy
partially—partly
participate—take part
particularize—state in detail
peculiar—odd, strange
peevish—cross
pendulous—hanging, swinging
penetrate—pierce
penitent—sorry
penurious—stingy
peremptory—positive
perforation—hole
peripatetic—walking about
periphery—outer edge
permanent—lasting
permission—consent, leave
perpendicular—upright
perpetrate—commit
(in) perpetuity—forever
persevere—persist
perspicacious—keen
perspicuous—clear
perspiration—sweat
persuade—win over
pertain—refer

pertinacity—spunk
pertinence—fitness
peruse—read
petulance—bad humor
phantom—ghost
pharmacist—druggist
phlegmatic—sluggish
pinnacle—peak
placate—soothe
plaintive—sad
plebeian—vulgar
plenary—full
plurality—greater number
poignant—sharp
polemic—dispute
possess—own
posterior—rear
postpone—put off, delay
powerful—strong
practicable—can be done
preachment—sermon
precept—rule
precipitant—hasty, rash
precipitation—rain, dew, or snow
preclude—shut out
precursor—forerunner
predestination—fate
predilection—liking
predisposition—tendency
predominant—superior
preeminent—top
preparedness—readiness
preponderant—chief
preposterous—senseless
prescience—foresight
present—give
presuming—bold
presumptuous—forward
prevaricate—lie
primordial—primitive

principal—main, chief
probability—chance
problematical—doubtful
procedure—way, method
prodigious—huge
prodigy—marvel, wonder
proffer—offer
proficiency—skill
proficient—expert
profligacy—vice
profound—deep
progeny—children
prognosticate—forecast
project—plan
promulgate—proclaim
propagate—breed
propensity—bent
prophesy—foretell
propitiate—appease
proposal—plan
propriety—fitness
proscribe—outlaw
proselyte—convert
provoke—vex, stir up
proximity—nearness
puissance—force
punctilious—exact
punctual—prompt
pungent—sharp
purloin—steal
pursue—chase
pusillanimous—cowardly
putrefaction—decay

quadrilateral—four-sided
qualified—fitted
quarrelsome—cross
quarry—prey
querulous—fretful
quiescent—still, quiet

radiant—bright
radiate—give out
ramification—part, branch
ratification—approval
recapitulate—sum up
reciprocal—mutual
reciprocate—give in return
recognize—know, accept
recollection—memory
recommendation—praise
reconciliation—settlement
recondite—obscure
reconnaissance—survey
reconstruct—make over
recover—get back
rectify—make right
recuperate—get well
redeem—buy back
redundant—extra, not needed
refractory—stubborn
refrigerate—cool
regimen—rule
regulation—rule, law
rehabilitate—restore
reimburse—pay back
reinforce—strengthen
rejoinder—reply
related—akin
reliance—trust
relinquish—give up
remainder—the rest
remedy—cure
remiss—slack
remonstrate—protest
remorseless—cruel
remunerate—reward
remuneration—pay
repentance—regret
replica—copy
reprehend—blame

reproduction—copy
repudiate—reject, disown
repugnance—distaste
requisite—needed
rescind—repeal, cancel
resemblance—likeness
residence—house, home
resilience—bounce
resolute—firm
respite—lull
restrain—check
resuscitate—revive
reticent—silent
retrench—cut down
retrieve—bring back
retrogress—move back, get worse
reversion—return
revocation—repeal
ridiculous—absurd
righteousness—virtue
rigidity—stiffness
rigorous—harsh, strict
risible—funny
rotundity—roundness
rubicund—ruddy
ruminate—ponder

saccharine—sweet
sagacious—wise
salacious—lewd
salient—striking, main
saline—salty
salutation—greeting
sanitary—healthful
satellite—follower
saturate—soak, fill
savory—tasty
scandalous—shocking
scepticism—doubt
scintillate—sparkle

scrutinize—inspect
sebaceous—fatty, greasy
segment—part
segregate—set apart, separate
selection—choice
semblance—likeness
sequestration—removal
serpentine—twisting, sly
shortcoming—fault
similar—like
similarity—likeness
simulate—pretend, feign
sincere—frank
sinecure—easy job
singularity—oddness
situated—placed
slovenly—untidy
solicit—ask for
solicitous—anxious, eager
solitary—alone
spacious—vast
speculate—reflect
stimulate—excite
stratifications—layers
stringent—strict, tight
stultify—make foolish
stupefaction—stupor
stupendous—immense
subjugate—subdue
subjugation—conquest
sublimity—majesty
subsequently—later
subservient—servile
substantial—real, strong, large
substantiate—prove
subterfuge—trick
sufferance—consent
sufficient—enough, ample
suffocate—smother
suitability—fitness

sumptuous—costly, rich
supercilious—proud
superlative—top
supersede—replace
suppurate—fester
surreptitious—secret
sustenance—support

tabulation—table
tantalize—tease
technicality—detail
tempestuous—stormy
tenuous—thin
terminate—end
terminus—end
tertiary—third
titillate—tickle
tortuous—twisting
tranquillity—quiet
transcendent—superior
transcription—copy
transpire—take place
transpose—shift
trenchant—sharp, keen
trepidation—fear
tribulation—trouble
tripartite—three-part
triplicate—triple
triviality—trifle
tumultuous—noisy
turpitude—baseness

ulterior—hidden
ultimate—last, final
unadvisedly—rashly

unassuming—modest
unavailability—lack
uncertainty—doubt
uncivilized—savage
uncommonly—rarely
uncompromising—firm
uncultivated—wild
undisguised—frank
undulations—curves, waves
unequivocal—clear
unfaltering—firm, steadfast
unfavorable—harmful
unfounded—baseless
ungovernable—unruly
uniformity—sameness
unmistakable—plain, evident
unnecessary—needless
utilize—use
utilization—use

vacillate—waver
vacuous—empty
validity—truth
valorous—brave
variation—change
vehement—eager, forceful
venomous—spiteful
ventilate—air
venturous—bold
vigilance—caution
vindicate—defend, uphold
visualize—picture
vitreous—glassy
vociferate—shout
voluminous—bulky

Index